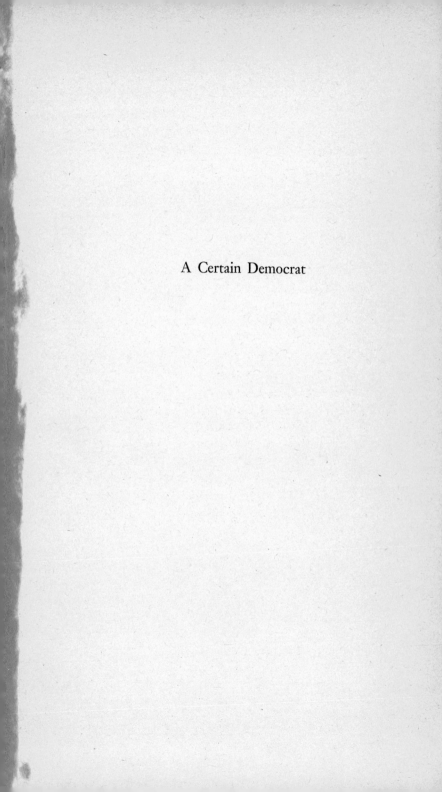

A Certain Democrat

A Certain Democrat

Senator Henry M. Jackson

A Political Biography

by
WILLIAM W. PROCHNAU
and
RICHARD W. LARSEN

PRENTICE-HALL, INC.
Englewood Cliffs, N.J.

To
LANI *and* DEANIE

●

A Certain Democrat: Senator Henry M. Jackson, A Political Biog-
raphy by William W. Prochnau and Richard W. Larsen

Printed in the United States of America *T*
Prentice-Hall International, Inc., London
Prentice-Hall of Australia, Pty. Ltd., North Sydney
Prentice-Hall of Canada, Ltd., Toronto
Prentice-Hall of India Private Ltd., New Delhi
Prentice-Hall of Japan, Inc., Tokyo

●

Library of Congress Cataloging in Publication Data
Prochnau, William W , date
A certain Democrat.
1. Jackson, Henry Martin, 1912   I.   Larsen,
Richard W., date   joint author.   II. Title.
E748.J22P7   328.73'0924 [B]   74–37158
ISBN 0-13-123158-8

FOREWORD

THIS IS NOT a standard political biography and it is not intended to be one. Rather, it is an effort to describe and, hopefully, to provide better understanding of a public man who played a unique role in a special period of American political history. The focus is on the man, Senator Henry M. Jackson, and the times. Thus details of his involvement in some congressional issues are omitted or referred to only briefly—particularly his work on resource development in the Columbia River Basin and elsewhere in the Far West, his work on behalf of Alaska and Hawaii statehood legislation and other issues which arose, particularly, out of the committees on which he has served.

Many persons were helpful to us in our research. They include citizens of Everett, Washington; many employees, past and present, of the senator's office and committee staffs; Mrs. Jackson, and many friends and political foes of the senator. To each we extend our gratitude.

We are especially grateful to Senator Jackson who frequently took time away from his busy schedule to grant the many interviews which we sought.

—The Authors

CONTENTS

CHAPTER 1

THE LAST OF THE COLD WAR LIBERALS

June 11, 1954 . . .

The scene is the Caucus Room of the Old Senate Office Building, a massive marble room that exudes the feeling of imperial Rome. Muscular stone pillars bull upwards almost forty feet to support a scrollwork ceiling. The voices of the senators, the statesmen and their lessers soar up to the scrolls, then carom back down with a strange hollow echo.

Even the most insular tourist, wandering in off the hot streets of Washington, would have trouble avoiding the skin-prickling feeling of past triumph and tragedy in the huge vault of the Caucus Room.

Off to the left stood banks of the brutal-white lamps of early-day television. To the right were those more traditional illuminators of Washington's instant history—the working press, sweating under the accursed lamps, elbowing each other for room to use their blunted pencils.

In the back, where the public is invited to watch American democracy at work, every chair was filled, as was every standing-room slot along the white-gray marble walls. The United States Army, which was on trial, had its own observers, as did a United States Senator, who also was being tried. As they had been for thirty-two days, the spectators

1

once again had been warned sternly that "no audible manifestations of approval or disapproval of any kind at any time" would be allowed. No emotion was to be shown in the Caucus Room.

In the center, at a small witness table, sat Joseph R. McCarthy, a senator from the state of Wisconsin. At his left sat Roy M. Cohn, a scowling 26-year-old New York lawyer, whose activities on behalf of the senator had made him the darling of the American Right, the scourge of the American Left.

The senator and his lawyer sat facing a long table and a phalanx of familiar, if not friendly, faces. They belonged, after all, to members of McCarthy's own committee—the committee he had used as a vehicle for his crusade to root the Commies out of the State Department, the Army, the Information Agency, and out from under all the government's beds. It had been a strange, unholy crusade. He had wreaked fear, used it, nurtured it, served his cause with it. Even the panel facing him now, his colleagues, had felt it. Joe McCarthy had compiled a dossier on each of his fellow committee members. But they felt the fear less now. Joe McCarthy's glory days—those file-folder-waving glory days—were on the wane. The political self-immolation of Joseph R. McCarthy—the long trial of the Army-McCarthy hearings—was almost over.

At the center of the long table was Karl Mundt, the cherubic conservative from South Dakota, who sat in for McCarthy as temporary chairman. Off to his right were the uneasy Republicans—Everett McKinley Dirksen of Illinois, Charles E. Potter of Michigan; to his left, the antagonistic Democrats—John L. McClellan of Arkansas, Stuart Symington of Missouri, and Henry M. Jackson of Washington. Behind Jackson sat Robert F. Kennedy, the skinny,

2

abrasive, 28-year-old counsel to the Democratic members of the committee.

It was the end of a long Friday afternoon and Jackson was probing now, asking McCarthy about a document that had been written by one of his favorite Communist-chasers, young G. David Schine. In thirty-two days of national television, Jackson, like the others in this high drama, had become a political celebrity. Columnists and housewives alike compared him to Jimmie Stewart—an unemotional, methodical, Western good guy, always on the side of the angels, the good, liberal angels. Jackson, square-faced and earnest, was a fledgling in the Senate. Twenty months earlier, as he had struggled to get into that most exclusive club, Joe McCarthy had gone out to Seattle to warn the people that Henry Jackson was a little too pink, too soft on the Communists, to be trusted in such a high place. But now he was there and McCarthy was squirming, while Jackson interrogated him about G. David Schine.

The Schine Plan for the eradication of international Communism had been submitted to the State Department for "immediate execution." It had not been executed because, even in these days of the Red Menace, the mind could be pushed only so far. "The broad battlefield is the globe and the contest is for men's souls," Schine had written in his almost childlike prose. "We can fill their bellies, as we must, but man does not live by bread alone. We require of the free men of the world, their hearts, their consciences, their voices, and their votes. How to do this?" Schine had concluded that we could create a Deminform (Democracy/Information) to combat Cominform and get overseas Elks Clubs to help out; we could propagandize through pinups and distribute democratic bumper stickers for European cars.

3

Jackson's questions came rapid-fire, prosecutor-style, ridiculing. The white-hot lamps were punishing and there were beads of sweat on McCarthy's brow. Roy Cohn, tight muscles in his neck, sat glowering, first at the earnest Jimmie Stewart prosecutor, Jackson, and then at the aggressive aide de camp, Kennedy, who fed questions to Jackson.

On the right, at the press table, the reporters were scribbling furiously. Deminform. *Really, Senator McCarthy?* Fight Commies through the Elks. *Are there any Elks Clubs in Pakistan, Senator McCarthy?* And pinups. *What in the world will you do with pinups, Senator McCarthy? In all seriousness, senator. In all seriousness.*

"As to pinups," the senator from Wisconsin replied, flustered and hurrying a glance at Cohn, "I don't know what he is referring to as a pinup."

"We can all laugh on that one, I think, Senator," Jackson said. Over Joe McCarthy's shoulders, from the back of the room, the laughter rumbled and he slumped slightly. Senator Mundt rapped the gavel at this audible manifestation from the public. And Cohn half rose out of his chair, the glower turning to a hate-stare.

Then Mundt was pounding the gavel again. The hearing would recess until Monday. Cohn was out of his chair, protesting. Schine was his buddy, his Commie-chasing buddy, and McCarthy was his boss, his Commie-chasing boss, and they had been ridiculed, humbled.

"I would like my round," Cohn insisted, "to ask some questions which might develop true facts about some of the things which Mr. Jackson said here this afternoon."

The gavel came down again. The questions could be asked Monday. The hearing was in recess. In the back of the room, the observers began to mill out—first those standing shoulder to shoulder by the marble walls, then those seated, scraping chairs, moving out through the great oak doors, past the uniformed Capitol Police. The press stood, then moved toward the committee table to question Jackson, the antagonist. McCarthy shuffled off toward his left. Bob Kennedy picked up his papers and his files and his notes and then, arms laden, moved around the committee table, down around the press table and off toward the doors. Roy Cohn shoved documents and notes and the Schine Plan into the briefcase at his feet and, a file-folder under his arm, rose and moved off toward the press table. The great television lamps still were on, full flare, and they illuminated the scene.

Bob Kennedy and Roy Cohn, both still in their twenties, met, at a course determined by Cohn, perhaps a half-dozen feet in front of the press table. Jackson stood nearby talking to the reporters—Potter of the *Sun*, Marder of the *Post*, Edwards of the *Chicago Tribune*.

Cohn reached Kennedy and the anger was so deep he spoke through a slit-mouth, through clenched teeth.

"You'd better tell Jackson," he spat the words at Kennedy, "we're going to get him on Monday." *For being soft on Commies. For things he has written that show he is soft on Communism.*

Cohn and Kennedy stood there chin to chin and they would have come to blows if Kennedy's arms hadn't been full. *Do you want to fight now?! Don't threaten me, Cohn! Don't threaten a United States Senator!* The press milled around and Cohn backed off, flourishing the file-folder which was marked in red, "Jackson's Record." But Cohn never would get Jackson, never even make the attempt, not on Monday or any other day, for the great Rightist orgy of McCarthyism was all but over and file-folder-waving was out of vogue.

5

Still, the hate mail came in, dirty, no-good, traitorous, Kremlin-worshiping, Commie-coddling, Left Wing senator from Washington . . . . "You can't tell these kids on campus now that there was this decade of fear," Jackson would say years later. "I mean fear, just plain fear."

July 11, 1970 . . .

The scene is a large storage room behind stage at the Spokane Coliseum, where the biennial tumult of the Washington State Democratic Convention was being played out once again. It was a nondescript room—cinder-block functional. Sawhorses and odd pieces of lumber were stacked randomly, forming a low barrier between a garage-like area for delivery trucks and the main part of the room, which opened onto the stage.

Shortly before nine o'clock in the morning a sedan drove into the room and deposited a powerful United States Senator, 58-year-old Henry M. Jackson. He was met there by an equally powerful colleague, 65-year-old Warren G. Magnuson. Both represented the essence of the American political Establishment. They were members of the Senate's Inner Club. Political longevity had granted both the power of committee chairmanships. They were intimates of Presidents and policy-makers. Jackson had arrived through the garage door for security reasons.

For Henry Jackson, still youthful despite graying temples and thirty years in the Congress, it was an election year. So far, it had not been a very good year. For a decade, Jackson had been one of the Vietnam hawks. The war was winding down now, but Cambodia and the shootings at Kent State had reignited the issue. On campus, antiwar students had pelted the senator with marshmallows. The hecklers had shoved insulting signs under his nose—Pentagon Puppet,

6

Pentagon Pimp—and harassed his quiet, Barbie-doll-beautiful wife. But the supreme political insult had been made just two months earlier in Seattle. There, at the Democratic county convention in the largest county in his state, the delegates had voted to spurn their powerful Democratic senator, the greatest vote-getter in the history of Pacific Northwest politics. They had voted instead to endorse Jackson's opponent in the Democratic primary, a flamboyant, New Left peace candidate named Carl Maxey.

Now Jackson was at the state convention and, beyond the storage room, the delegates were filing into the vast Coliseum hall. In Washington State, political conventions do not nominate candidates. This year the state convention would not even endorse candidates because the hierarchy had counted noses and, at best, Henry Martin Jackson, the most popular politician in the state, could get only a slim majority of the Democrats in the hall that day.

Jackson clambered over the lumber barrier and, followed by Magnuson and their two wives, strode into the main part of the storage room. There were about two dozen off-duty policemen in the room, some of them sitting at a long table, playing poker. All of them wore identical short-sleeved, white sweatshirts. Emblazoned across the chest in black were the words, "Pigs Is Beautiful." Jackson, in the way of all politicians, gave them a short talk before moving through the door and onto the stage.

This would be Jackson's only appearance at the convention. In better years he would have gone down onto the floor, milled among his friends, the delegates. But this year there were too many strange faces down there, waving the two-fingered peace sign, some so hostile they might lower one finger.

In his brief appearance Jackson planned to introduce

7

Magnuson, the keynote speaker. There would be a demonstration by Jackson's partisans. But there was an electric tension in the air. The peace delegates had let it be known that they planned a counter-demonstration and, in these days of Left-versus-Establishment confrontation politics, no one was exactly sure what that meant.

Abruptly, the session began and a party functionary was introducing Jackson. Beneath the stage, in the orchestra pit, a five-piece band struck up "Happy Days Are Here Again." The Jackson delegates, about half the crowd, rose, chanted and began their serpentine surge around the hall. Jackson, a tense smile frozen on his broad Norwegian face, moved to the front of the stage, followed by Magnuson and their two wives.

Below them the floor of the Coliseum convulsed. The peace delegates were marching now, too, intermingling with Jackson's people, jostling occasionally, shoving their placards up and down among the Jackson placards. The din grew, "We Want Jackson!" clashing with a unified chant of "Peace! Now!"

Jackson surveyed the swirling scene. There had been greater convention confrontations and noisier convention shows. There had been the Depression conventions when the cops had come in with firehoses to clean out the Left-Wing dissidents. And there had been the glorious tumult of the national convention in Los Angeles in 1960, when Scoop Jackson, the good liberal, almost, almost, had been chosen as John Kennedy's running mate. But the swirl now was around Senator Jackson, the warhawk.

The band blared on, *happy days, happy days, happy days*. The demonstrators pressed forward into the area below the stage where the small band sat, and Jackson leaned over to shake hands, selectively. Then the crowd pushed up onto the stage itself. The senator was amid the demonstrators, friends, foes, and they moved their conflicting standards up and down, piston-like, in his face. Intuitively, a handful of Jackson volunteers and non-uniformed security men formed a ring around the senators and their wives.

A delegate elbowed his way to the microphone and, capturing his strategic target, amplified the peace chant. Briefly, the sound of the Jackson Establishment was overwhelmed by the thunder of the dissidents—a cadenced "Peace! Now!" that protested against an awful stream of events—the killing of John Kennedy, the killing of Martin Luther King, the killing of Robert Kennedy, the killing in the streets, the killing on the campuses, the killing in the ghettos, the killing in the muck-jungles of Southeast Asia.

For a moment, Jackson was lost from view in the crowd of bodies. Then the hierarchy cut the microphone's power and the band ended its happy-days exultations. Gradually the roar subsided; the demonstrators left the stage and settled back into their seats.

Jackson moved to the lectern and, unemotionally, began his introduction of Magnuson. "We meet here today in the proud tradition of our great party. . . ."

Then Magnuson was up and the cheers were unanimous, coming from both factions in the hall. They called him Maggie and they loved him, all of them. Over the years he had fought all the good Democratic fights and, lately, he had taken some pointedly anti-military positions. When Scoop Jackson was championing the antiballistic-missile system in the Senate, Magnuson was voting against it.

Magnuson, in a rambling style of mixed metaphors and worn homilies, preached the impossible—unity. Don't take your bat and ball and go home, he instructed the dissidents.

You've sent a great Democratic team to Washington. Send it back again.

Finished, Magnuson backed away from the microphone amid cheering. Jackson and others quickly moved to his side. In the excitement, Magnuson, unpredictable Maggie, had forgotten his principal political task: He had failed to give an outright endorsement to Scoop Jackson.

As the applause ebbed, Magnuson hurried back to the microphone to shout, "And when I said team, I meant Senator Jackson, too." There was an added roar, mixed with some booing, and the senators retreated from the stage, moving back toward the storage room.

A reporter sprinted after Jackson. As the newsman reached a door to the backstage area, it was closed and being locked behind the departing senators. Inside the door stood two beefy, off-duty policemen, the words "Pigs Is Beautiful" written across the chests of their sweatshirts.

Throughout 1970 the hate mail came in, dirty, no-good, war-mongering, sabre-rattling, militarist, Right-Wing senator from Washington. . . .

Senator Jackson . . . is an uninhibited wearer of the liberal label.

—St. Louis *Post Dispatch*
April 18, 1954

Jackson has not changed. He has not become less progressive than he was. But his party, his state and his nation have become more progressive. They have moved and he has remained set in his ways.

—Bill Hall in Lewiston, Idaho, *Tribune*
August 3, 1969

We don't know whether to applaud Jackson's consistency or condemn his stubbornness. One thing is certain, he is getting farther out of step with the voters each week.

—The Seattle *Argus*
May 9, 1969

JACKSON'S LANDSLIDE BREAKS 1964 RECORD
—Headline in the Seattle *Times*
November 4, 1970

For most of a generation—the Jackson generation of New Deals and Fair Deals and New Frontiers—to have been liberal was to have been where the action was. It was a generation in which a nation was pushed, shoved and tugged from *laissez faire* capitalism to paternal big-government federalism. Power shifted from capitalist New York to federalist Washington. Businessmen changed their allegiance from conservative Herbert Hoovers to populist Lyndon Johnsons. It was a generation in which, at the beginning, Franklin Roosevelt could complain with some justification about a carping conservative press and, in the end, Richard Nixon could complain with some justification about a carping liberal press.

Through it all, Jackson surely had been where the action was. As a young man, he had formed a Roosevelt First Voters' League. As a young Democratic politician in the Pacific Northwest's militant Left days of the Great Depression, he had artfully maneuvered his way through thickets of Communist-controlled unions in his radicalized home state. James Farley had gone to Washington State at the time, observed the imbroglio of radical Democratic politics and concluded that "there are 47 states and the

11

Soviet of Washington." In 1940, at the age of twenty-eight, Jackson went to Congress and veered left, voting against the Communist-chasing activities of the House Un-American Activities Committee. The Americans for Democratic Action sought him out for his liberalism. Joe McCarthy went after him and there was no better way to have one's liberal credentials polished up.

Those were the halcyon days. It was liberal to be for those big western dams because the conservatives said it was socialism and everyone knew what that led to. In the 1950s Jackson was suspicious of the Russians. But what was illiberal about that? Strengthening the national defense was a Democratic theme through the Eisenhower years. The idea was to stop the Communists with missiles, not by brandishing State Department files. Kennedy, Mansfield, Symington, and Jackson all were sounding the same horn then, warning about a missile gap.

But times change and liberalism is built on shifting sands. If it once was liberal to be for the dams because they were federal, it now is liberal to be against the dams because they are dams. And national defense? That sort of liberalism apparently went out with the agony in Southeast Asia.

In 1954, when the Vietminh took Dien Bien Phu from the French, and about the time McCarthy fell, too, Jackson warned that American troops might be needed in Vietnam. In 1961, when President Kennedy started boosting the level of America's corps of "military advisers" to Saigon, Jackson warned that more would be needed. He stuck with that all the way through the awful sixties, all the way through the awful war. *Hawk, Superhawk, the Senator from Boeing*, the liberals started calling him. *Hateful man, willing to feed fodder into an endless war*.

And all the way through the sixties, Jackson's voting

12

record—on everything but defense—was one hundred percent liberal, more liberal than a McGovern or a Gene McCarthy.

Times change. But not Henry Jackson. He believes what he believes—what he always believed—and it bothers him that the liberals don't call him a liberal anymore.

"The attempt here is to say that we'll test our credentials only in the area of foreign policy," Jackson said, as the liberals left him. "I mean, why don't they go around and denounce Fulbright with his totally reactionary domestic record? No, they won't do that because he is in tune with them on foreign policy."

By the end of the sixties, Jackson had become the last of the Cold War liberals—a man who continued to view the Russians with deep suspicion but also continued to vote for almost every progressive domestic measure that came before the Senate. But all the political labels—hawk, dove; Right Winger, Left Winger; liberal, conservative—had begun to lose their meaning after a decade in which a disheartened country often made unkind caricatures of its leaders. Henry Jackson also became a caricature, to the antiwar activists, at least—a Mars-god symbol, Cold Warrior-Hot Warrior, clutching missiles in each hand and willing to bomb Hanoi back into the Stone Age.

"But it works both ways," Jackson said with a perplexed smile. "When I am in an area where the people are conservative, they call me conservative. It's incredible. Because I've taken a tough position on foreign affairs, they forget my whole record on domestic affairs. Four years ago, they'd have given me a kick in the pants."

In July of 1970, at about the time of the Spokane convention, John Kenneth Galbraith, the intellectual gadfly of

13

the Democratic Left, published an article in *Harper's* entitled *Who Needs the Democrats?* The article was a minor sensation in Washington. In effect, Galbraith called for a purge of those Democrats who have failed to join the leftward-intellectual stream of new liberal thinking.

"History, in fact, has played a nasty trick on the Democrats," Galbraith wrote.

It has made politically commonplace all of the major policies for which the party has stood in the past thirty years. The one important exception is foreign policy which it has made aggressively damaging. The men who occupy the positions of power and influence in the party (with some notable exceptions) are still deeply committed to these policies or deeply identified with their own past. So, to borrow General Westmoreland's best word, they have become conservatives by attrition. Not that many would admit it. Being a liberal is like being an Episcopalian: If you have once been well and truly confirmed, you are allowed to consider yourself a communicant for life. You don't have to practice.

Throughout the article, Henry M. (Scoop) Jackson was not mentioned by name. Jackson later said:

Well, Galbraith attempts to arrogate to himself the authority to determine who is a liberal and who is not a liberal. There's a certain amount of arrogance in this. He thinks that when he speaks, he speaks *ex cathedra*, that he's infallible in these things. It seems to me that, above all else, the real test of a liberal is a sense of tolerance and appreciation of the right of disagreement and dissent. I believe this, but others of this new school do not. They tell you what *is* and what *is not*. They want to deal in absolutes. This is the heart of arrogance.

14

After the Spokane convention, political life did not grow easier for Jackson. In the old days the antagonistic Right had contented itself by painting red hammer-and-sickle insignia on his billboards. The antagonistic Left was more physical. Regularly, one finger of the peace sign *was* lowered. He was splattered with overripe fruit. He was threatened with assassination.

Still, by the end of the no-holds-barred Democratic primary campaign, it was clear to almost everyone, even Jackson's aggressive peace-candidate opponent, that the senator could not be defeated. Cut down to size, perhaps, but not defeated. "If nothing else," Carl Maxey said on the eve of the September primary, "we've wrecked Jackson's stated ambitions to be a Presidential or Vice-Presidential candidate by pointing out what a phony liberal he is."

When the returns had come in, Maxey appeared to have been wrong. Jackson had overwhelmed him with eighty-seven percent of the vote in the Democratic primary. Later, in the general election, Jackson cruised almost serenely past his Republican opponent, winning with 83.9 percent of the total vote. It was the most crushing landslide in the political history of his state, a state with a strong two-party tradition. Jackson's majority was far greater than that of his party's leading Presidential contenders—Ed Muskie in Maine, Hubert Humphrey in Minnesota, and even Ted Kennedy in Massachusetts.

The year had been a supreme test for Henry Jackson, for he was, somewhat by his own choice, identified with an ugly war. The new extremists, as he called them, had put him down as "the most hateful of them all." But there was deep, if unintended, irony in that. If there was anything that Henry Jackson was not, to those who knew him after a thirty-year career in Washington State, it was hateful.

15

Reporters, probing the Jackson phenomenon in the isolated corners of his diverse state, could find Wallace voters who were for Jackson and Gene McCarthy voters who were for Jackson. They could find many voters who disagreed with him on the hot war and the Cold War, but not many voters who disliked him. He still was what he had been when he came to the Senate and perhaps what he was when he came to the House—a quiet, methodical man, immensely likable albeit stubborn as a bull ox. "People don't vote for you because of the way you vote in the Senate," he had said long before the war became an issue. "They vote for you out of respect. If they think you're a damn fool, your vote isn't going to change their mind." Jackson, throughout thirty years in public life, had been the man on the white horse—untainted by the hint of scandal, hard-working, almost a civics-book example of the ideal public servant. The recriminations from the disaster in Southeast Asia might unhorse some, but not Scoop Jackson in his far-from-conservative Pacific Northwest constituency. By the end of 1970 he had earned what almost every politician seeks but rarely attains—the freedom to stand stubbornly for an unpopular cause without serious risk of political extinction.

There were those who made the point, with accuracy, that Jackson's overwhelming victory was more a tribute to his straight, unflappable, good-guy personality/image than it was a vindication of his considerably more controversial philosophy on world affairs. But, whatever the case, it definitely did thrust Henry Martin Jackson onto the Presidential stage . . . .

It is a muggy day in May, 1971, and on the parkway outside Washington Rennie Davis's rag-tag street army is retreating from the May Day antiwar demonstrations. Senator Henry M. Jackson, now interested in leading an army of his own, is pulling out, too, his car racing down the parkway toward Friendship Airport and an airplane that will take him to Dallas for some politicking.

Along the road a boy and a girl, uni-sexed in blue jeans and long matted hair, are walking north. They are carrying one bedroll. Bringing the government to its knees, ending the war, quite naturally had meant mating in the government park, too. It was part of the logic. *You offend us by murdering in Vietnam; we offend you by screwing in the park.*

Scoop Jackson is a rather conventional man, born of immigrant parents in a Northwest mill town, reared in the strong American work ethic, a believer in the old values. He has trouble absorbing the logic. "Jeesuz," he says, "one of those girls took her clothes off on teevee. Did you see that? Took her clothes off."

In May, 1971, Jackson's Presidential campaign is not yet a real Presidential campaign. He has been describing himself, almost with a half-wink, as an official noncandidate. He has not geared up and neither has the public. He bolts through the Friendship terminal, carrying his own bag, and not a single eye turns toward him. Aboard the plane, the stewardess, training-school efficient, mechanically asks for his name and then inscribes JACKSON, H. on her clipboard.

As usual, Jackson spurns the proffered booze and, settling into his first-class seat, he leafs through *The New York Times*. The pauses are long over the datelines—Moscow, Cairo, Hong Kong. Jackson still is an internationalist, while the rest of his party seems to be creeping in another

17

direction. That bothers him, this neo-isolationism, especially from fellow Democrats like Senator William Proxmire, the Pentagon critic from Wisconsin.

"He's got a midwestern isolationist hangup like Gerald P. Nye," Jackson says.

But Jackson also has been accused of hangups. "You can't have enough security for Henry," Eugene McCarthy has said. "If he had his way the sky would be black with supersonic planes, preferably Boeings, of course."

Two hours later the Boeing 727 bumps around a hailstorm, ducks toward Dallas's Love Field—from Friendship to Love—and arrives with the senator from Washington, a liberal at ease in the South. At the airport Jackson is met by Warren (Woody) Woodward, a vice-president of American Airlines, president of the Dallas Chamber of Commerce, and an old L.B.J. hand. There is a brief airport news conference and then they are in a limousine heading downtown. The big, black car cruises past Dealey Plaza and Woodward points out where J.F.K. was shot. ". . . he turned the corner and Lee Oswald was up there, in that building."

Jackson cranes his neck and says nothing. He hasn't been in Dallas since 1960 when he was John Kennedy's national chairman, a good western protestant chairman to balance off the candidate's eastern Catholicism.

It is evening now, almost night, and the last stop is a Dallas television station, WFAA, for a TV taping. Brian Corcoran, the senator's press secretary, is hovering about, trying to get the proper camera angle. Jackson has a "heavy eye"—the left one—and like Claudette Colbert he photographs better from one side than the other.

As a television performer, Jackson is old-fashioned and he doesn't dig McLuhan. Jackson still believes in content over form. People *should* listen. His words *should* have more impact than the ethereal image. So his aide worries about the camera angle and the image. On the monitor the ethereal image is that of a very serious man, concerned about very serious problems. The questions are coming at him about the Russians. No smiling matter. The form becomes dour, the brow furrows. . . . *the strategic balance is tilting toward Moscow. The Russians will use their advantage for nuclear blackmail. We are facing difficult times, difficult times indeed . . . .*

Jackson is the Senate's student of national security, a man who probably has studied the Russians more thoroughly than anyone on Capitol Hill. Politically, this is both his strong and his weak point. Before Jackson became interested in 1600 Pennsylvania Avenue, Richard Nixon described him as "a man who understands the threat to peace and freedom as well as any man I know." Senator Proxmire calls him semi-hysterical.

In the TV studio the words roll on . . . *one thousand and forty land-based missiles . . . forty-one Polaris submarines . . . the adversary . . . strategic balance . . . the Kremlin . . . tilting . . . blackmail. . . .* "This may not be popular—people may not want to hear it—but it's true," the senator intones.

Later, the limousine deposits Jackson, Woodward, and Corcoran in front of their hotel. Woody spots a friend and pulls him over to meet the senator. Jackson smiles broadly, shakes his hand, small-talks for a moment, and then the man walks off.

"Senator," Woody says, a big grin splitting his face, "you don't know it but you just met the world's largest landowner. Not the United States' largest landowner. The world's. I said to him, 'Come on over, I want you to meet

19

Senator Jackson.' He said, 'I know Senator Jackson. He's conservative, isn't he?' And I said, 'Yessir!' We just changed your image."

"Well," the senator says with a wry smile, "people see what they want to see."

The next morning the senator is up early, as always, and being on the high-protein diet, breakfast is just steak. Today is military-industrial-complex day, although Jackson probably wouldn't describe it that way. There will be a speech to the Dallas Council on World Affairs, helicopter-assisted tours of the Bell and General Dynamics plants in nearby Fort Worth, then a speech at one of those woozy-boozy political dinners—this one for Jim Wright, the Democratic congressman from aerospace-oriented Fort Worth.

Back in the limousine, heading for a conference with the editorial board of the Dallas *Morning News*, Jackson is talking with the driver. Both are Masons and Jackson muses that he started in DeMolay. Corcoran, a Catholic convert, breaks into a laugh. "I was in DeMolay *and* the Knights of Columbus," the press secretary says. "Top that."

"Hell, he ought to be the one running for office," Jackson interjects. "Remember the DeMolay oath? You find any Catholics, you cut their heads off? How times change."

How times change . . . . The *Morning News* is a very conservative newspaper. When the liberal, Catholic President came to Dallas in 1963, the *News* published a black-border, Right-Wing ad condemning him. Now Jackson is there, chatting, and he seems uneasy, being a Kennedy liberal.

Someone asks him if he *really* thinks a Democratic convention would nominate Henry Jackson, the hawk.

"Well, who's to say," the senator responds. "The extremists took over the Republican party in 1964 and now the New Left is trying to take over my party. The convention process does not necessarily reflect the beliefs of the people of the party. Last year, my own party convention repudiated me and I won the election by eighty-seven percent."

And he is asked about Lieutenant Calley and the war-crimes trials. It is a curiosity about Jackson that when his audience veers too far left, he often speaks to the right, as if to instruct them. When it veers too far right, as now, he speaks to the left. It is the heritage, perhaps, of a career of battling the political fringes, right or left.

"The fact that Lieutenant Calley murdered people in a war that is very frustrating is no defense," he says, and the conservative editors look at him strangely. "We can't allow soldiers to depart from their role and, in premeditated fashion, execute innocent civilians."

Jackson the liberal. Jackson the conservative. Voted against HUAC. Voted for the war. Accused Rennie Davis. Accused William Calley.

Jackson whisks through the World Affairs Council speech . . . *Russian imperialism, the balance is tilting, not popular but true* . . . and through the helicopter tours of defense plants. Then, in late day, the helicopter is hurrying him over burnt fields to the Green Oaks Motor Inn, English tudor with a Japanese garden and a pitch-and-putt golf course. The marquee is lit up for the visiting dignitary. "We've got a Scoop. Welcome Henry M. Jackson." Beneath the marquee is an Eldorado with a bumper sticker. "War Is Good Business. Invest Your Son."

That evening, Jim Wright's dinner is set up at Ben Hogan's golf club, the Shady Oaks, and the crowd is overflowing to hear the man who wants to be President. Wright has just taken an informal poll of Texas Democratic congressmen and their leading choices for the Presidency are Wilbur Mills and Scoop Jackson. "Oh, Jackson has a lot of support down here," a Fort Worth reporter acknowledges. "His trouble is with the liberals."

By the time Jackson arrives, the bar has been open an hour. Making the rounds, he grins boyishly every time he gets a badly slurred question. Jackson has no compunctions about booze for anyone else, he just doesn't drink much of it himself. But he has the political wisdom to know that the Shady Oaks is not the place for a formal talk so, even before he sits down, he has thrown away his prepared speech.

Eventually, the waitresses are clattering the trays away and Jim Wright is up to introduce the senator. He might be making a nominating speech. Senator Jackson "is not an easy man to stampede . . . .

"In the hysteria of the 1950s he opposed the Right-Wing excesses of McCarthy . . . .

"In the hysteria of the 1970s he opposes the Left-Wing excesses of those who take to the streets . . . .

"In both positions he sometimes has been lonely, but in both positions he has been right."

The applause is loud and Jackson, after the throwaway lines, warms easily to the Wright theme that here is a man who has fought the extremists, Right and Left, and has sought the truth in the great American middle. First he talks about Joe McCarthy . . . .

"He moved in a way in which people literally were denied the Bill of Rights. We had people in this country who didn't dare speak out because of fear. This is a devastating

22

technique because, of all the forms of tyranny over the mind of man, fear is the worst . . . .

"Thank God America rose up in its righteous wrath—liberals, conservatives, middle-of-the-roaders, all of us had our stomachs full of that."

Then he shifts to the Rennie Davis street extremism of the 1970s . . . .

"But what we now see is another denial, an interference, an attempt to intimidate people in public life who have a responsibility for making decisions, decisions which should be the will of the majority. People have a right to march, a right to protest. But they should understand that when they come out in large crowds, they run the risk of that crowd being incited by extremists.

"What is an extremist? An extremist, whether that person is of the right or the left, is a person who would take the law into his own hands. And there is no place in America for an extremist of any kind . . . . "

The applause rumbles through the room and Jackson is satisfied with himself. He stands at the lectern, sober visage, one arm uplifted . . . *Innocent people get caught up in crowds . . . crowds become mobs.* And mobs, he reminds these Texans, have perpetrated lynchings. *Mobs led to the rise of Mussolini and Hitler.*

"A mob, whether it is incited by the right or the left, is a threat to our freedom. Rule by mob is not in our tradition. Let us never become a banana republic where decisions are made by those who can bring out the largest mob . . . .

"This is something Americans must reflect upon carefully and thoughtfully because the difficult decisions that we must make should be based on reason . . . . "

23

But, say the Rennie Davis street people, *war is not based on reason. You offend us by murdering in Vietnam; we offend you by screwing in the park and lying in the streets and bombing your banks and telling you to fuck off.*

It is ten o'clock at night and Jackson, back at the Green Oaks Motor Inn, is standing in his underwear, brushing his teeth, and listening to a tape of the speech.

From downstairs, the strains of *Moonlight Serenade* waft up. The country-club kids of Fort Worth are having an old-fashioned prom—girls in their anachronistic, mother-chosen chiffon formals, boys in boutonnieres, spit shines, and barber-clipped haircuts.

On the parkway outside Washington, the street army still is straggling home.

From Glenn Miller to Rennie Davis . . . . Such a short hop, this 1970s radicalizing process. A photo in a high-school annual—innocent eyes, gyrene crewcut, retouched acne, Sears suit. A photo on the front page—defiant eyes, snarled hair, clenched fist, combat khakis.

From Swing to Aquarius, with all the good liberal Democratic politicians following. Almost all of them . . . .

In Jackson's suite the tape recorder is droning on. ". . . in the hysteria of the 1970s he opposes the Left-Wing excesses of those who take to the streets . . . the difficult decisions that we must make should be based on reason. . . ."

24

THE HOBNAIL BOOT

"WE HAVE TO *take first things first,*" the last of the Cold War liberals said again and again as his country turned inward in the 1970s. *"We're dealing, after all, with survival.*

"You can't talk about a better United States, if the country can be destroyed. Look at what happened to Norway. Norway had a thousand years of freedom. The Norwegians had clean air, clean water, clean land, a great environment. They had one of the highest standards of living in the world. They had one of the first national health programs, dating back to the turn of the century.

"What good did it do them when the hobnail boot took over in the spring of 1940?"

A confiscated German Fokker bomber, its steel wings flapping like a seagull's, droned low over the Oslo Fjord with a young but important American visitor to Norway in December of 1945.

Outwardly, Norway had not suffered as badly as other nations from the march of the hobnail boot. Oslo was poor and drab but physically intact. The Norwegian people had had their thousand years of freedom interrupted for five long years, but, on a spartan diet of fish and black bread, they remained healthy and now were in good spirits. Henry Jackson, making his first visit to the land of his parents, had seen much worse. The past spring he had been to Buchenwald, where the emaciated bodies of the Jews were stacked like cordwood. During the summer he had trailed along behind American landing forces on the bloody, coral beaches of the Pacific.

But Jackson, a 33-year-old congressman with five years in the House of Representatives, would make two discoveries in Norway that would shape his thinking for the rest of his life.

On his first night in Oslo the young congressman became feverish and, when the Norwegian doctors arrived at his hotel room, they had to peel the paper bedsheets off his body. For forty-eight hours Jackson hovered near death with pneumonia. The Norwegian government devoted one-tenth of its supply of the new wonder drug, sulfa, to save the American visitor. The American Air Corps flew in a vial of even more precious penicillin, the first penicillin ever used in Norway.

Jackson spent ten days in the hospital and, when he left, his bill was just $15.44 under the Norwegian national health-care program.

Years later, Jackson would recount that story when he talked about the need for a national health program in the United States. In the early sixties, when Medicare was a white-hot political issue, Jackson would tell the story to doctors' groups in the most conservative parts of Washington State. The doctors, rigid in their opposition, would sit there stone-faced while Jackson preached to them that they would be better off if the people were better off.

After he left the hospital, Jackson moved into the recently reopened American Embassy to regain his strength. The ambassador was a rather patrician upstate New Yorker named Lithgow Osborne, an old family friend of

Franklin Roosevelt and a man who, even at this point in time, was alarmed by the postwar activities of the Russians.

The Red Army, like the armies of all the Allies, had a contingent in Oslo. Primarily, the Soviet soldiers were there to handle the repatriation of thousands of Russian prisoners-of-war, but, like Russians everywhere after the war, they were slow in going about their business and were in no hurry to abandon their beachhead.

As Jackson recuperated, he and Osborne would sit around an open fireplace in a cramped, little den in the embassy, talking away the long, Norwegian winter nights. Osborne found the congressman somewhat shy, very intense, and a particularly good listener—unusual qualities, he thought, in an American politician. Each night, as they relaxed in large overstuffed chairs, the talk invariably turned to the Russians.

Downtown in Oslo, the Russians were strange allies—uncommunicative, secretive, suspicious even of their own captured soldiers who were being repatriated. Recently, Osborne had gone to a railroad-station ceremony with the Russian commandant, General Ratov, to watch the liberated POW's board a train for their return to the Soviet Union. It was a poignant scene, Osborne told Jackson, with Ratov standing there, his barrel-chest draped with medals, watching the men, some of them not at all happy about their repatriation, being herded aboard the railroad cars.

Toward the end of the war the Russians had come into the north of Norway and engaged in some bloody battles with the German occupying forces. But the Red Army never reached Oslo—until after the war. The Norwegians were uncomfortable, but scrupulously diplomatic, about the lingering presence of their giant neighbor. Elsewhere, postwar governments were having far more trouble. All of Eastern Europe had dropped behind what Winston Churchill soon would describe as an Iron Curtain. The Baltic states had been annexed and the Red Army still occupied chunks of Finland. Elsewhere, Persia, Turkey, and Austria were having trouble with Russian tenacity.

Osborne had concluded, just months after the end of the war, that the West was in for serious trouble with the Soviet Union. During those long nightly talks in the embassy, Osborne's fears had a profound effect on the recuperating congressman. It was then that Jackson also began to believe that in the coming generation the Russian bear might prove to be even more threatening than the hobnail boot had been.

"I've used the occupation of Norway as an example of people getting mixed up on their priorities," Jackson said after 25 years of the Cold War. *"What good did it do when the hobnail boot took over in the spring of 1940?*

"People are saying today that we've got all these problems at home, that we have to solve our problems here because there are so many things bothering us.

"Well, that's hard to disagree with. It has great appeal, and especially politically. It's great when you want to demagogue and say we'll think of our own first. There are not many people outside the United States who vote in elections here. But the fact remains that a great majority of our people really do recognize that we are living in a limited area and that we have responsibilities that we can't shirk. If we do, it's only a matter of time until we lose our freedoms.

"Therefore, the first priority is survival. If you don't take care of that one, you can't take care of the other things. I

28

feel we have the resources to do both. Life is not either-or. Every day I have problems. I have them in my office and in my family. If we all just said, 'Well, it's this or it's that, it's black or it's white,' life would be a pretty simple thing. But it wouldn't work very well, would it?"

CHAPTER 2

VIETNAM

THE PRESIDENTIAL CAMPAIGN of 1960, like so many American elections, was largely a campaign of non-issues. There were almost meaningless arguments over the little Chinese offshore islands of Quemoy and Matsu and heated debate over a nonexistent missile gap. Both were all but forgotten within months after the election. But the 1960 campaign was distinctive in one very specific way: It was the last American Presidential campaign for at least a dozen years in which an already fifteen-year-old war in Vietnam was not a major, emotional, headline-grabbing issue.

When John F. Kennedy took office in January of 1961, the United States had just 685 military advisers in South Vietnam, their presence almost unnoticed by the American people. But if Vietnam were not yet a major public concern, it already was a major private concern of the new American President.

Within days after his inauguration, President Kennedy called Senator Henry M. (Scoop) Jackson down to the White House to talk about a pressing Cold War issue—a nuclear-testing moratorium that both the United States and the Soviet Union had been observing. Jackson was a natural choice for the Presidential consultation. After eight years in the Senate, the Washington Democrat was an acknowledged expert on atomic weaponry and the Cold War. And, until just days earlier, he had been the chairman of the Democratic National Committee.

The snow from a crippling blizzard still lined the streets of Washington as Jackson drove to the White House, contemplating the warning he would give the President that the Russians, then flexing their Cold War muscles, almost surely would break the nuclear moratorium and resume open-air testing.

"I started to talk about the atomic side of the picture, the moratorium," Jackson said later. "But the President said, 'Look, the problem is Vietnam. I've just been talking to Maxwell Taylor and this thing is a real mess. I'm terribly disturbed—Taylor is and I am—about the developments out there.' What was clearly on his mind was Vietnam, not what he was planning to talk to me about. He was worried, really worried. He felt very strongly that the developments in Southeast Asia, in Vietnam in particular, could have an impact on a much larger area."

Jackson offered the President little advice about Vietnam on that day in January of 1961. But, unlike most Americans and even most American senators, he already had been watching events in Indochina for more than a decade.

As early as 1949, Jackson expressed concern about coming trouble in Southeast Asia. In 1954, when Dien Bien Phu fell and the French gave up their ill-fated military operations in Vietnam, Jackson warned that American intervention might be necessary. "We cannot afford to allow too much of the (Asian) land area and population to fall under Communist domination," he said in an interview at that time. "This probably would be a consequence if Indochina should fall. The Communists soon would be right up against Australia and the Philippines. They would have the sources of materials and tremendous new populations and industrial capacity to use in their crusade for world domination." In the same interview he added, "If it is necessary to move into Indochina, I'll support it." Jackson hedged somewhat by warning that there should be a "realistic chance" of success for an American move. "We don't want to be trapped in action that can result in nothing but a disastrous lost cause," he said, unaware of his grim prophecy.

Fifteen weeks after the White House conversation with Jackson, John Kennedy took the first small step in the long, painful escalation of American involvement in Southeast Asia. The President announced to a mostly disinterested American public that he was adding one hundred Special Forces counterinsurgency experts to the small corps of military advisers already aiding Saigon.

Jackson was in Roswell, N.M., speaking at a Democratic dinner, when the announcement was made. He had had no advance notice from the White House, but he said almost exactly what he had said when the French lost Dien Bien Phu seven years earlier. If American troops are needed in Vietnam, he somberly told reporters, "we must pay the price." If there was little reaction in the United States, the response was immediate from North Vietnam. The next day Radio Hanoi charged that the Kennedy administration had "embarked on armed intervention in South Vietnam." The Hanoi broadcast added that "Senator M. Jackson [sic], member of the military committee of the United States Senate, revealed that 'the United States must pay whatever price is necessary to hold South Vietnam. If U.S. troops are required to defend South Vietnam, the U.S. must also pay that price.' "

That would not be the only time that Jackson would

receive notoriety in the Communist-bloc media. Regularly, after that, Tass and Radio Moscow identified the senator from Washington as one of the "gray-haired militarists" who were pushing the world to the brink of war. Jackson and Barry Goldwater were the favorite targets and some liberals began to mutter that, even in the Communist press, Barry Goldwater was strange company for the former Democratic national chairman to be keeping.

Throughout the fifties and sixties, Jackson viewed the Vietnam struggle in an almost classic Cold War perspective. Returning to Seattle from his first visit to Saigon in 1955, Jackson made this view crystal clear. "If we don't stop Russia in Southeast Asia, we might as well sign a quit-claim deed to the balance of Asia and grant Soviet entry into the United States," he said.

After a visit to the war zone in 1962—and a two-hour talk with South Vietnamese President Ngo Dinh Diem—he concluded that the situation was deteriorating but that the Cold War importance of the outcome was unchanged. Vietnam, he wrote on his return, "is a great psychological, political, economic, and military prize . . . . The country is rich in natural resources and Vietnam is the key to that part of the world.

"If we lose Vietnam, we may well lose Laos, Cambodia, and eventually all of Southeast Asia to Communist domination. This struggle is just as much a fight for freedom and our own security as the conflict in Berlin, Cuba, or elsewhere."

Years later, as Americans masochistically sought to assign blame for a decade of disaster, this kind of almost simplistic Cold War thinking would come under sharp attack. But it was much more difficult to challenge in the era of Soviet-American confrontation that was reaching its peak as John Kennedy took office. It was a time of show-down in Cuba and Berlin, a time when falling-domino theories were not only believable but perhaps accurate. The great Communist leaders—Mao, Ho, Khrushchev—talked openly and boldly about a world strategy involving long "wars of national liberation" which would exhaust the patience of the affluent West. John Kennedy met Khrushchev in Vienna and found no reason to disbelieve that they were involved in a deadly chess game on a world board. In Southeast Asia the chess men became dominoes: If Vietnam fell, her obscure little neighbors would fall, too, like a row of dominoes, and Communism would have expanded to the shores of the Philippines and Australia. The domino theory was controversial and widely debated, but Henry Jackson believed it and so did John Kennedy. "I believe it, I believe it," the President said of the domino theory. If Vietnam were lost, Kennedy added, "it would give the impression that the wave of the future in South-east Asia was the Communists. So I believe it."

In the spring of 1971, almost exactly a decade after his first White House conversation with John Kennedy, Henry M. Jackson concluded, along with most of the nation, that it was time to get out of Vietnam. But Jackson, as he did so many other things, did it with a difference. Unlike most of his Senate colleagues, he did not produce private memoranda to show that he had been a secret dove throughout the long, awful years. Nor did he conclude that American involvement was a mistake. The tactics—the long war of attrition—may have been a mistake. But not the decision to get involved.

Jackson's stance was not popular. By 1971 the people—hawks, doves, and many others—were looking for scape-goats and demanding public confessions. But if the people wanted an admission of sin from Henry Jackson, they would be very disappointed. "I guess I'm just stubborn," Jackson said, "but I won't bend. I think we tried to do the right thing out there."

In the decade of the sixties, the United States went from no reaction to over-reaction on the war in Vietnam, from indifference to self-hate. Few Americans had felt it at first. It was a nightly living-room show—bloody and ugly, to be sure, but no bloodier and no uglier than the standard fare. At some point the fiction-image of the living-room television screen finally converted into the reality of broken, mauled bodies a half-world away. And the result scarred the American soul. Many Americans started talking about a sick society and began lamenting a dirty, immoral war.

Henry Jackson is an extraordinarily disciplined man, a man who prides himself on his rationality and steels himself against emotionalism. He seems almost pained when asked about the morality of the war, as if that *cannot* be an issue. He could never buy the idea of a sick society or accept the self-hate theory that the Vietnam war was, by its nature, more immoral than other wars.

"Now, two wrongs don't make a right," he said, as the war appeared to be ending. "But when one starts to get into an argument about morality in a war it seems to me that one can pick his own options. They talk about civilian casualties. Goodness gracious, in World War II, the fire-bombings of the cities, who were they directed at? Where were the outcries then? Now, two wrongs don't make a right . . . but in Vietnam, with a few exceptions, conscious efforts were made to avoid civilians . . . . "

Americans are a cosmeticized people, often seeking to

35

obscure reality. They cosmeticize their blemishes to make themselves look beautiful and cosmeticize their dead to make them look peaceful. But there was no way to cosmeticize the long, televideo war of the sixties. The reality of Hiroshima and Nagasaki and Dresden had not been forced upon them. The reality of Dakto and Mylai and countless, indistinct, burned villages and countless, indistinct, tortured faces *was* forced upon them.

By the end of the decade of the sixties, the theories about falling dominoes and thwarting the Russians and blocking the Chinese were fading into the rhetoric of the past. The Communists *were not* at the shores of Australia and the Philippines.

And the people, many of them, right or wrong, had concluded that the war was immoral—perhaps that all wars were immoral.

In 1964, both Henry M. Jackson and President Lyndon B. Johnson stood for election. This time, indeed, Vietnam was an issue. But it was, in many ways, a typical election campaign for Jackson. In the Democratic primary he was opposed by a peace candidate who attacked him on Vietnam. His Republican challenger contended that he didn't take the Communist threat seriously enough.

"A Democratic opponent calls me a warmonger and one on the Republican side says I'm soft on Communism," Jackson reflected during the campaign. "I must be following a pretty good middle road."

In 1964, of course, it was not too difficult to take the middle road, because it occupied most of the territory. To the left was the peace faction, still just a fringe group of little political consequence. To the right was Barry Goldwater who, while his war policy was not too far removed from what soon would be American policy, had completely horrified most of the public with offhand statements about the use of tactical nuclear weapons. To stay in the middle, a politician had to remain to the left of Goldwater and to the right of the pacifistic peace fringe.

Throughout the 1964 campaign, Jackson warned the voters that the United States was in for a long war in Southeast Asia. "We cannot expect to end this in a short time unless we want to commit a half-million forces in the field and I'm against that," he told a campaign audience in Bellingham, Wash. "We don't want another Korea."

Events soon would alter that declaration, just as events soon would make nonsense of much of the rhetoric of 1964—a year in which Lyndon Johnson stood as the candidate who was "not going to send American boys nine or ten thousand miles away from home to do what Asian boys ought to be doing for themselves."

Even though he was an outspoken congressional leader and a member of the Senate Armed Services Committee, Jackson never was involved in war-policy-making during the Vietnam decade. The American system permits advice on foreign policy—but not policy-making itself—from the Senate. And the advice of an individual senator invariably carries less clout than that of a Presidential adviser. Much of Jackson's advice—very hawkish advice—was rejected by Lyndon Johnson during the crucial Americanization of the war in 1965 and 1966. Jackson had three strong feelings about Vietnam: First, American involvement not only was justified, but it also was essential to the country's interests. Second, the American public would support a protracted war only if the war were kept small.

Third, if the war had to be enlarged, American forces should go for the North Vietnamese jugular and get the war over in a hurry.

The great historical debate over the events between, roughly, the Gulf of Tonkin episode in 1964 and the total Americanization of the war by 1967 is likely to rage for years. No effort will be made to resolve it here. But, shortly after the election of 1964, the American effort in Vietnam shifted gears—and shifted in a major, world-shaking way. The war became very big and very American. And Jackson's emphasis shifted to his third point, going for the North Vietnamese jugular.

As the methodical troop buildups began in 1965, Jackson became his most hawkish. His Vietnam speeches became almost didactic, seeking to instruct and bolster the will of his audiences.

"As for American policy, we can be grateful for the way President Johnson is demonstrating a cool and resolute determination to block the Communist effort to subjugate all of Vietnam," Jackson said in a 1965 speech to the American Legion. "His firm determination is backed by the firm will of the American people.

"We are committed to do what must be done to help the people of South Vietnam defend their freedom. The commitment will require us to do more than we have done or have yet been asked to do."

But then Jackson made it clear that, privately, he was asking the White House to go much further. "How long should we wait before making the shoe pinch in North Vietnam by destroying key economic installations there?" he asked the Legionnaires. "To do too little, too slow, may be the most costly way of bringing about a substantial improvement in the military situation."

38

Constantly during the massive American buildup Jackson's refrain was that it was going to be hard, long, and tough for the American people. He supported the White House unwaveringly, but it riled him, and riled him deeply, that the refrain was not the same from the Johnson administration—and particularly from Defense Secretary Robert F. McNamara. In closing his speech to the Legion he got off some mild, but perceptive, criticism of McNamara's string of optimistic, light-at-the-end-of-the-tunnel statements about the dilemma in Vietnam.

"To arouse great but unjustified expectations may quiet a few critics today," Jackson said, "but it will only sharpen their doubts and disillusion tomorrow."

The doubts and disillusion already had begun to set in. If the critics were a tiny fringe group during the 1964 elections, they were becoming an increasingly important force as the United States edged into a major war in 1965. Jackson viewed them accordingly and this began his series of showdowns with the New Left.

"Once again the so-called 'peace movement' is gaining adherents on many campuses," Jackson said in a May 1965 speech at Boston College.

In addition to writing letters to the editors, you aren't really with it these days unless you have advised the President by carrying a placard up and down in front of the White House . . . .

I wonder sometimes whether the so-called 'peace movement' may not be related to our American tendency to neglect the study of history. I wish every student could be exposed to a thorough study of that fascinating but shameful decade when Hitler was building the German war machine while the democracies were preaching disarmament and neglecting their military preparedness.

39

Hitler's strength was our weakness, and World War II was not the product of an arms race but of the failure of the West to use its superiority to call a halt before Hitler could do what he said he was going to do.

It is not a pleasant fact to recall, but the truth is that the peace movement of the thirties helped to bring on World War II, not to prevent it. And it is a fact that the well-intentioned advocates of immediate withdrawal of our armed forces from Vietnam should ponder . . . .

The true champions of peace today, as in the thirties, are those who understand that power must be used, with restraint but also with assurance, to keep the peace . . . .

Shortly after Henry Jackson, the hawk, returned from his third trip to Vietnam in 1965 he met a full-fledged, circa 1960s, American peacenik. The man's name was William L. Hanson. He was an attorney from Seattle. He was a Quaker. He was devoted to peace. He was, by almost anyone's definition, a beautiful man—quiet, peaceful, but tough, in his way. He was, of course, not typical of the antiwar faction. But who was? Abbie Hoffman? William Lewis Hanson, the dove, signified as much about what is wrong with the American political-labeling system as did Henry Martin Jackson, the hawk.

Hanson and Jackson met in the senator's subdued Capitol Hill office, and it was an awkward meeting, at first. Hanson, in his way, was expecting calloused horns on Jackson. Jackson, in his way, expected a man carrying fragile flowers. Each was wrong.

Jackson talked persuasively about policy and Hanson talked persuasively about morality. Jackson talked persuasively about the Chinese threat and Hanson talked persuasively about the plight of the Vietnamese peasants.

At the end of the forty minutes they were, it seemed, almost liking each other, for both were eminently likable people. Jackson, just back from Vietnam, suggested that Hanson ought to go over and take a look for himself. He would try to make the arrangements with the State Department, the senator said. Hanson, a wry smile on his face, nodded.

It is typical of Jackson that the suggestion was not a political dodge. Later that same day, when Hanson arrived at the White House for another meeting, an aide to Lyndon Johnson had a memo about the proposed trip. But Hanson, by then, was having second thoughts. He concluded that a trip to Vietnam, under those auspices, would be tainted.

Years later Hanson would recall that the meeting burnt one thing into his mind: Jackson acknowledged, quite candidly, that the United States was in Vietnam because of the great chess game of world politics. All the falderal about building democracy in Southeast Asia, all the talk about a better life for the Vietnamese, was secondary. The United States was there because of its own Cold War interests.

To Hanson, this was sacrilege. To Jackson, it was just plain, simple logic. In forty minutes of intelligent conversation William Hanson and Henry Jackson never got on the same wave length.

But, by 1966, this was becoming a common American problem.

While he was in Vietnam in 1965 Jackson had a long session with General Westmoreland, the American commander. As Jackson recalled later, the conversation was disturbing.

41

I told him that either we bring the war to an early conclusion or we simply could not tolerate what I was then given to understand was to be the strategy and which he confirmed at the end of our discussion—namely, a war of attrition or a protracted conflict. This is what really bugged me. I could just see that we would have to make some drastic, dramatic moves if we were going to bring this conflict to a conclusion. Otherwise, it was going to be extended indefinitely.

What Jackson had in mind as drastic, dramatic moves included the blockading or mining of the Haiphong harbor, which was the supply-line port through which Russian aid flowed to Vietnam; accelerated bombing of other ports, as well as petroleum and power sources; and a highly controversial plan known informally as the Inchon-landing proposal. The Inchon-landing proposal, named for a similar operation in the Korean war, involved landing an American attack force just above the demilitarized zone in North Vietnam. Its objective would have been to cut across the narrow southern edge of North Vietnam, into Laos, and block the Ho Chi Minh Trail supply lines to the south.

Actually, the Inchon-landing proposal already had been rejected by the Defense Department and the White House, as being far too risky. It was, surely, a drastic proposal, calling for an invasion of North Vietnam. But it tells much about American conduct of the Vietnam war to note that soon thereafter Defense Secretary McNamara tried to do with technology what politics would not allow him to do with men. With great fanfare he announced a plan to build an electronic sensory "barrier" near the DMZ in an effort to block infiltration. The plan quickly slipped into obscurity.

"We talked about this (the Inchon-landing proposal) at the White House," Jackson said later. "What it always came down to was the question of whether the Chinese or the Russians would come in. This is the way those arguments would always end up. I was never convinced that they would come in. Of course, there was a big argument in the intelligence community, but the general agreement was that the Chinese would not come in. The Russians were not about to start World War III over this kind of situation."

After his return from Vietnam, Jackson was somber about the outlook and his public comments reflected his feelings. In Seattle, he called for a doubling of the American troops in Vietnam, from 200,000 to 400,000. "The sooner we get on with this business," he said, "the sooner the major part of this conflict will be over and the sooner we will begin saving lives."

Throughout the crucial year of 1966 there was an almost plaintive repetitiveness to Jackson's public statements. He compared Vietnam to Czechoslovakia in the 1930s—*Czechoslovakia went down the drain and we had World War II.* He warned the people to have patience—*The main question still is the one asked by Winston Churchill: Are the American people willing to stay the course?* He praised President Johnson—*I think the President has followed the right course despite the doubting Thomases.* He called for more troops, more bombing, a limited call-up of the reserves, and de-mothballing of part of the Navy fleet.

By this time Lyndon Johnson was getting into deep political trouble. His critics were coloring him *black*, labeling him *superhawk*. But, in actuality, he was a flustered man, making war policy by compromise, with events cascading down on him. In the Senate, the Fulbrights and

Morses and Gruenings were bombarding him with doubts about not only the efficacy of his policy but also the morality of what he was doing. More privately, the Jacksons and the Russells and the Stennises were pushing him to do more of it and get it over faster. Throughout the land, the rumble of discontent and disillusionment was growing and Lyndon Johnson, the consensus politician, tried to steer a middle course. *Let us reason together . . . . But*, replied the street people and growing numbers of others, *war is not reasonable.*

"The basic mistake that was made was in trying to find an in-between position which could only lead to an in-between outcome," the Cold War liberal, Henry Jackson, would say later. "There are certain things in life, when you're involved in the decision-making process, that you can't settle by compromise. The compromise here meant a protracted conflict. I couldn't get this out of my head at the time. I could never buy it. I was trying to relate it to what I thought, as a politician, the public would stand."

What the public would stand was being rapidly surpassed in 1966 and 1967. American involvement in the Second World War had begun and ended in less than four years—the time that transpires between Presidential elections. American involvement in Vietnam already had run almost through two Presidential terms and, eventually, it would run through at least one more.

As the public's disillusionment grew, the little darts of criticism that Jackson had felt throughout his long career became arrows. In some ways the issue of Vietnam isolated Jackson as he never had been isolated before. Those who disagreed with him—some of the leading war critics

44

—were old friends. Robert Kennedy, his buddy from the McCarthy days, the man who had fought to get him the Vice-Presidential nomination in 1960, now was soul-searching in public about the morality and the wisdom of the war. William Fulbright, one of the few colleagues whom Jackson entertained socially during his first years in the Senate, was a bitter critic. In the Pacific Northwest Jackson was surrounded by doves—Morse and Hatfield in Oregon, Church in Idaho, Gruening in Alaska. Even his old comrade-in-political-arms, Warren Magnuson, was beginning to question what was becoming a quagmire in Vietnam. A young Seattle congressman whom Jackson had helped elect in 1964, Brock Adams, was one of the first, articulate war critics in the House. They all asked a basic question: Is it worth it? Are all the maimed, mauled, scarred, napalmed, bloodied, broken bodies worth it? The stark contrast between those men and Jackson, the un-emotional Cold Warrior who had concluded that it was time to make a stand, was dramatic, painful, and often unfair.

Those who stand closest to power often are the most tolerant of a person's right to disagree—even on the most basic issues. Jackson, for example, might lambaste Wayne Morse during Vietnam debate in the Senate, but in 1968 he went into Oregon to try to help Morse save his threatened Senate seat. And the relationship between Jackson and Kennedy might seem antagonistic in a public forum, but privately they remained friends. "How's my old reactionary friend," Kennedy would greet Jackson—with heavy irony, for, back in the Joe McCarthy days, the liberals viewed *Bob Kennedy* as the reactionary.

Relations between Robert Kennedy and President Johnson, never good, were deteriorating badly by March 1967.

They did not improve as a squad of Kennedy's aides spread the word around Washington that he was preparing to make a major Senate speech calling on L.B.J. to halt the bombing of North Vietnam.

An hour before Kennedy's speech Henry Jackson received a telephone call from Lyndon Johnson. He was sending over a letter explaining his position on the bombing, the President told the senator. Jackson could make whatever use of it that he saw fit. In the code language of official Washington there was no doubt as to what the President had in mind. The letter arrived, hand-delivered by a White House courier, minutes before Robert Kennedy began his speech.

Kennedy's speech was an impassioned one, watched from the press galleries by scores of reporters sensing the inherent drama in a showdown between John Kennedy's brother and John Kennedy's Vice-President. As Kennedy spoke, aides to Jackson, their arms laden with xeroxed copies of Lyndon Johnson's letter, bustled onto the little subway car connecting the Old Senate Office Building with the Senate. Before Robert Kennedy was finished, the aides had distributed the President's reply in the Senate press gallery. And, when Kennedy sat down, Henry Jackson rose on the floor of the Senate to offer Lyndon Johnson's rebuttal. The odd twist of fate and, in a way, the sadness was obvious to the most casual Jackson observer.

"There are some who still speculate that if Bobby had had his way on that fateful day in 1960, Scoop Jackson, not L.B.J., would be sitting in the White House today," a reporter for the Seattle *Times* observed the next day.

But now, these many years later, there was Jackson, rising on the Senate floor as L.B.J.'s anointed defender in the latest round of Mr. Johnson's dispute with the brother of his martyred predecessor.

The reporter, however, would have been mistaken if he had read anything personal into that incident. Three days later Robert Kennedy invited his old friend, Scoop Jackson, up to New York to speak at a $500-a-plate Kennedy fund-raising dinner. "I'm neither a hawk nor a dove," Jackson said in liberal New York. "I'm just interested in seeing that we don't become a pigeon out there."

If those closest to power were tolerant of the differences among themselves, however, the public was becoming less so. Jackson, throughout his career, had taken more darts than most politicians. But they had come from the political fringes, Left and Right—from the extremists. As patience wore thin on Vietnam, the darts *did* turn to arrows and they started to come from some discomforting directions.

In three decades on the public stage, Jackson has had an unusually easy relationship with the press—particularly in his own state. He was a liberal, so he stood well philosophically with the working reporters; but he also understood and was sympathetic to the problems of business and management, so he had the ear of the publishers. The press corps in Jackson's home state, if anything, has been scrupulously and unselectively kind to the powerful Democratic senator. But Vietnam changed many things in American life and, to some degree, it changed that, too.

Occasionally, Jackson almost seemed to offer himself as a target for the arrows. Once, during a torrid Senate debate over Vietnam in 1966, Jackson warned that Hanoi might misinterpret the heated arguments and added that "foes, in particular, have never understood the meaning of loyal opposition." It was a highly dubious proposition, an implication that the Senate should change a tradition of open debate because a far-off enemy might not understand. The press, both in and outside Washington State, pinned his ears back.

In late 1966 Jackson made his fourth and last trip to Vietnam and was aboard the U.S.S. Manley when the ship was struck by North Vietnamese artillery. For a politician in a war zone, there is nothing more fortuitous than to find yourself accidentally—and safely—caught in the middle of the action. But Jackson's reception when he returned to Seattle was not all that he might have expected. He was greeted by, among other things, a bitter-comic column by Ed Donahoe, the acid-tongued iconoclast who edits the Pacific Northwest's most prominent labor newspaper, the Washington *Teamster*.

I'm still not sure whether Senator Hotspur, who votes like LaFollette and thinks like Cromwell, was actually hit and more important, where? God only knows what is going to happen to that Gook Cong artilleryman when word gets out that he almost winged a live United States Senator who got closer to the rumble of gunfire than the occasional newsreel film at the Bijou. And when Henry Martin Jackson pays another self-serving visit to Vietnam, them gooks will get back a little of their own iron, so help me Mendel Rivers. . . .

For better ways to heat up World War III, look for Super Senator Jackson to fire the first volley—with his gatling mouth.

One has to understand Ed Donohoe's very special role in Pacific Northwest journalism to put his column in proper perspective. His *forte* is to stick needles into sacred cows—and no politician was more sacred than Jackson, both to Donohoe's labor bosses and to the working stiffs, too. That, of course, made it all the more painful.

But if Jackson really needed proof that the times were changing, it came a few months later. In August 1967 the Everett *Herald*, the gray, conservative daily that Scoop Jackson had peddled in his home town almost a half-century earlier, gently chided Everett's favorite son about the agony in Vietnam.

"Senator Jackson is usually well-tuned to public sentiment and therefore must be aware that a significant change is taking place," the *Herald* wrote. "Many people, if not the majority, now feel that the Vietnam effort has become senseless, is a stalemate, and must be halted or abandoned."

In 1967 Jackson was midway between Senate elections. Still, being a total politician by nature, he regularly made the cross-country flights back home to his Washington State constituency. It did not take the most sensitive political antennae—and Jackson's were sensitive—to perceive what his hometown newspaper was talking about. There was a cumulative effect to a decade of televised, seemingly pointless war. Slowly, it had even radicalized unpretentious housewives in the affluent suburbs that sprawl in the hills around Seattle, and it had polarized the students on the same University of Washington campus that had produced the lawyer/politician, Henry Jackson, more than three decades earlier. It rubbed nerves raw on the docks along Puget Sound and dropped sparks in the tinder box of Seattle's small, but volatile ghetto. Some businessmen even were beginning to question what the war might do to Seattle's fragile economy. It was an economy that had skyrocketed in booms and nose-dived in busts ever since the Great Alaska Gold Rush at the turn of the century. In

1967 it was an economy that was thriving on the sale of commercial jet-liners to the world's air lines and lumber to the nation's home-builders. Nothing would gut both markets more than tight money and high interest rates—and the war was beginning to produce both. Some would speculate that Seattle's huge Boeing aerospace plants would prosper in a war economy. But the opposite was true. Boeing made no Vietnam weapons in Seattle.

The tiny political faction of antiwar activists that always had harassed Jackson was becoming embittered, emboldened, and enlarged. Jackson would land at Seattle-Tacoma Airport and the photographers would capture him—broad and smiling face, arm waving, a new father, diaper bag slung over his shoulder, the perfect political picture of a senator/father. But often, they would capture more than Washington State's smiling white-knight senator: In the background in the airport lobby would be the placards, *Defoliate Jackson*, and the unsmiling faces of those who saw their senator as anything but a white knight.

Late in the year, with the national bitterness boiling just beneath the surface, Jackson made an almost plaintive plea for understanding in one of his regular Vietnam speeches on the Senate floor.

"The war in Vietnam cannot be brought to an end by attacking each other here at home, but it can be lost, rather, it will be lost, if we destroy our confidence in each other," Jackson said.

"We are in for serious trouble indeed if our tempers become frayed and our understandable unhappiness with a long and difficult and costly war leads us to impugn one another's motives and to make charges that, if true, could only mean that our leaders do not merit our confidence as men of integrity and dedication to the national interest.

"We are facing a most serious test of our national character and democratic processes—a debate over our policies and purposes in the midst of a war and a national election campaign. We are, or ought to be, engaged in reasoning together, not in cutting each other up."

Years later George Ball, the senior dove in the Johnson White House and a man whose views were almost diametrically opposed to Jackson's, would argue much the same thing—that there were no devils among the Vietnam policy-makers. The policy-makers had seen Vietnam as a pawn in the Cold War, as a war to be fought to avoid a larger war. Henry Jackson had argued that the bombing was necessary to *save* lives. Dean Rusk had argued—and believed to the end—that American policy *was* saving lives. "The overriding moral question," Johnson's Secretary of State would say after his career was in near-ruin, "is how to avoid World War III." But, to growing numbers of Americans by 1967, that kind of old Cold War logic was becoming a classic example of situation ethics—a warped justification of the methodical mauling of a tiny nation of peasant-innocents. Hawks and doves alike overdrew their cases and created caricatures of each other as the nation prepared, unknowingly, for an emotional and physical blood-letting.

Cold War necessity or immoral disaster, the public could take its choice. But, in either case, the war in Vietnam was becoming an American tragedy. The coming year, 1968, would be one of the saddest and most traumatic in the proud history of a proud nation—a year in which all the agony of the muck-jungles of Southeast Asia would come home and spill over into the streets of America.

CHAPTER 3

THE AGONY COMES HOME

IT WAS THE time of Gene McCarthy, a new McCarthy, and snow hugged the hills and hollows of New Hampshire, hiding Yankee warts, painting the countryside serene. White clapboards formed box churches, bleak calvinistic shrines with sword-point spires pointing the way toward salvation, and a God who was, by most current accounts, either dead or hiding out in Argentina. It was going to be a bad year.

A half-revolution of the world away, in the tortured forests and blood-polluted paddies of Vietnam, it was the time of Tet, a religious holiday during which the gods who look over that part of the globe appeared to be hiding out, too. Or fuzzed off, crapped out, dead, the soul gone, sucked out the way a lizard cleans a cockroach and leaves the shell there. It was going to be a very bad year.

In Washington, Robert Kennedy was agonizing over the war and pondering the Presidency. Martin Luther King wanted the fighting to end, even while he was struggling to control a nonviolent movement that almost inevitably had to go violent. But the bad year, 1968, would stop both of them, brutally and harshly.

In the White House Lyndon Johnson was having nightmares. The big commercial airplanes would roar down over his house at night and the President would be startled half-awake, under attack. Lyndon Johnson, strange, complex man, also was agonizing, although he would get less credit for his agony. The year would stop him, too.

It is unwise to slide too easily into the quick fashions of the day—the talk about a sick society, for example. But 1968 would be enough to convince anyone that the world was teetering on the brink of a nervous breakdown, the country edging into national neurosis.

How else to explain the temporary insanity of the cops in Chicago? How else to explain the paranoia of white suburbanites arming themselves for the black revolution? How else to explain the mass madness of the black rioters? The psychoses of the looters, the stoners, the snipers? The neuroses of the night-stick wavers, the tear-gas launchers, the FBI men with their insidious, invidious cameras? The obscene hecklers? The assassins? The kids opting for the cop-out world of Mary Jane? Priest challenging Pope, student challenging teacher, child challenging parent, everybody challenging the fuzz?

What in heaven, or hell, was going on?

"I knew of no precedent for anything like this, other than the Great Depression, when we had riots—but for food, for bread," said Henry Jackson, a man who held tight reins on his emotions.

The thing that troubled me the most was my own inadequacy in trying to get reasons for these things. You could talk to a friend and he would say this is because of so and so and then you talk to someone else and he'd say it was something else.

I must say that I really felt, for the first time, an inability to truly comprehend the nature of the trouble. Very honestly. One could understand it if there were a lot of unemployment and other things going on to justify this kind of human response. I had a general feeling of frustration—as a politician. For really the first time in my political career, I didn't even have *some* kind of an answer. I just felt honestly lost in trying to explain to those who would ask me about it. And I couldn't explain it to myself. Whenever I tried to come up with an answer, why I soon found it was no answer at all . . . .

For the most part, through the long, awful year of 1968, Henry M. Jackson would preserve the rigid shield of self-control that he had set up for himself decades earlier. But, once or twice, at moments of great national and personal agony, the shield would crack and the public, if it cared to, could obtain a brief look inside at raging emotions. The crack would be short, and quickly patched, but it showed that the torture also was there in the methodical, rational senator from Washington.

The Tet offensive began in late January. The elite troops from the North and the battle-hardened insurgents from the South came out of their jungle refuges and into the cities—into Hue and Pleiku and Bien Hoa and Can Tho and even into the heart of Saigon itself. The televideo image of the war changed abruptly—from elephant-grass skirmishes with an elusive enemy to World War II-style, house-to-house street combat. The enemy pushed into the heart of South Vietnam's secure zones and suddenly there seemed to be no secure zones at all.

Tan Canh is a little village in the Central Highlands of South Vietnam. Two years before Tet, 1968, it had been just another quiet village on the twisting, dirt road to Laos.

54

But in the great American military buildup, the 4th Infantry Division of the United States Army built a combat post on the outskirts of Tan Canh, and the village changed. Tan Canh girls went the route that girls go in war. The boys became beggars. The young men left to fight with the V.C. The old men stayed home to wash clothes—G.I. khakis. During Tet, Tan Canh was left smoldering in ruins. The girls and the beggars and the laundryman-fathers went out of business. The village was on the periphery of a major American military base, but it was beyond protection, beyond help. The V.C., the sons of Tan Canh, came in one night and exorcised the guilt of the parents and the sisters and the little brothers by razing their village.

Within thirty days the insurgents had pulled back into their jungle refuges, but the war never would be the same again. In Washington a few Pentagon diehards argued that the Tet offensive had been a failure, that, in fact, the allies had decimated the enemy's best troops. General Westmoreland, the American commander, asked for another 206,000 troops—which would have pushed the total to more than 700,000—to go now for the jugular. But this was a political war and political Washington, hawks and doves alike, shuddered at Westmoreland's suggestion.

On March 13, in the wake of Tet, Senator Jackson told the press that the Johnson Administration was at a crossroads on Vietnam and was conducting what he called an A to Z study of the war policy. He declined to say which way the study was leaning—toward further escalation or toward deescalation. But, behind the scenes, the Johnson government was moving toward an inevitable decision to finally turn down the war.

The powerful members of the Senate Armed Services

Committee—Russell and Stennis and Jackson and Mrs. Smith—were called in for conferences with the President and his new Defense Secretary, Clark Clifford. Unanimously, they had supported all the troop buildups of the past three years—and usually had asked for more. Now they were given the military alternatives once again another massive troop increase, possibly an invasion of North Vietnam. One by one, the senators turned their thumbs down. Their patience, like the patience of the American public, had expired. Jackson confided to friends that the United States was hopelessly bogged down and more troops would only deepen the mire.

Still, while momentous decisions were being made at the White House, the nation was sliding into the quadrennial emotional binge of a Presidential election. Johnson may have been turning quietly dovish in Washington, but he was being painted as anything but that in the wintry-white hamlets of New Hampshire. There, Richard Nixon was running for the Presidency and promising that he had a plan to end the war. Eugene McCarthy, the senator-poet from Minnesota, also was there, directly challenging Lyndon Johnson on the war. McCarthy was neither kind nor did he believe in leaving personalities out of his crusade. The difference between Johnson and Nixon, he said, was the difference between vulgarity and obscenity. Already, it was becoming *that* kind of year.

Jackson, as is his nature, spurned the rising tide of emotionalism. In a speech on the eve of the New Hampshire voting, he hinted that it was time to begin peace negotiations, but then he attacked the new political rhetoric of 1968. Some politicians were "engaged in constructive criticism" of the war, he said, but others "are engaged in nothing less than slander of the United States."

"Nervous prostration is not a policy, nor are bald-faced political appeals unsubstantiated by the remotest hint of a plan."

When the returns came in from New Hampshire, Richard Nixon had won the Republican primary, as expected, and Lyndon Johnson had won the Democratic primary—but not exactly as expected. The seemingly Quixotic venture of Gene McCarthy had given him forty-two percent of the Democratic vote. Johnson received forty-nine percent, but the result still was a stern repudiation of a sitting American President. Briefly, in Establishment circles, the meaning of the outcome was debated because, after all, Lyndon Johnson *had* won the primary. But the debate was half-hearted. Like the Tet offensive, the result may not have been totally conclusive, but it was the final political straw for Lyndon Johnson.

Four days later, on March 16, Senator Robert F. Kennedy pushed his way through a mob of reporters, bystanders, and "Kennedyphiles" and entered the huge vault of the Caucus Room in the Old Senate Office Building. As a young man, Kennedy had hovered behind the senators, whispering questions to Henry Jackson during the showdown of the Army-McCarthy hearings. Then, in 1960, Bob Kennedy's brother, John, had entered the same room and declared that he would seek the Presidency of the United States. On this day, in March 1968, Bob Kennedy announced that he, too, would seek the Presidency, challenging Lyndon Johnson for the Democratic nomination.

The next day Scoop Jackson was asked how he viewed the candidacy of his old friend.

"My support for President Johnson has been announced previously and is reaffirmed," Jackson said. "At another time and under other circumstances I could have supported

Senator Kennedy, but in this period of great danger to our country we must stand with the President."

The relationship between Jackson and Johnson went back to the early 1940s, when both were young members of the House. But it never had been close. They were too much unlike—Johnson an effusive, volatile Texan and Jackson a subdued, almost shy Northwesterner. At times, when both were in the Senate in the 1950s, Johnson would call late in the day and invite Jackson over to the Majority Leader's office for bourbon, branch water, and good Texas man-talk. Jackson, never one of the boys, almost invariably begged off.

But, with Vietnam moving crushingly in on Lyndon Johnson during his days in the White House, the calls to Scoop Jackson were made more often. *Scoop, get on down here. There's something I want to talk to you about.* At the White House, the senator and the President would go into a tiny annex off the Oval Room. No bourbon-and-branch-water now, but the President had a passion for diet soda. They would sit in the little annex and it would be Fresca after Fresca after Fresca and interminable talk about the dilemma in Vietnam.

The personalities may have been different, but now there was a grim mutuality of interest between the two—both liberal/populist/federalists and both under sharp attack for a war which they didn't like but they believed in. On campuses, they were anathema, seen as unfeeling men with mail fists. At the University of Washington, the students were buying Henry-Jackson-suffers-from-a-military-industrial-complex posters in the university bookstore.

One day in 1966 Jackson received an unusual telephone call. The President and Lady Bird, the drawling Texas voice said, would like to come over for dinner. The call began a series of quiet, completely private and unpublicized dinners for the President and his wife at the Jacksons' home in the gracious Spring Valley section of Washington. There was a pattern to the dinners: never more than ten guests, the seating capacity of the Jacksons' dining room; a calculated mix of Jackson friends and prominent news personalities, some of them selected by the President; and a guest of honor who was consumed by a single subject—Vietnam.

The Secret Service would come before each dinner and Helen Jackson recalls that, before the first party, she was artfully compelled to make a long-overdue purchase—blinds for the kitchen windows, which she hurriedly bought at a dimestore.

There was a pattern to the Presidential performances at the dinner parties, too. He was a commanding man, who dominated the conversation. But he was moody, and his moods seemed to change with the tide of the war. In 1966, at the first party, he was defensive and one guest recalls that he seemed to have documentary proof of his views stuffed into every pocket. A *New York Times* editorial was pulled out to make a point to Chet Huntley, a Senate vote count was flourished to prove something to Edward P. Morgan. By 1967 Johnson was aggressive, antagonistic toward the press, and he lashed out at Martin Agronsky, the C.B.S. newsman. By mid-1968, when Lyndon and Lady Bird Johnson came over to the Jacksons' for the last time, the President seemed at ease, relaxed, laughing—the burden lifted.

At one of those dinners, after the men had pulled off alone into the Jacksons' tidy little library, the talk turned to the 1960 Democratic convention when Johnson had been chosen as John Kennedy's Vice-President. "Hell, Scoop," the President said, leaning his huge frame against the fireplace mantle, "they didn't want me. They wanted you. It was the old man who wanted me." Jackson, who had been Bob Kennedy's favorite for the Vice-Presidential nomination, shrugged, grinned, and said nothing. Old Joe Kennedy, the patriarch of the Kennedy clan, was a realist. So was Scoop Jackson, who realized that Johnson, with his strength in the South, improved the 1960 ticket far more than would a senator from the politically impotent Pacific Northwest. Jackson would say later that, *well, the fact is, if I'd been chosen, maybe John Kennedy wouldn't have become President and Lyndon Johnson wouldn't have become President and Scoop Jackson wouldn't have become President. Maybe we'd have Richard Nixon as President.*

On March 31, 1968, the President of the United States made another of his periodic television addresses to the nation. The subject, as usual, was Vietnam, but this was not a usual speech. The President was ordering a partial halt to the bombing of the North. He was asking the North Vietnamese and the indigenous rebels, the Viet Cong, to come to the negotiating table.

Still, in the despair and disbelief of 1968, more was required. Lyndon Johnson, in an appendix to his speech, announced that he would not run for re-election, that as a mark of his sincerity he was withdrawing from the White House.

It was a thunderclap that stunned the nation—surely not the first stunning event of 1968, but sadly not the last.

Jackson watched the President's performance on the monitor in a downtown Washington television studio. Like the nation, he was startled. But he could understand the decision, the pressures that led to it. Several hours after the speech, back at his Spring Valley home at about midnight, Jackson's phone rang and it was Jim Whittaker calling from Los Angeles. Whittaker was a Seattle man, a mountain-climber, the first American to reach the summit of Mount Everest. He was an old Kennedy friend, having led Bobby to the top of the isolated, unclimbed Canadian peak which had been named Mount Kennedy after the assassination of his brother.

Whittaker's question was simple and direct: Now that Lyndon Johnson had withdrawn, and Scoop Jackson's commitment to him was void, could he see his way clear to supporting Bob Kennedy? Jackson replied that he would wait and see.

The next day, with reporters hounding everyone on Capitol Hill for a reaction to Lyndon Johnson's spectacular announcement, Jackson responded that "the Vietnam war laid heavily on his mind; he was determined to do what he thought was right, regardless of political consequences." The day after that Jackson said that "in all likelihood" Bob Kennedy would be nominated by the Democratic party in August. To a whole generation, who viewed Scoop Jackson and Bob Kennedy only in terms of the war in Vietnam, Jackson's comment was astounding.

Three days later, on April 3, another Jackson was invited to the White House on a purely social matter: Young Peter Jackson, the senator's son, was celebrating his second birthday. The President was in rollicking good spirits and he got down on the floor of his Oval Room office and played with Peter, five-year-old Anna Marie Jackson, and the Johnsons' grandson, eight-month-old Patrick Lyndon Nugent. After about ten minutes of the tightly scheduled fifteen-minute break in the Presidential day, a teletype clattered in one corner of the Oval Room. The President stood up, lumbered toward the machine and read the message—Hanoi's carefully worded acceptance of Johnson's offer to go to the peace table. Solemnly, Johnson tore the message off the machine and handed it to Jackson. Neither the President nor the senator said a word.

Later, Jackson told the press that there was reason for "cautious optimism" about Hanoi's response. But he quickly warned that "this is the year in which one makes predictions only with the greatest potential hazard. Monday was April Fool's Day and this is only Wednesday."

On Thursday, on a walkway outside a second-floor motel room in Memphis, a rifle bullet crashed into the jaw of Martin Luther King. On Friday the smoke from Washington's burning black ghettos billowed over the Capitol Dome and turned the sky brown over the White House.

Henry Jackson flew to Atlanta for the funeral of Dr. King. There were few, if any, men in the Congress whose voting records were any better on civil rights. But Jackson had been a follower, not a leader, in the great civil-rights battles of the fifties and the sixties. And, as the movement radicalized in the late sixties, Jackson became increasingly uncomfortable.

With blacks rioting in a dozen major cities after the assassination, Jackson sternly warned that grief over the tragedy "exempted no man from the responsibility for his own acts." And he took a back-handed slap at the press for giving too much attention to the more militant black spokesmen. "There is something out of whack when a hoodlum can call a press conference to spout hate into every living room in America. I propose that we no longer give to these extremists the attention they do not deserve."

It is typical of Jackson, however, that once the passions had died down he made one of the strongest civil-rights speeches of his career—and to a most unlikely audience. Just as once he had preached Medicare to the arch-conservative doctors in his state, now he preached civil rights to his state's businessmen. "We have started down a road," he said in a speech to the Association of Washington Industries two weeks after King's death. "There is no turning back. There is no stopping short of full membership in American society for all Americans." There were no ringing phrases, no flamboyant rhetoric—just a pointed challenge to the businessmen to get off their butts and do something about jobs for blacks.

Bob Kennedy's Presidential campaign was having problems. It was a strange campaign, but then this was a strange year. The bulk of the Democratic political establishment steered clear of him, despite the family aura, and waited for this new prince of the Kennedy legend to prove himself. The activist kids and the most strident of the antiwar people accused him of opportunism and stayed with their poet-soldier hero, Gene McCarthy. Bobby went into the streets, the awful, tense streets of 1968, for his political sustenance and, to some degree, he found it there. America's ghetto-dwellers—the blacks, the Chicanos, the hungry, the deprived—reached out for him, pulled at him, this new Boston Brahmin who spoke their language with an Ivy League accent.

But, in 1968, success in the streets did not translate easily into success at the polls. Late in May, Kennedy was defeated by McCarthy in the Presidential primary in Oregon. It was the first political defeat for anyone in the star-struck

Kennedy family in a string of thirty elections. Bob Kennedy gamely acknowledged that his quest for the White House would be over if he didn't bounce back with a victory in California the next week.

On June 4, after a bone-punishing political blitz, Kennedy won California by a razor-thin margin and his hopes climbed again. At a victory celebration in Los Angeles' Ambassador Hotel he flashed the victory sign and his infectious rabbit-grin. A continent away, in Washington, Scoop Jackson pondered the results and concluded that Kennedy's chances now depended on the decisions of the big-city Democrats—men like Richard Daley of Chicago.

Shortly after four o'clock, Washington time, on the morning after the California primary, a United Press International reporter dialed Henry Jackson's unlisted home telephone number. The insistent ringing jolted Jackson out of a sound sleep and, momentarily, there was a dream-like, nightmare-like quality to the conversation. Bob Kennedy, the disembodied voice of the reporter said, had been shot while leaving his California victory celebration. Jackson, numbed and in a dream-reality limbo, groped with the meaning of the words. "Oh my God," he finally sobbed, "the world has gone mad . . . . "

. . . It was a hot summer night in 1964 and the vast hall in Atlantic City was jammed for the last session of the Democratic National Convention, when the party would pay an emotional tribute to the martyred President, John F. Kennedy.

Scoop Jackson, the stolid Nordic man who had been chosen by the Kennedy family to perform this task, stood at the lectern and droned on. . . . *join now in this memo-rial tribute to a man we loved . . . a spirited man . . . a rational man . . . a compassionate man . . . .*

The great convention hall buzzed, as all convention halls seem to buzz, as Jackson went on. The crowd was there, as Jackson easily understood, waiting for the man he would introduce—the brother, Bobby, who sat on the back steps of the stage, hunched out of view, head in his hands, dreading what was ahead.

After a moment, Jackson stopped and made the introduction. As Bob Kennedy came up off the back steps, the emotion thundered through the hall in an overwhelming wave of sound. There were no balloons, no confetti, none of the artificial pizzaz that goes with political conventions —just a thunderous, cascading roar.

Kennedy had tears in his eyes and his head was cocked to one side, oddly, like the head of a puppet. He looked frail, although he hardly was that, and the sound seemed to buffet him physically. A minute went by and he wanted it to stop. "Mister chairman," he rasped, plaintively, into the microphone. Jackson, standing at his side, counseled, "Let it go, Bob. Let it go."

Seven times Kennedy tried to interrupt the roar, but it reverberated, in waves, for thirteen minutes. Then, finally, it died away to silence—an eerie kind of total silence. Kennedy spoke just briefly and introduced a film tribute to his brother—an alive, vibrant film of lilting Cape Cod scenes and fatherly romps with the children. Midway through the showing, Bob Kennedy turned his eyes away from the screen. In the convention hall, a woman knelt and prayed in the aisle and only the sniffling broke the silence.

When it was over, Bobby left quickly and Jackson came

65

back to the lectern. "There is nothing to add," he said. "We have our memory. We shall cherish it. Now it is time for the living to go on . . . . "

Jackson had been deeply troubled when his friend, Bob Kennedy, began the reach for the Presidency. The emotionalism of it bothered him, as emotionalism always did. The year was so tumultuous, with passions boiling in the streets, that Jackson, with only an occasional lapse, steeled himself even more strongly against giving way to his personal feelings. It was the kind of year in which Jackson believed the wise statesman-politician would act as a buffer against the passions, struggling to pull the nation back toward rationality. But Bob Kennedy seemed to be riding the waves, floating with them, using them for propulsion.

At first Kennedy sent some of his speeches over to Jackson and Jackson scrawled comments and suggestions on them before sending them back. But that ended after two or three efforts. Bob Kennedy was on his way down a very special road and Jackson couldn't travel it.

Still, to the end he *wanted* to be able to go with Bob Kennedy. Jackson had no use for Gene McCarthy's caustic, acidic anti-Establishmentarianism and, while he liked and respected Hubert Humphrey, there was no personal tie or real political mutuality there. It was Bobby that Jackson watched. "I hoped that after California was out of the way he would have moderated his position," he said later. "This is what I was hoping for, frankly. I understood his political problem. He was trying to stave off Gene McCarthy. McCarthy had won in Oregon. He was fighting McCarthy and all my sympathies were with Bobby in the California fight. My friends were supporting him out there. Maybe it was wishful thinking. Only time could have answered that question, that he would have moderated his position so that I could have supported him."

After Kennedy died—and after that brief emotional lapse on the telephone—Jackson pulled the barriers back around him.

In the wake of two political assassinations within two months, Congress was deluged with a wave of gun-control proposals. But even though his second Kennedy friend had just been felled by a gun, Jackson opposed all but the most modified anti-firearms plans. "I think there is danger in the emotion of the moment to assume that by simple legislation you can resolve what is indeed a highly complicated problem," Jackson said. Jackson's home state is a state of hunters and outdoorsmen, but, even so, he was heavily criticized by some who argued that gun controls *at least* were a start toward curbing American violence.

Time and again, Jackson had the sick-society theory put to him and he rejected it. "I do not agree with those who choose to characterize our age as the era of violence or our nation as a sick society," he said. "I reject this view and believe that it will be rejected by historians. I believe instead that history will record our era as one in which unprecedented opportunity and prosperity were achieved and, hopefully, extended as never before to the entire population. We are dismayed—rightfully so—that these ends are not being achieved without the terrible and tragic cost of recent years—violence, political assassination, civil disorder, student revolt, militancy, racism, social protest, and cynicism toward traditional values."

But those did not seem to be marketable views in 1968 and as the year progressed Jackson became almost isolated, lost in the swirl of crazy, convoluted events. Occasionally, he would surface but always on some issue that ran against the great emotional tide of 1968. He would emerge and *defend* the American conduct of the war, emerge and *defend* Lyndon Johnson, emerge and *defend* the antiballistic-missile system.

Just days after Bob Kennedy's funeral . . . *now it is time for the living to go on* . . . . Jackson was on the Senate floor, leading Lyndon Johnson's battle to build the highly controversial ABM. It was a year for spurning weapons, the emotions cried, and turning attention to the national soul. The liberals skewered Jackson and some called him a war-monger.

"I have a liberal voting record in the Senate," Jackson replied almost plaintively in a Senate speech on the day of the ABM vote. "My personal record of sponsorship and support of liberal and humanitarian causes—in both the House and the Senate—rates second to that of no other senator. And there is a humanitarian aspect contained in the pending legislation. We are talking about saving twenty million to thirty million American lives. Is not that something worth considering, when we are talking about the life and death of the Western world?"

But, if the swirl of national attention was moving around other senators talking about other issues in 1968, Jackson was having a quietly productive year in some areas. As chairman of the Senate Interior Committee, he was moving landmark legislation covering what would become one of the commanding issues of the 1970s—the environment. Over the heated opposition of Western lumber interests, Jackson worked out the careful compromises that led to approval of two major new national parks—the Redwoods in California and the North Cascades in his own state. Perhaps even more significant was a Jackson victory over the oil interests. He bulled through legislation that tapped

68

federal revenues from offshore oil and added the money—
$200 million a year—to the Land and Water Conservation
Fund for purchase of park and recreation lands.

In July, Jackson organized an environmental colloquium
on Capitol Hill and it was attended by half of Lyndon
Johnson's Cabinet as well as some of the nation's leading
environmental scientists. They talked about the degrada-
tion of the air and the land and the water, warned about
how little time was left to stop man's fouling of his own
nest. Out of that colloquium grew Jackson's idea for a
National Environmental Policy Act—a sweeping idea that,
when it was enacted into law less than eighteen months
later, forced the federal government to examine the environmental consequences of almost every one of its actions,
whether it was to build a supersonic transport or to carve a
barge canal. But the public's attention span was limited—
riveted on war, assassination, and the agony spilling into
American streets. The environment was not yet an issue
and the response to Jackson's colloquium told a lot about
the national mood in the awful year of 1968.

Not a single newspaper reporter attended and not a
single newspaper article was written.

Six days before the Democratic National Convention in
Chicago, Russia invaded Czechoslovakia and Jackson, in
Seattle, said this should show the world that Moscow cannot tolerate "even a little bit of freedom." He predicted
a stiffening of American public opinion against the Soviets
and, once again seeing Vietnam in a Cold War context, he
speculated that the Democrats now would "find it less
difficult" to write a tough war-policy plank into their platform in Chicago.

Henry Jackson rarely engages in wishful thinking. But

69

his forecast for Chicago turned out to be a pure flight of fancy.

Jackson did not go to Chicago. On the eve of the convention he received another middle-of-the-night telephone call—this one from Everett, Wash., informing him that his elder sister, Gertrude, had cancer and almost surely was dying. Jackson had been closer to no one in his life than he had been to this favorite spinster sister. He spent the week of Chicago in Seattle hospital rooms, catching only occasional glimpses of the new televideo war—the war in the streets of a tortured American city.

By the time of the convention the nation's mood was as black as her ghettos. The country peered nervously inward —at her core, Chicago—waiting for the neurosis to burst out of control. The events in the streets of Chicago may not have been rational, typical or readily understandable. But they were significant for, as much as the Vietnam war itself, they appeared to radicalize a generation of Americans. It was, in many ways, the climactic emotional binge in a year of raging emotions.

There were no heroes in the streets—surely not among the street-army antagonists of the Establishment and just as surely not among the baby-blue-helmeted guardians of Establishment morality. The cops were baited, insulted, tormented, provoked, taunted with obscenities, and pushed to the very brink of their rationality. But they went over the brink. Then there was a cop clubbing a girl—sister, daughter, scruffy little long-haired hippie girl—and a cop belting a priest and squads of Chicago's Finest lashing out at the long hairs and all they seemed to represent. The derelicts and the drunks came out of the bars along Chicago's side streets and applauded, cheering on the cops as if they were the home team. But perhaps they were, for most of the nation was applauding, too.

Strange, bleak year. The sons of Tan Canh had exorcised the guilt of their kin and now the Chicago cops were doing the same thing.

The election campaign and the hum-dum-a-dum beat of the sloganeering that followed seemed a hollow anticlimax to everything that had happened earlier. The country was worn out, bored with its leaders. *Time for a change!* But with Nixon? *Stop the war!* But with Humphrey? *State's rights!* But with Wallace?

At the beginning of the decade of the sixties, if someone had tried to peer into the future and had assumed a certain amount of orderliness in American affairs, that person easily might have concluded that 1968 would be Scoop Jackson's year. As the decade began, Jackson was catapulted onto the national stage by his near-miss of the Vice-Presidential nomination. The same sort of near-miss in 1956 had served to thrust John Kennedy forward. On stage, Jackson was welcomed as likable, honest, clean-cut, and all-American. Because of Jackson's virtues—his unquestioned integrity, his native caution, and his almost total lack of vices—it would have been predictable that the senator from Washington would not stub his political toe. Jackson's power would grow, through seniority and knowledge, in the Senate. Presumably, he would carve out spheres of interest and influence that would enhance his position on the national stage. He would speak out on the issues. By 1968, John Kennedy would have served two terms as President and the Democrats would be shopping around for a new standard-bearer. Henry Jackson would be fifty-six years old, an almost ideal Presidential age, and he would be a seasoned, experienced political leader.

Indeed, as the 1960 convention closed in Los Angeles, and Jackson graciously accepted his Vice-Presidential setback, one California reporter wrote that he had "emerged as the most exciting figure in the Democratic Party, next to John F. Kennedy himself. He must, today, be rated as a real contender for the Presidential nomination in four years, should this year's ticket lose, or in eight years should Kennedy serve two terms."

But fate was not kind in the sixties—neither to Jackson nor to the country. Jackson did speak out, because he is an outspoken man. He did develop spheres of interest and power, because that is the way to get things done in the Senate and within the American political system. But Jackson's sphere was national defense and, by 1968, he had become almost the last of what had been a common breed at the beginning of the decade. He still was a Cold War liberal and it puzzled him that his critics didn't agree that the defense of the United States was the issue, the only real issue.

Had he come to the Senate and national prominence during the Depression, Jackson once said, he would have devoted his attention to social legislation. But he came to prominence during the Cold War and he reacted accordingly.

"It was clear to me that the Cold War was going to be the great challenge of my time," he said. "Just as the challenge in the thirties was the Depression, now the predominant issue was the survival of the Western world."

In 1968, when all the agony came home, Scoop Jackson was *not* the most exciting figure in the Democratic Party. For the first time since he had come to the Senate, sixteen years earlier, Jackson was not included in *any* of the speculation about the national Democratic ticket.

Yet Jackson still was what he always had been. . . .

72

4

THE SMELL OF SAWDUST

THIRTEEN-YEAR-OLD Henry Jackson's newspaper route began at the Everett *Daily Herald* office, then serpentined around several blocks of the mill town, moving always toward the waterfront.

His first delivery was at the J. C. Penney store, just across the street from the *Herald* office. Then came a succession of smaller stores and shops, like Jilg's Delicatessen. Many of the merchants greeted him by name: *Hello, Henry.* Some knew him by his nickname: *Hi, Scoop.* The Scandinavian merchants knew him, particularly, as Pete Jackson's boy. His route was a mixture of stores and houses. He tossed papers onto the porches of the little pinched-together, look-alike frame houses where the millworkers lived. And he delivered a paper to the stately big house owned by Joe Irving, one of the men who gained wealth in the early logging-boom days of Everett.

Inwardly, the boy admired his own, businesslike precision. From the canvas bag slung from his shoulder he pulled a newspaper, folded it swiftly into a tight roll—with a tuck at the bottom—and lobbed a perfect strike—*thup*—onto the porch. He liked having satisfied customers, so if there was a threat of rain and there was no cover for the porch, he tucked the paper against the doorknob. For

three years in a row he earned the *Herald* award as the
carrier boy with the fewest complaints: He had none. He
arranged that by asking customers to telephone him at
home if there was a complaint: Thus the newspaper office
never had a record of an unhappy subscriber on his route.

Sunlight fell onto the streets as a dull, red-orange glow,
filtered through a smoke haze. Thirty years earlier Everett's civic leaders had given a boastful name to their town
beside Puget Sound: "The City of Smokestacks." The
town deserved the title. Smoke and cinders rose steadily
from the burners of the mills along the waterfront and,
when there was an onshore breeze, the pall spread across
the town.

Rockefeller wealth was attracted here from the East in
the early days, because there were empire-builder dreams
that, with the railroad arriving, and with the availability of
mineral ores and abundant forests, the port settlement
would grow into an industrial center. The railroad came
to Everett but it also moved southward the twenty-eight
miles to Seattle, where the big population and business
boom occurred. Everett's hopes for a smelter died when
the ores in the mountains didn't prove out. But the forests
remained—they would be there forever, it seemed—and
Everett settled noisily into its role as a mill town. Slow-
growing, it was creeping toward a population of 30,000 in
the mid-twenties. No one objected to the smoke and the
smell of sawdust from the lumber and shingle mills along
the water: Those were the fragrances of Everett's economic well-being.

Scoop Jackson's paper route moved onto Hewitt Avenue, the town's main east-west street, which begins at the
Snohomish River to the east, rises through the business
district, then slopes downward again to the docks and

tracks at the saltwater bay. One of young Jackson's sub-
scribers on Hewitt was an upstairs whorehouse. When he
opened the door on the street it triggered a bell to alert the
madam. He loped up the wooden steps while the plump
woman in heavy makeup, her hair in a short bob, bustled
down a corridor, approaching him. She doubted it would
be a customer at this hour of the afternoon. She nodded and
smiled. He laid the evening *Herald* on the small registration desk near the head of the stairs, and quickly retreated
back down to the outside door. Once in a while he saw
some of the women who stayed there, or he could hear
their muffled talk and laughter from behind the closed
doors along the hallway, but he had no great curiosity.
Everett was a town with an easy understanding that the
longshoremen and loggers occasionally needed a few beers
and a woman.

Henry's route sloped downhill toward the waterfront
where the smell of sawdust grew heavier and the saws
whined in the Weyerhaeuser mill. He passed the vacant lot
below Nassau Street and glanced at the derelicts. They
were men in old working clothes. Some of their faces had
purplish blotches. Bleary-eyed, they huddled unsteadily
over the task of straining alcohol from canned heat. Filter-
ing it through a wool shirt yielded a drink, even if it was
barely sublethal.

When these men became drunk, they became desperately
drunk. One of them reeled into a monstrous stagger, a sidewalk wide. He thumped against the wall of a building and
leaned there, groaning. Henry walked at the edge of the
sidewalk to get around the man. These men were harmless,
except occasionally, in their blind reelings, they bumped
into passersby.

Young Jackson had a detached understanding of these

men with their distorted faces and their canned heat. But he felt a neck-prickling discomfort when he walked through the door into the warehouse on Grand Avenue. He delivered the newspaper there to the Smathers Transfer Company office. He was a non-talkative boy but he absorbed sights and sounds. He noticed the cases stacked along one wall of the warehouse and he noticed, too, that the men who sat in the office talking and laughing with the Smathers brothers were city policemen and deputy sheriffs. They paid no attention to him as he left a newspaper and departed. There were articles in the Seattle papers and conversation around town about the rumrunners who were moving bootleg liquor from Canada into Seattle. Henry's older sister, Gertrude, said she was sure that the police were mixed up in it, and some of it had to be coming through Everett.

Near the foot of Hewitt Avenue, the docks were in sight, the tugboats lodged in their berths. To the right a ship with the red-and-white flag of Japan lay beside the Oriental dock, taking on her cargo of Japanese squares—logs which had been sawed only enough to give them four flat faces.

Young Jackson dropped off a newspaper at Monroe's grocery store and the canvas bag was much lighter as he approached the railroad tracks above the docks. He entered the Bayview Hotel, walked across the lobby and pushed open some swinging doors. The first time he had entered the room he had been startled by the sights. The dominant fixture was the long mahogany bar. Along its length were some prominent townspeople, talking, laughing, and drinking. There were no signs outside, but it seemed that everyone knew how to find their way to the room. They had glasses of liquor *right out in the open*. . . .

. . . Right out in the open. Decades later Henry Jackson's brow rises as he says that, still with boyish, gee-whiz wonderment. "I don't have strong convictions about somebody taking a drink. That didn't bother me. I'd had a little wine as a kid. But what really bothered me was the illegality of the thing."

Miss Ellen Repp, his junior-high-school civics teacher, talked about the prohibition law. Miss Repp was no prude. Her point was that it was a law that was being violated, widely and openly. It was corrupting public officials. And when the public found it comfortable to violate one law, why not violate other laws? *We talked about it in class and then, along the newspaper route, I could see it.* Jackson, the man, can recall with dispassion the whores and bums. But there still is the startled tone, even after a quarter century in public life, when he talks about the mass public violation of law in the 1920s. *Right out in the open. . . .*

Young Henry placed a *Herald* on the shiny dark wood of the bar, managed a weak smile when the bartender nodded toward him, then left. Across the street he walked through the stately old railroad depot, left a paper with the ticket clerk and paused to buy a candy bar at the confectionery stand. That was a rare self-indulgence, reserved for the end of his route. He nibbled the candy as he walked southward along the tracks, watchful for the fast freights, especially the silk trains. They seemed to explode out of the smoky twilight, shaking the earth as they roared past Everett, carrying silk from the Oriental ships at Seattle's docks to the garment manufacturers back East.

He kept an eye on the hobos loitering along the tracks waiting for a slow boxcar. Unlike the poor drunks with their Sterno, the 'bos could be trouble. He scrambled

down from the gravel railroad bed to take a *Herald* into
the Weyerhaeuser mill office. The second shift had just
gone to work now and here, on the dock at the mill gate,
the tart smell of pitch blended with the aroma of sawdust.
His final delivery was at the city dock and, as he glanced
toward the dark water, he mused that this is where all the
men had been killed. . . .

. . . Henry Jackson was only three years old—going on
four—on the day of the Everett Massacre. But he was certain he could remember something from that day. Just a
memory fragment. Raised voices. A stir of excitement in
the neighborhood. Men had come out of their houses carrying guns. Sounds of apprehension from his mother. His
father didn't join the other men.

That was in 1916. The millowners and the union were
locked in a bitter controversy. The union had struck the
mills, but the tough millowners, influenced by William Butler, the most powerful banker in town, decided to fight.
Strikebreakers were hired and, with the protection of city
police and hired goons, the mills went back to work. The
union men found themselves outside the gates in frustration, smelling the smoke and sawdust of mills operated by
strikebreakers. The union men sought wages at 1916 levels
being paid in other mills around Puget Sound, but Butler
argued, and the industrialists of Everett agreed, that higher
wages would trim profits too thin.

Members of the International Workers of the World focused on the labor strife in Everett. Theirs was a loose
alliance of all kinds of dislocated, frustrated men—the
Army of the Downtrodden, they called themselves. Theirs
was not truly a labor union: It was an unkempt social

78

labor movement, its mission to speak out against the capitalists who exploited the men in the woods and in the plants. Often an impassioned speech against the tyranny of the industrialists provoked a swinging police club. So a split lip and a missing tooth became the badge of honor of an I.W.W. member, a Wobbly.

One group of Wobblies, arriving to protest the oppression in Everett, was seized by Sheriff Donald McRae and his men. The Wobs were taken to the woods at night, stripped of clothing and beaten until the ground was blood-soaked. Incensed, Wobbly leaders in Seattle issued a call for volunteers to join their greatest crusade: They would go to Everett *en masse* and hold a free-speech rally.

Banker Butler and other leaders of the Everett establishment sent out word to Everett citizens that their town might be attacked by the rabble. Butler had a spy at the docks in Seattle the morning of November 5, and the agent telephoned word that about 150 Wobblies were boarding a boat, the *Verona*, the first of two passenger boats carrying crusaders north to Everett.

A mill whistle summoned Everett men to the defense of the town and, about two hundred, many of them armed, converged around the city dock. Many had fortified their courage for the event with swigs of moonshine whiskey.

As the *Verona* entered Everett's harbor, spectators could hear the Wobblies singing. Wobs found strength in song in their frequent moments of crisis. But they grew silent as the boat approached the dock. A quieting sight met them. The sheriff stood there waiting, a pistol in each hand. Nearby was big Joe Irving, the tough chief lieutenant of banker Butler. Behind, in irregular formation, were armed men. The surliest looking ones were the strikebreak-

79

ers and goons hired by the millowners to keep order. Hidden from the Wobblies' view were other armed men, aboard nearby tugboats and in a nearby warehouse.

The *Verona* slipped into its berth. A line was secured to the dock. The first of the Wobblies moved to disembark. The sheriff shouted a question. "Who's your leader?" "We're all leaders," they replied. Hundreds of curious citizens had gathered on the hill above the harbor, watching the scene. They gasped at what happened. There was a shot. Then there were volleys. A murderous crossfire sprayed across the deck of the boat. Men fell. Others scrambled toward what protection could be found inside the cabin or behind it. As the panicked Wobblies fled to the far side of the *Verona*, the boat listed abruptly. It almost capsized. Bodies, trailing blood across the deck, slipped over the edge. Some of the living plunged into the water. As they thrashed in the cold water below the dock, they made perfect targets. Even a marksman with a moonshine-blurred sighting eye could pick one off.

When the shooting at last ended, they counted more than thirty men aboard the boat who had been hit. Five were dead or dying. No one ever determined with certainty how many died in the water beside the dock. It was a dozen or more.

Everett citizens who had watched the horror from the hill shouted angrily at the trigger-happy vigilantes. Sheriff McRae, who took a bullet in the leg during the wild shooting, became the target of hatred for citizens after that, although Butler and the millowners blamed the Wobblies for the incident. Later the I.W.W. opened a headquarters in Everett. One night some men removed all the books and documents and burned them: The ashes were noticed the next day, with an American flag lying over them.

Everett had its heritage of labor turmoil and bloodshed, but as though by some communal repression, the event quickly was forgotten. The Wobbly Massacre was seldom discussed in Everett, never taught in the history classes of the schools. The sense of class struggle in time left the waterfront as millowners and unions settled into a grudging accommodation with each other. Everett became a strong union town, as the economic and political influence of the millowners declined. But Butler, the tough-minded, aloof banker continued his power ascendancy, always stubbornly hostile to labor. . . .

. . . Henry Jackson, toting his empty paper bag, headed up Hewitt toward the newspaper office where he had left his bicycle in the bike rack. Everett was changing in 1925. Old wooden frame buildings were being replaced now by brick and masonry. His father was busy at his concrete work because there was need of basements and retaining walls.

Many of the streets in town were named for men of wealth and influence. Colby, Hewitt, Hoyt—all were names of early-day capitalists of Everett. Sometimes Henry bicycled out Rockefeller Street toward the Jackson home at the southern end of town. The front door of the two-story, narrow frame house at 3602 Oakes Street pointed north, but the view was to the east. Beyond the railroad tracks and the Snohomish River Valley below the hill, the wooded foothills rose to the Cascade mountains. Those miles of evergreen forests helped keep Everett's mills going.

There was a solid though not austere Lutheran discipline in the Jackson home and each of the four children—Arthur, Gertrude, Marie, and Henry—learned the virtue of industriousness. The girls often were noisily dominant of others and Arthur chafed at their incessant orders. "Mother, I just can't stand living with those girls," he sometimes complained. But the occasional bickering among the children seldom involved Henry. He was the youngest—born in a back bedroom of the house May 31, 1912—and the one with the most docile personality. He had ways to please his mother: She liked him to be busy and he kept busy with his paper route and other jobs. And she loved chocolate mints so, when he arrived home from his newspaper deliveries, he often brought a bagful of her favorites from Holmes' Candy Shop. She loved sweets of all kinds and, as a result, she was a very plump Norwegian mother.

Pete Jackson, a tall, quiet Norwegian, prided himself on his life of hard work. The years of labor put only a slight bend in his six-foot-plus frame. His hands were heavy-knuckled and calloused. Peter Gresseth was his name at birth, but before leaving Norway he adopted the given name of his father, then added *son*, a Norse tradition. Most Norwegian sons of John became Johnson. Perhaps for individuality, Pete Anglicized the process, choosing to be the son of Jack. He was content to be the quiet smiling parent in the family background. Mrs. Jackson did the talking for both of them. She did the disciplining of the children and made most of the family decisions.

The Jacksons had met and married at the Lutheran Church in Everett, which was the first meeting place of most of the early immigrants from Norway. Pete disliked Montana where they had moved in his search for work during their early married years. Like many poor, unskilled Scandinavians, he had labored at the sweltering, heavy jobs in the Anaconda smelter. Because he was an uncomplaining, reserved man, the children particularly recalled the bitterness in his voice when, lapsing into a heavy accent, he re-

membered that *damn company town*. Live in a little
company house. Buy at the company store. The rent and
food money is taken out of your pay before you are paid.
And if a poor frugal man tried to save a little money by
spending less at the store, the company men seemed angry.
The Jacksons were happy to return to Everett.

Some of the other men around Everett sometimes talked
admiringly of Pete Jackson: Old Pete, they said, was a hell
of a man. He worked during some early years as a police-
man. His special assignment was to pick up the drunks who
fell or were thrown—sometimes face down—into the deep
mud of the street. Pete could pick up a drunk, toss him
over a shoulder and carry him to jail as easily as toting a
fifty-pound sack of feed.

Now Pete, at fifty-seven, hoisted cement bags with the
same ease. He worked for years as a laborer around concrete jobs. Later he became his own boss, contracting for
some of the smaller jobs around town. A union man, but
no radical, he regularly was elected financial secretary
for the Plasterers and Cement Masons Local 190.

Arthur, ten years older than Henry, had their father's
wiry, dark, jut-jawed look. Some of the neighbors thought
Arthur was as smart as anyone in the family, but, because
it was expected and necessary, he quit school to go to
work. Arthur labored with his father and together each
morning they left the house, pushing a wheelbarrow, clattering with its load of shovels and other cement-work tools.
Arthur was destined to be crippled for life. A swift, severe
arthritis struck him in the 1930s. He would spend a long,
lonely life, aloof from other members of the family.

Henry had the look of his mother; square body frame
and short legs. Like Gertrude, his head seemed slightly
oversize for the body. When he was playing with neighbor

boys one day he put on Trigve Klockevold's cap and, as it perched ludicrously above his high brow, the other boys laughed uproariously.

Scoop was his nickname with almost all the friends, although his mother called her son Henry. Sometimes the family talked about the nickname and where it originated. They usually agreed that Gertrude had given it to him, inspired by a comic strip in the newspaper. A little cartoon newspaper reporter named Scoop maneuvered others into doing jobs for him. *That's our Henry*, Gert exclaimed. When he was four years old he fell from the porch and broke his arm. For months afterward, when asked to do a chore, he piped a favorite excuse. "I can't—my sore arm."

Mrs. Jackson presided over an ambrosial kitchen. The neighborhood youngsters knew it as an exotic place of warm cookies, rhubarb pie, richly-frosted cakes, and occasional Norwegian specialties, krumkaken and fattigmand. One year the local electric company, Puget Sound Power and Light, held a pie-baking contest and a cake-baking contest and Mrs. Jackson won first place in each, with a lemon-meringue pie and an angel-food cake. One prize was an electric stove. Arthur was especially grateful: That meant less wood and kindling to chop and Arthur did such chores around the house.

Henry was born late in Mrs. Jackson's life—she was forty-three—at a time when life was financially easier for the family. Gertrude and Marie took on many of the duties of rearing their younger brother, so his mother had the leisure to indulge him. When she baked apple pie, she spooned an extra measure of whipped cream onto Henry's warm serving, then beamed as she watched him devour it.

There probably was disappointment within Mrs. Jackson that none of her children married happily at an early age and brought grandchildren home to her. Gert and Marie never married. They spent most of their lives at home. Arthur had a brief, unhappy marriage. Henry would wait through years of preoccupation with politics and she always wondered if he ever would marry. Mrs. Jackson fretted most about Marie, the insecure, dark-haired daughter who developed a furtive reliance on alcohol.

Yet Mrs. Jackson's life in Everett was more comfortable than was life for most other women in the mill town. The Jackson family had to learn frugality, but even in the lean years when the mills had to close at times, the Jacksons got by. The harbor, the boats, the forests, and mountains of Everett reminded the parents of their native Norway. Each made a determined effort to speak English around the children and they encouraged the Americanization of the household. Still, Henry and the other children learned to say grace and bedtime prayers in Norwegian. Mrs. Jackson, an earnest though not pious person, was a founder and one of the hardest-working members of Our Savior's Lutheran Church where Reverend Carl Norgaard—tall, stern, brilliant—delivered God's word both in English and in Norwegian. Henry was baptized in that church, given the middle name Martin, inspired by Martin Luther. He went to Sunday school there, too, but when his mother had a disagreement with the minister, Henry was abruptly enrolled in a Presbyterian church. Mrs. Jackson disliked the authoritarian manner in which Rev. Norgaard had decided it was time to build a new church. *That was a decision which should be left up to the members of the church*, she lectured the children at the dinner table. Mrs. Jackson was a stolid Nordic civil libertarian. When one of the neighborhood children referred to the Jewish junk man as a kike, she grew furious: *Don't you ever use words like that.*

Henry Jackson grew up in a matriarchy, with his mother as the captain and Gertrude as the chief lieutenant. They were the strongest forces in the family and some of the neighbors complained that Gertrude was the strongest force in the neighborhood. She gratuitously advised neighbors when their lawns needed mowing, when their dogs barked too often, or when their children needed discipline.

Mrs. Jackson and her daughters weren't really busybodies, but they had a compulsive sense of involvement and a curiosity about people and events. And the girls, particularly, were assertive. One Everett friend remembered a blistering attack from Gertrude during one of Jackson's election campaigns. She had seen a sign in the yard, supporting the Republican candidate. She was incensed. *What are you doing with that Republican's sign in your yard?* He explained: "Gert, it's a duplex and the sign was put out by the man living in the other apartment." *Well, you go get him to take it down,* she ordered. *And get one of Scoop's up in your yard.*

Jack Dootson, one of Henry's childhood acquaintances, recalls that a visit to the Jackson home almost always invited a stream of questions. "Sometimes Gert and Marie and Mrs. Jackson were all asking questions at the same time." Who was visiting your house the other day? How are you doing in school? Where are you going on the Fourth of July? How's your mother feeling? It was a constant barrage of interrogation, but, Dootson said, "It was O.K., though, with three of them asking, I just picked out the questions I thought were easiest to answer."

Gertrude was a teacher at Garfield School and she was regarded as one of the best educators in Everett. Tall, with a large, masculine face and build, she was awesome to many of the students. But they learned from her and most of them liked her. Garfield was the school attended by the poor children and, during Everett's lean years, Gertrude described to her family the sight of children coming to school without shoes. Emotionalism was not a family trait but Gertrude's compassion surfaced occasionally. One day just before Christmas vacation she noticed William Gissberg, one of her students, leaving the school, carrying his newspaper bag. He was startled as she approached him and took his hand. "Have a Merry Christmas, Billy." She slipped a dollar bill into his palm.

Scoop Jackson's family enjoyed the flow of compliments he earned from neighbors and others. *A nice boy. Always so busy. Nice, quiet boy.* Jackson's was a newsboy-Cub Scout-Boy Scout upbringing. He missed the bruised knees and scraped elbows of the other boys' sandlot baseball games or football scrimmages. He wasn't a natural athlete and, besides, he kept busy at other things. When he was eight he was a door-to-door magazine salesman, peddling *Colliers* and *Country Gentleman*. As did other kids in town, he learned to swim in the saltwater bay where Pigeon Creek emptied below the Weyerhaeuser mill. Among his few light chores around the house, his principal job was the care of the rabbits. One day he suffered the little-boy shock of learning the rabbits had been butchered for the family table. He skipped that dinner.

The most memorable boy-becoming-a-man impacts occurred outside the home. Below Mount Baldy, in the Cascade Mountains, his Boy Scout troop was encamped one June. The tough camp director gave an early-morning order: Everybody into the lake. Their whoops and yelps echoed off the mountain's rock faces, but the boys went in. . . .

. . . *The camp commander had been a platoon leader in World War I and he ran the place like a military operation.*

*There was ice in the lake. Ice floes drifting around . . .
And we had our chores to do . . . He really put the blocks
to us. The greatest thing in the world.* Jackson, as a man,
still glows when recalling that Viking morning.

The family expected and appreciated industriousness, so
Scoop Jackson's busy-business was a matter of course.
Then it became gratifying of itself, as his bank balance
climbed. He became a young tightwad. At hours when he
wasn't walking his *Herald* route, he hawked papers at a
news stand on the downtown corner of Hewitt and Colby.
The chauffeur occasionally bought a newspaper from him
for Mr. Butler, the banker. Then one day young Jackson
had a chance to see Butler in person. The elegant capitalist
walked across the street from his bank, extracted a coin
purse from an inner pocket and asked the boy for a Seattle
paper. . . .

. . . William Butler was from the East and he was the
financial czar of Everett. He dominated the town's economy and for years he had major influence on its politics.
Butler had his banks and he controlled many of the mill
operations. The local newspaper understood that it was
never to print anything about him.

His brother was Nicholas Murray Butler, famous president of Columbia University who once was a candidate
for the Republican nomination for President of the United
States. The brothers shared a steadfast conservatism which
they discussed and savored in their exchanges of letters. The
fact that William Butler lived in Washington State did not
alter the fact that he was very much of the Eastern elite.

He and Mrs. Butler lived in the great colonial house far
out on Grand Avenue. The mansion, with its view of Puget
Sound and the Olympic Mountains to the west, had been

given a colonial elegance appropriate for Mrs. Butler who was a Virginia blueblood. Townspeople sometimes caught a glimpse of the banker or his dowager wife in the back seat of their long, dark, chauffeur-driven limousine when it appeared on Everett's streets.

The banker's days were rituals of precision. At breakfast he read the Seattle newspapers, *The New York Times* and other publications appropriate for a man of such diverse interests. By nine o'clock each morning, Butler arrived at his bank. He was a short man, but every inch the grand capitalist. His white moustache was perfectly clipped. He wore high collars and dark suits. His vest strained to encase the pot belly. With frugal flicking of his cane, he strode through the bank entrance to disappear into his private office in the innards of the building.

There were other rich men in Everett who extracted wealth from the mill town. But many of those industrialists had callouses on their hands. They were visible men who could often be seen around town and on the waterfront. Mr. Butler remained royally aloof in his office, making decisions about sales, leases, loans, interest rates, and other matters which determined the future of Everett. . . .

Cameos of the boy-heading-for-politics appeared sparsely through Jackson's early years. Mrs. Dootson, his third-grade teacher at Longfellow School, asked each student what they wanted to be when they grew up. Jackson replied, "President of the United States." Word of that got back to his family, because the Dootsons were neighbors. So the nine-year-old, head down, blushing, endured some dinner-table kidding. His mother talked seldom of politics except when the politicians did something to her dislike, then she grumbled that they're all a bunch of crooks.

Jackson's emergence began when he joined the junior-high and high-school debate teams. One spring day in high school he strolled around the block during the lunch hour with Fred Moore, another student. They talked over a debate topic: tariffs. Jackson was to argue in favor of increased tariffs, and, amidst the conversation, he interjected: "I think one day I'll be a senator."

The Jackson family and other parents assembled in the Everett Theater downtown one day in the spring of 1930 to watch the high school graduation exercises. Henry was not quite at the top of his graduating class, but, because of his skill on the debate team and his academic energy, he was chosen as one of the four commencement speakers. There was a pastoral mood to the program. A girl sang *Daffodils*. The girls' quartette sang *I Hear a Thrush at Eve*. But there was nothing idyllic about Henry Jackson's speech. His subject: Law Enforcement. In his tense tenor, he lectured about the trouble in a society which winks at its laws and allows a tolerance policy: That, he said, breeds corruption in public officials and disrespect for other laws.

He had worked hard preparing his speech, but he found ample source material. Newspapers were carrying stories about bootleggers and cops who were receiving payoffs.

He might have seemed the all-American boy hero to his Norwegian immigrant family, but when he arrived at the University of Washington in the fall of 1930, Scoop Jackson seemed a gawdawful seedy sight to the more urbane collegiates. His hair was shaggy: He wore an odd sweater —his DeMolay club sweater—from high school. But it was a meager year for pledges along fraternity row, so the Delta Chis took him. "He seemed to have a good head on his shoulders," Lloyd Shorett, one of the Delta Chis, recalled. Promptly one of the members was appointed as a committee of one to take the kid down to the University district to get him a haircut.

Money was to be a problem through college. Dollars saved from his newspaper route had gone into the bank. With his mother's advice, he had earned some profit from an investment in Puget Sound Power and Light Company stock. He had sold just before the market tumbled. But his savings wouldn't pay his way through school in fraternity-life style, so he spent most of his university days living at home in Everett, commuting to classes with a friend who owned a car.

The thirties were long, bleak years around Puget Sound. Men stood outside the Everett mills and the longshoremen-hiring hall, waiting in vain for a few hours' work. In Seattle there were soup kitchens and long lines of hungry people waiting outside commissaries. Seattle had its Hooverville—a sad, rambling collection of shacks made of tarpaper and packing crates, its population of men scrounging in the cold rain for fuel and food. At night they huddled inside the shacks, coughing in the smoke of warming fires built inside gallon cans—their makeshift stoves. Jackson walked along Forty-fifth Street in the University district and watched women picking through garbage cans outside restaurants and markets. He remembered the shame on their faces.

Jackson returned to the Delta Chi house during his final year of law school. For board and room he waited on tables and washed dishes. He found inner satisfaction in the long hours of work. Arising at six o'clock to ready the dining hall for breakfast, the day of studies, washing dishes into the evening hours were solid disciplines.

He finished law school, barely in the top one-third of his class. There had been nothing brilliant about him, his professors concluded. But they had no doubt he would do well. No one had more driving determination. Forced to squeeze studies into hours of outside work, he had picked up a knack for absorbing facts rapidly and storing them for ready recall. That would be a great quality for a lawyer —or a politician.

Jackson had months to wait before he knew the results of his bar examination. Meanwhile he needed a job. He found one in Snohomish County's biggest industry in 1935: Relief. He went to work in the Everett welfare office and renewed his acquaintance with John Salter.

Salter, a short, skinny, dark-haired Irishman, had first met Jackson in Providence Hospital. They were fellow twelve-year-old tonsillectomy patients in adjoining beds. Although their homes were only a few blocks apart, they had not been fast friends through their school years. Salter went away to prep school in California, then entered a seminary. Within a few months he would have been ordained a priest, but Salter left the seminary and returned to Everett. It was just as well. Salter was not conspicuously qualified to be a priest. He was destined for politics. Wily and Irish, he was a perfect partner for Jackson, the serious Norwegian.

Salter and Jackson asked the necessary questions of the poor people who walked into the relief office where they worked in Everett. They filled out the forms and criticized the red tape. Some days they traveled into rural parts of the county, investigating the applicant's depth of poverty. They were touched mostly by the humiliation in the eyes of the older people who, through lives of hard work, had set aside some money for their later years but now were destitute. They weren't failures, but the institutions had failed them. Savings had been wiped out by bank failures or a prostrate stock market.

America, the voice said, must begin "a great national crusade to destroy enforced idleness." The country needs new laws on banking, more job programs and the Congress should enact a program of social security for older people. Jackson and Salter listened intently to President Franklin D. Roosevelt's fireside chat on the radio. They talked enthusiastically about the bold ideas of the New Deal.

Snohomish County in 1936 was solidly Democratic. The Depression erased the old establishment Republican dominance of Everett politics. Jackson and Salter, eager young politicians, formed a local chapter of the Roosevelt First Voters' League. They had no members, but Salter issued a press release to the *Herald*, anyway. The story, naming Jackson and Salter as officers of the new group, provoked a quick reaction from the long-established Young Democrats organization. Alarmed that a rival group was beginning, the Young Democrats made an overture for merger. His League was a paper organization only, but Salter played a bluff hand in the negotiations. It worked. The merger was transacted and, as part of the deal, Jackson became president of the combined Young Democrats and Roosevelt First Voters' League. Salter was treasurer.

One press release had produced a political coup and Salter remembered the technique.

Henry Jackson, at twenty-six, was a budding political personality and he also was, at last, a practicing attorney. Lloyd Black, one of Everett's most respected lawyers, had taken him into the office. Jackson adored the older man whose integrity was so immaculate. Black became a second father to Jackson and, in time, his political counselor.

They talked together one day about Al Swanson, the Snohomish County prosecuting attorney. In earlier years Swanson had been a popular political personality, but now there seemed to be a seaminess about him. Swanson was drunk much of the time and, in the faltering image of the rotund Swanson, Scoop Jackson saw a political opportunity.

Jackson sought Black's advice about running for prosecuting attorney. The county had never elected a 26-year-old to such high office before, but, Black said, the office of prosecuting attorney deserves integrity and Jackson had that. Jackson reasoned that a change would be good for the Democratic party. Swanson was a Democrat, but he was vulnerable. If another Democrat didn't knock him off in the September primary, a Republican might win the office in November.

Jackson decided to run and Salter eagerly became the campaign manager. Co-workers in the welfare program and former high school chums were recruited to help. Gertrude, in her gruff, aggressive way, became her brother's most effective campaigner. There was no saying no to Gert when she proclaimed, "My brother's running for prosecutor and you're going to help him, aren't you?"

The politician in him awakened, Jackson hustled the streets, handing out his card to everyone in sight. Even old-time Democrats were impressed by the eagerness of "the kids."

Swanson was swept out of office. The youthful politicians exulted in the margin of victory: Jackson 14,582, Swanson 4,407. The Republican was easily defeated in November and Snohomish County had a 26-year-old prosecutor, who suddenly was effervescing in the sheer joy of politics.

Joe Hart and the others who ran the gambling operations around Snohomish County guessed that they'd have to make some new arrangements. The new prosecutor had given campaign lectures on law enforcement and the illegality of gambling. Hart planned to send word to Jackson to think things through before doing anything drastic.

But there was no time to talk. Jackson, soon after taking office, delivered an ultimatum to pinball operators: Get the machines out of the county within thirty days. Then began a series of raids. Jackson, his deputies and state liquor investigators began hitting the whorehouses first. Sometimes they raided two or more at the same hour, the strikes synchronized like a military operation. Bootleg liquor was the target. Occasionally a prostitute or a madam was run in. But the objective was to dry up the flow of illegal booze and to discourage the other criminal activities which flourished around the houses.

The Ranch was a night club in the south county on Highway 99, close enough to Seattle to attract big crowds of fun lovers from the city, but located in Snohomish County where county officials always were understanding. The Ranch had the best dance orchestras, the best food, the best floor shows, and the biggest, most wide-open gambling action in the Pacific Northwest. In a side room blackjack, dice games, and roulette—no-limit games—went full blast.

Wanda Smathers Owens, ex-wife of one of the Smathers of the Everett Transfer Company, owned the night club. A strutting, well-preserved, middle-aged blonde, she expected raids to happen now and then. But they were ceremonial affairs and she always received a friendly warning by telephone long before the police arrived. There always was time to get the gambling gear out of sight.

She didn't get a friendly advance call the night the new prosecutor pulled his big raid. Jackson waited outside while some deputies slipped into the crowd. The Ranch, however illegal its operations, was a widely-accepted institution in the county and several prominent people were gambling. One of the deputies noticed with horror that the man with the hot dice at the crap table was Sam Manus, the magistrate. Manus had only hours earlier signed the warrant which authorized the raid. Not even he had anticipated Jackson's sincerity. Without the prosecutor's knowledge, the deputy eased Manus out a side door before the raid was announced, a necessary act of selective law enforcement because Manus was the judge who presided the next day over the trials. The Ranch was closed down.

Meanwhile Hart, the pinball king, was hauling in his gambling devices. He concluded there was no doing business with Soda Pop Jackson. The prosecutor had a new nickname, stemming from the implausible fact that he was a non-drinking politician in Snohomish County. Hart sent word to Jackson that the pinball machines were withdrawn from the cardrooms, poolhalls, taverns, and other places. Where are they—Jackson wanted to know. Hart sent word they were stored in a warehouse. Is the warehouse inside the county? It was. "Get them out of the county," Jackson insisted. They went.

That summer Jackson went on a fishing trip with some of his Delta Chi fraternity brothers. The young men had a boat well provisioned with beer. Absorbed in conversation, Jackson sipped one beer, became sick, and fell asleep. The others stacked empty beer bottles around his sleeping form and someone suggested taking a photo of the proper, crusading young prosecutor, unconscious, surrounded by evidence of his debauchery. "Don't waste the film," one of them said. "With Jackson, nobody'd ever believe it anyway."

Jackson was eager to return from that trip because he had new political ideas. Congressman Mon Wallgren had told him he was thinking about quitting the House of Representatives to run for the Senate. Wallgren told Jackson he would be an able replacement in Congress. But Jackson later discovered that Wallgren had given the same encouragement to some other Democrats. Pat Hurley, a well-known popular Democrat, decided to run. So did Howard Bargreen, who also was well known and who was a Scandinavian, an important credential in the district. On the final day of candidate registration, following days of indecision, Jackson filed. Six Democrats were in the race.

Jackson had name familiarity because of his gambling crackdown as prosecutor and he had the successful 1938 campaign team working again. But of all the candidates, Jackson was the least exciting personality, his campaign workers conceded. His speeches were carefully reasoned, humorless, and boring. Laboriously, he preached to restive audiences of the need of an old-age-pension act and other measures which Roosevelt then was seeking from Congress. "I think we should provide free training to young people," Jackson said, "so they can be beneficial to our country in our national defense program." He never seemed to know how to end a speech, so a campaign aide often was stationed in the back of the hall to give a signal when it appeared that the audience had enough. But Jackson's dry oratory had a subtle effect on the audience. A politician so dull, they concluded, had to be honest.

It was known that if Jackson went to Congress, the politically charged Salter would go with him as his assistant. That produced an advertising slogan for the opposition: "Don't Send Two 28-Year-Old Kids to Congress." Salter capitalized on it. He sprinkled press releases with new adjectives: *"Energetic, young* Henry M. Jackson, *a new face . . . ."* The criticism of Jackson's youth became a plus and the more the opposition used it the better. During the campaign Jackson received a $250 contribution from the Democratic Congressional Campaign Committee. He kept the "best wishes" telegram which came with the check. It was signed Rep. Lyndon Baines Johnson, the committee chairman.

Youth prevailed again in 1940. Voters gave Jackson more than a 3,000-vote margin over the nearest other Democrat, Bargreen. The general election was easy. With Roosevelt on the ticket, Democratic margins were big and Jackson overwhelmingly defeated a Republican named Payson Peterson.

Before leaving for Washington, Jackson received word that one of his constituents wanted to see him: William Butler, the banker, invited the 28-year-old congressman-elect to his office in the bank.

Butler had come through the Depression unchanged, either in his conservative viewpoint or his status of power in Everett. The thirties had slowed his accumulation of wealth, but Butler remained the millionaire recluse, the mystery man. The banker had made all the foreclosures necessary and had called in the notes when it was financially responsible to do so. They called him the meanest son-of-a-bitch in town. One industrialist, anguished by financial losses, had carried a gun around town, promising to shoot Butler if the old man ever foreclosed on him. But no one ever got around to shooting Butler. He was an inconspicuous target, because he still kept to himself in his office or in his mansion overlooking the Sound.

The banker received the young politician with stiff pleasantries. Butler was now seventy-four. Jackson remembered selling a newspaper to the banker once and now he was fascinated to talk with him. Butler—the last of the *laissez faire* capitalists. He looked strikingly like J. P. Morgan, Jackson thought.

Butler got to the point. He was worried about what the federal government was doing to Everett. Paine Field, begun as a WPA airport project, now was being enlarged for the Army Air Corps. What worried Butler were the extremely high wages the government was paying to workers out there. If that sort of thing continued, the federal government would force wages up all over the county. That, Butler explained, would bring inflation and put an awful burden on the private businessman who, God knows, was always hard pressed to make his needed profits.

So banker Butler, indeed, had not changed. During the 1916 strike he knew it made no sense to pay higher wages to millworkers. The same sensible conservative economics were as valid in 1940 as they had been in 1916.

The 28-year-old congressman-elect carefully sorted his thoughts before he replied. Perhaps, he told the banker, if wages did go higher, people might have more money to spend, then business and banks might even enjoy more prosperity.

That night, sitting in his mansion, Butler must have reflected on that conversation: All these new young men with their rampant socialism—all galloping after that madman Roosevelt—might just take this whole great nation over the cliff of ruin.

Less than four years later banker Butler would be dead.

And in the decade of the sixties there would be a new

owner of the Butler mansion, who while showing friends through the elegant house, would exclaim, "Wouldn't old Mister Butler turn over in his grave if he knew that a Democrat—the blockheaded son of Peter Gresseth, an immigrant Norwegian laborer—owned his big house?"

CHAPTER 5

. . . YOUR SON IS A COMMIE

I HAVE SAID *this before, but I shall say it again and again and again: Your boys are not going to be sent into any foreign wars . . . The purpose of our defense is defense.*

President Franklin Delano Roosevelt had said it during his campaign for re-election in 1940. Wendell Willkie, the Republican, had made approximately that same pledge that fall. They made their peace and neutrality covenants with the people that autumn, but now it was January, 1941—an ominous time, with most of Europe overrun by the totalitarians and Britain fighting daily for survival.

Even the January wind had an ominous bite in it, as it whipped around the sunlit dome of the Capitol and swept across the plaza, chilling the crowd of people bundled in heavy overcoats and mufflers. The wind ruffled the bunting on the stand where President Roosevelt took his inaugural oath again. Four years earlier he stood in this same place and spoke of the crisis of the banks, poverty, unemployment, and the other agonies of a nation in the spasm of the Depression. That pain was not fully gone and so he referred to it again: "The hopes of the republic cannot forever tolerate either undeserved poverty or self-serving wealth."

But grudgingly the nation was being carried into events

abroad. Roosevelt spoke of the world crises and the American response. The real peril, in a world threatened by aggressors, he said, is inaction. "We risk the real peril of isolation," he told the shivering crowd. Only days before, a great new issue had arisen to confront the Seventy-Seventh Congress: Lend-Lease, a program to sustain besieged Britain. That Roosevelt proposal, Senator Burton K. Wheeler of Montana had said, means "war—open and complete warfare" which will "plow under every fourth American boy." Roosevelt had been infuriated.

Now Roosevelt's words, ringing out of the public-address speakers over the Capitol Plaza, told Americans: "In the face of great perils never before encountered, our strong purpose is to protect and to perpetuate the integrity of democracy. . . ."

From the special section on the Capitol steps reserved for congressmen, the youthful Nordic face of Henry M. Jackson beamed at the President. Bareheaded, shoulders hunched in his heavy overcoat, Jackson joined enthusiastically in the thup-thup-thup applause of gloved hands.

Jackson had been sworn in only seventeen days earlier as a Member of Congress—a freshman, age twenty-eight. One newspaper story referred to him as "the baby of the Seventy-Seventh Congress." One reporter had flattered him by asking what he thought were the priorities of the Congress. "To keep America out of the war and help Great Britain all we can," he replied. And to make certain there were adequate air and shore bases to defend the Pacific Northwest.

Jackson had, like many of his contemporaries, moved into politics on the tide of public concern about unemployment, hunger, and misery among Americans. There still were those nagging problems in some areas, but the great new issues arising to face Congress now were international matters and Jackson would be an international man.

"This is London . . ." said the familiar deep voice on the nightly broadcast. Jackson never missed the evening radio news. The voice was that of Edward R. Murrow and Jackson mused that Murrow was a constituent of sorts. The newsmen came from Skagit County, in the Second Congressional District in Washington, from a small town where Murrow's father ran a railroad locomotive on a logging-spur line. The Murrows, father and son, had been members of the radical International Workers of the World —the Wobblies. In a future year, Ed Murrow would be attacked by Senator Joe McCarthy for that radical background. But in the 1940s, Murrow was the man whose voice brought to Americans a dramatic description of the hour-to-hour survival of Great Britain.

Jackson voted against the initial Lend-Lease proposal. He held out for a tightening of the original bill: It should have stronger restrictions, he said, to ensure against another national frustration like that which occurred from the unpaid war debts following World War I. Pro-British emotions were rising, but Jackson disdained emotionalism in making public decisions. Later he voted for a Lend-Lease bill with the protections he wanted.

A new uneasiness was simmering within the nation: un-Americanism. Patriotism was moving toward a new, historic crescendo. The Nazis and Communists were threats to a free world and yet, to newspaper readers, they seemed to be freely at work here at home—particularly the Communists. American Communists were not phantoms to members of the Washington State delegation in the House of Representatives. Communists—most of them politicized social radicals embittered by Hooverville shacks and soup

kitchens; others dedicated, doctrinaire Marxist-Leninists—
were fiery forces in Washington State Democratic politics.
Hugh DeLacy, the Seattle congressman, was a graduate of
that strident political school. Another was Representative
John Coffee. Washington State had its firebrands.

During his first weeks as a Congressman, Jackson heard
Coffee castigate the Dies Committee, the House Committee
Investigating Un-American Activities. "A bogey-chasing
expedition," Coffee called it. During debate on the floor of
the House, Coffee asked, "Why establish a committee, the
chairman and members of which can march into your state
and into mine, sit around a table surrounded by newspaper
reporters and motion picture photographers and receive
endless publicity designed to mitigate or curtail all independent thinking? Communism! Why, it was suggested on
the floor of this House that because the Plymouth Rock
was desecrated the other day with red paint, ipso facto, it
must have been done by the Communists. . . ."

Representative Martin Dies of Texas, chairman of the
investigating committee, fought back. His committee,
searching out those of dangerous ideology or committed to
subversion, had produced testimony invaluable to the well-
being of the national security, he said. Un-American organizations had been named. Un-American men had been
identified. "Had we not widely publicized their aims and
purposes, many Communist-inspired and -instigated strikes
would have already crippled our national-defense industries. Through exposure we have frustrated their plans.
. . . We have shown that Communists are entrenched in
positions of leadership and we have publicized the names
of these Communist leaders. . . ."

Overwhelmingly, the House voted to continue the Dies
Committee. Jackson voted *yes*. But repeatedly in years to
follow, he voted against funding it. Its star-chamber pro-

cedures, its violations of civil rights, were contrary to his civil-libertarian, legal senses. As a young prosecutor he had fussed extensively over the legalities—the constitutional rights—involved before sending his deputies off to raid a whorehouse.

Jackson, the quiet kid who had won the newsboy carrier award for his diligence, was a quiet, methodical man in the House of Representatives. He gave few speeches on the floor. He disliked the political rhapsodizing for the *Congressional Record* so appealing to other junior Members. He fretted about his attendance record, was dutiful in committee tasks and did his homework. Thus he captured the attention of Sam Rayburn. Stern Sam Rayburn, Speaker of the House, seemed foreboding to most junior Members of Congress, and many old timers. But one day he gave Jackson the high compliment: "You're going to be around here a long time." The sanctum of the Speaker's office—so remote a province for so many—had an open door for Jackson.

Mister Speaker, Jackson learned in their occasional chats, was a man of the earth. He grew up with poverty, first in Tennessee, then in Texas, he told Jackson. Jackson was impressed by his feeling for people and his compassion for the poor: "A great liberal," Jackson concluded. He let Rayburn know that his parents were immigrant Norwegians—and that his father was a laborer—thus reinforcing their bond.

Jackson found it easier to establish friendships with the Southern congressmen who, he found, had the easy personal manner of Westerners. Estes Kefauver of Tennessee became an early, close friend. They held many common views, especially on the issue of public power—Kefauver a public-power advocate from the Tennessee Valley, Jackson, a public-power advocate from the Pacific Northwest where the energy of the Columbia River was just beginning to be harnessed. Few men would have a close personal relationship with Jackson, but Kefauver was one. . . .

. . . You know, there have been some great liberal Southerners, says Jackson. Of course today you hear the criticism of the South. But it's all on the race issue. There have been some great liberals out of the South. . . .

Rayburn had the inner toughness Jackson likes in people. And the Speaker was a man of the legislative system, the man who moved bills quietly, fashioning his workable consensus. Jackson learned the style. When the House Committee Investigating Un-American Activities was without a chairman in 1945, Rayburn offered the chairmanship to Jackson, a third-termer. But Jackson declined: "A man who's voted against funding the committee shouldn't be its chairman." In the future Jackson would enjoy some far more important dividends from Sam Rayburn's friendship—membership on the Appropriations Committee—which gave him a strong statewide political base, with all the public works back home in Washington—and the Joint Committee on Atomic Energy, an assignment which would thrust Jackson into the role of a congressional authority on the atom and defense.

Soda Pop Jackson. That was his nickname during his days as prosecuting attorney. Preoccupied with politics and his job, he had no time for girls. He took a proffered cocktail once in a while, but only if the social situation required it. He may have been one of the most eligible bachelors in Everett, but, said one Everett girl, "he was the worst date in town." Sometimes he and Phil Sheridan, a deputy prosecutor, dated girls together. At the party, Jackson drifted off into the crowd, chatting about politics. Sheridan always was left to replenish the drinks and find potato chips for both girls.

Jackson grew more mature in Congress. Washington girls saw him as a catch. For years he shared a newspaper-littered sixth-floor bachelor apartment with John Salter, his bachelor administrative assistant, on Northeast Capitol Hill, near the Supreme Court. During the evenings Jackson was absorbed in newspapers, magazines, and the radio news. There were occasional stories mentioning Jackson—one of the city's most eligible bachelors. But there were few gossip items. There was nothing really to gossip about.

Alice Frein Johnson, Washington correspondent for *The Seattle Times*, found him a talkative news source on congressional matters. But when she asked about girls he had been dating, Jackson turned crimson and mumbled vague replies.

"Scoop's idea of a hot date," said one girl in Washington, "is to take you to dinner at a steak house, then to the newsreel, and have you back on the doorstep by ten."

One girl, who had wearily been through that Jackson dating pattern too often, suddenly had her hopes raised one evening.

He brought her to her doorstep after the newsreel show at the Trans-Lux. "Can I come up to your apartment?" Jackson asked.

She excitedly agreed.

Her romantic fantasies were punctured as he explained: "I just want to hear the ten o'clock news on your radio."

In World War II Jackson had a brief military career, which did not extend beyond basic training. He was inducted as a buck private at Fort Lewis, Wash., in September 1943.

Roosevelt ordered Jackson and other Congressmen out of the military service and back to Congress about three months later. Jackson's brief service may have placated most constituents, but still there was criticism back home in the Second District: The two "28-year-old kids"—Jackson and Salter—who went to Congress in 1940 still were bachelors in Washington while other boys fought the war.

Salter reported from the political home front: "The heat's terrific. Hell, this is murder." He decided to make the supreme sacrifice: He would try to get into the Army.

Salter was the operator, the one who compensated for his congressman's steady disinterest in booze and women. Deft with the press release and the political action, Salter had a toughness Jackson admired. The exterior was a blend of acid and brass. Salter almost had a marvelous wartime career. Early in the war he had arranged to be an officer— better yet, a personnel officer—at The Presidio. "Great town, San Francisco," he reasoned: a lovely place for a bachelor to spend the war. But Salter flunked the physical examination because of poor eyesight.

The campaign heat at home in 1944 sent him seeking a new physical exam. The examining physician missed his visual handicap and Salter went into the Army as a private. His career lasted about three months. The training company headquarters at Camp Roberts, Calif., swiftly wearied of the steady stream of telegrams to Private Salter from Congressman Jackson. The messages asked the whereabouts of files, the status of projects, and other matters of seeming importance. When Salter was fitted for gas-mask lenses, his poor eyesight was discovered. The United States Army discharged him and both he and the Army were relieved.

With his administrative assistant away serving in the Army, Jackson won re-election easily in 1944. Thus Salter's military career had a measure of nobility, Salter concluded.

Postwar America was weary of austerity and rationing. It wanted sugar and nylons again. It was tired of price controls and you-name-it controls, longing for a quick escape from its olive-drab existence. Republican congressional candidates sensed the mood and moved in on the tide in 1946. Washington State was a nationally watched battleground that election year, because it had those conspicuous super-Left liberal Democrats. Hugh DeLacy was beaten. "If he isn't a paid-up member of the Communist party, he's cheating them out of their dues," they said. John Coffee, who had shouted on the floor of the House against investigations of the Communists, was defeated. Senator Hugh Mitchell, another liberal, was beaten by an exciting political personality, Harry P. Cain, a paratrooper just back from the war.

It was a debacle year for Democrats. In the Northwest states every seat in the House of Representatives went to the Republicans, except one: Henry M. Jackson narrowly won re-election. Jackson defeated the bland, pleasant Republican, Payson Peterson, whom he had beaten in 1940, '42, and '44. Peterson came within seven thousand votes of Jackson in 1946, and that was the closest any opponent would ever get.

Jackson was the survivor of 1946—a Democratic curiosity. Politicians watched his style. Later years would bring into American politics the television campaign, the image-makers, the charisma factor. But through the 1940s Jackson was putting together his own political foundation industriously, patiently, quietly—in much the same way his father built the concrete bulkheads around the town of Everett.

"I predict a long future for the Democratic party if it follows liberal principles. The people of the State of Washington are the most liberal of any state in the union." Those were the exuberant words of Jackson, as an eager, liberal freshman congressman in 1941. He stayed liberal. His voting record earned highest marks from the Americans for Democratic Action. He was right with labor down the line.

Yet Jackson parted from the suicidal liberals, as he viewed them—the radicals hellbent, chasing rainbows. The De-Lacys and Coffees reveled in the rhetoric which stirred a convention crowd, but they would, Jackson guessed, be shrouded in frustration if ever the causes came to success. They were the men who seemed to delight in outraging—never persuading—businessmen and editorial writers.

Jackson went to the plant gate, shook the hands of the men carrying lunch pails and talked on a first-name basis with their union officers. "My father was an immigrant laborer," he said. "And I worked with him." Then Jackson walked into the company office, too, and chatted with the executives. What's the outlook? He asked about production, transportation, and marketing. "You know, they called Grand Coulee Dam socialism. But where would we have been during the war without those airplanes Boeing built with that electrical power?" And the power would continue to flow. There are shortages now, but we'll get new dams going. He wanted to know about the company, its stock, and its future. There were handshakes, smiles, and he walked away with an annual report tucked under one arm. "Maybe he's a liberal," the executives said, "but he's no radical." His father was both an immigrant laborer and a contractor. His son saw a continuum of interdependence which stretched from the blue-shirted men on the

110

production line to the men wearing neckties in the office upstairs.

The rally, the roar of the crowd, was not the Jackson style. But he had been there, on the platform near the Washington monument in early 1946, the principal speaker at a "Save OPA Day" rally. OPA was a rising political issue, perhaps a tough one. But Jackson always had a fascination for wage and price controls. The savers, the people who had invested their few dollars in war bonds, will be hurt if price controls are lifted, he told the crowd. The economy is superheated. Lift the lid and inflation boils over. "When we asked them to invest in bonds for the future, we intended a future where the dollar would buy something." In a later year, he could say, "Hell, that was right, too." Controls were lifted and savers were hurt.

Regardless of what the Republicans said about such dangers, there was a Jackson easiness about the government taking care of things for people. Perhaps it was an ethnic view: "Norway," Jackson said, "has demonstrated that the only real and lasting answer to all forms of totalitarianism is social justice. Norway has found that if people have jobs and security, coupled with a devotion to the democratic way of life, they will maintain their freedom . . . The nationwide cooperation of labor and management has been an indispensable part of Norway's recovery since the end of the war. Labor is ready to exercise self-restraint and does, when it sees that excess profits and large-scale industrial combinations are controlled in the interests of all the people."

Bring-home-the-bacon politics became the Jackson style, too, even though his first try at it was a conspicuous failure. Salter set up, with a Barnum-and-Bailey flair, a spectacular first homecoming for his boss in 1941. Jackson had been struggling to persuade the War Department to establish

111

a repair depot at Paine Field. It would be a great start for a new congressman—announcing a fat new payroll at home. Salter planted "major announcement" speculation stories in the newspapers. The administrative assistant arranged a prestigious greeting committee to be there when the airplane carrying Jackson landed in Seattle. The mayors of Everett and Seattle agreed to attend. At the last minute Jackson telephoned from Washington that the airplane had mechanical trouble. Disconsolate, Salter called off his extravaganza. When the freshman congressman arrived the next day, a newspaper reporter was there to ask him about Paine Field. No comment, he said, gloomily. A senior congressman, Charles Leavy, had snatched the payroll for Spokane. Leavy was on the Appropriations Committee and thus had the political leverage. Jackson was determined to get into a like situation of influence in the House of Representatives, and with Speaker Sam Rayburn's help, he did.

In January, 1949, Jackson moved onto the Interior Subcommittee of the Appropriations Committee, where he had a chance to influence funds for Grand Coulee Dam and other reclamation and public-work projects popular across his state. He thus had a foundation for a statewide political race.

His other committee appointment was even more exhilarating: He went onto the Joint Committee on Atomic Energy. Less than a month earlier, Jackson had been in Europe where he witnessed the Soviet blockade's squeeze on Berlin. The United States must, he concluded, sustain the Berlin airlift "with determination." Within months, the Soviet Union would have the atomic bomb.

"It is no longer a secret that the Defense Department and the Atomic Energy Commission have gone far beyond the original bomb dropped on Japan. These new developments

112

in the near future may have both tactical and strategic military significance. . . . The Red Army may be forced to change its whole notion of warfare based on massing ground troops."—Jackson, February 9, 1951

"The recent atomic tests in Nevada had more effect on the plans of men in the Kremlin than all the propaganda and military warnings of western diplomats in the past twelve months. When it comes to dealing with the Russian leaders, atomic explosions often speak louder than words. It's no secret that we now have a device—a breeder reactor, or atomic furnace—that will produce more fissionable material than it burns and at the same time produce electrical power."—Jackson, February 26, 1951

Jackson quickly emerged as an informed congressional spokesman on the atom and national defense—critical, changing issues.

The stakes were high. The Soviet Union, possessor of the atom bomb since 1949, was moving, probing, menacing around the world. Soon there might be a Soviet hydrogen bomb. The United States began to reconsider its H-bomb project, shelved since the end of the war. Jackson became a member of the special subcommittee to examine the merits of renewing the project. He counseled often with the scientists—Ernest O. Laurence, Nobel prize winner for the cyclotron, and Dr. Edward Teller, as well as others. In the fall of 1949 he met with Dr. J. Robert Oppenheimer, invited him to dinner at the Carlton Hotel in Washington, and talked into the night about the H-bomb.

The bomb was impractical, Oppenheimer said. "If you should build one, it would be so big you couldn't deliver it." The Russians never will build one, he predicted.

"Well, I don't know anything about physics, and I don't

113

know anything about foreign affairs," Jackson replied, "but if I were a Russian I would seek to overcome whatever the United States has always been dominant in—and that's science and technology. That would be the logical direction for them to go." Oppenheimer disagreed. An American go-ahead on the H-bomb would only be fanning the arms race, Oppenheimer said.

"He was honest. I never had any doubt about him," Jackson said later. "I think he had a guilt complex because of his role in the Manhattan Project."

Through talks with the scientists, Jackson perceived an unexpected problem in the nation's quest for technical supremacy: McCarthyism. Many top scientists in the United States were Jews. They had joined anti-Nazi groups in the United States, many of which were taken over in time by the Communists. The scientists were intimidated by the damning investigations by McCarthy. Many of the scientists were wary of becoming involved in defense programs because a long-ago membership in such an organization could mean a subpoena. The man and his family would be the objects of the dreaded witch-hunt. "They all raised this question," Jackson reflected. "Here was concrete proof of the damage McCarthy was doing."

The anger persisted. There was a new war in Korea. McCarthyism was still on the rise.

". . . *The appeasing Democrats, always supported by YOUR Congressman, waited and appeased—waited until it was too late; waited until our ill-trained and ill-equipped green troops could be mowed down in mass murder . . . But Korea isn't all. The Red Terror is on the march. . . .*"

Your congressman was Henry M. Jackson. The hot words were from a 1950 campaign advertisement by Jackson's Republican challenger that year, Herb Wilson, an Everett businessman. Jackson . . . Commie-coddler, the man who resisted investigating subversives . . . fellow traveler, defender of General Marshall. George Marshall, the traitor.

There was special personal hurt that year. The telephone rang. Mrs. Jackson, now widowed at eighty-two, moved slowly to pick up the receiver.

Mrs. Jackson, did you know that your son is a Communist? The voice said only that. There was silence. Then the caller hung up.

The calls came often. The voices were different. Jackson was furious. Don't they know what they're doing? "My God, she's got a serious heart condition. This could kill her."

Gertrude, Jackson's older sister, who always campaigned for him, was a target too. They spoke to her on the street or in a store: *Your brother's a Communist. There goes the Communist's sister.*

The telephone calls persisted. *Mrs. Jackson, your son's a Commie.*

Jackson concluded there was little hope in trying to reason with people possessed by the fear of Communist subversion. *You could see it in their eyes. When you tried to reason with them, you found it just was no use.* Their emotions were rising on the stream of fear-inspiring events and public accusations: spy trials . . . secret documents moving to Russia . . . Communists in the State Department. It could all be fitted into a pattern with the proper kind of Right-Wing interpretation and, in that context, Jackson could be seen as the most dangerous kind of person. He gave lip service to the need for military preparedness against Communism in the world, but he seemed unable to comprehend—or, for some reason, unwilling to recognize—the real danger of subversion *within*.

The Washington State legislature, beginning in 1946, had its own subversive search. The Canwell Committee, led by a slightly-built, unblinking conservative named Al Canwell, a Spokane Republican, conducted a blitzing probe of Communists, former Communists, and persons who had belonged to groups considered to be Communist-front organizations. They were not hard to find. Radical activity had flourished in the state during the Depression. The hearings were sometimes raucous. Witnesses often refused to answer questions, indictments were handed out and some professors were summarily dismissed from the University of Washington for their refusal to answer questions. The agitation, recriminations, and doubts stirred by that committee boiled for several years in the state.

Jackson was troubled by the emotional atmosphere but his reflex response to public passions is a glacial calm. He delivered stern, unexciting campaign lectures: "The greatest issue facing America today is the struggle against world Communism. I believe that Communism is essentially an idea—a bad idea. We have a better idea—freedom, coupled with prosperity. Our most immediate job is to mobilize the full military and economic strength of the free world so that the men in the Kremlin will not start a World War III. This means continuing our programs of military aid to Greece and Turkey, the North Atlantic Pact . . . as well as our program of economic aid through our Marshall Plan."

He found a responsive way to talk about the menace of internal Communism with Scandinavian audiences: "Norway, which defeated its Communists at the polls, proves

116

that where there is prosperity and social justice, Communism withers and dies."

Wilson, the Republican candidate, was a feeble candidate and, after a season of uncertainty in 1950, Jackson won an easy victory. Democrats across the state rejoiced at this victory margin of more than sixty percent. They concluded that Jackson was the Democrat who in 1952 could slay the fire-breathing Republican dragon in the United States Senate: Harry P. Cain.

Jackson had been savoring that idea for years. He had a powerful desire to be in the Senate. He and a House colleague, John Kennedy of Massachusetts, had discussed their plans for Senate campaigns in 1952.

Senator Harry Cain was a thunderbolt of a man. As mayor of Tacoma he was considered one of the state's most exciting young Democrats. He went off to World War II, became a paratrooper colonel, and returned from Europe in 1946, just in time to be elected by a hero-worshipping state to the United States Senate—as a Republican. Some Democrats in the state thought at the time he was—beneath the Republican label—still a Democrat. Cain quickly shattered that notion. He became one of the most vocal conservatives and one of the most dashing Communist-hunters in the Senate.

Cain's voice was like thunder filtered through gravel. His personal appearance was electric. His speeches, delivered in a loosened-necktie, let's-get-down-to-business style, were almost hypnotic. His mobile face could change from an expression of joy to dark outrage in an instant. Always his hair was tousled. Just as he had jumped from airplanes into the action in Europe, he delighted in jumping into the midst of the political action, wherever it was. Often the action seemed to be around the issue of patriotism. Cain's friend was Senator Joe McCarthy, but it would be unfair to say that Cain was a disciple of McCarthy: Harry Cain had hit the Communists earlier and harder than had McCarthy. The two senators marched in cadence, on the same cause through the late 1940s and into the young '50s.

Cain was a political body puncher. He proved that in his 1949 attack on Mon Wallgren. Wallgren was the Everett congressman who in 1940 gave Jackson the notion to run for the House of Representatives. Later Wallgren served in the Senate, then was elected to a four-year term as governor of Washington. After his re-election defeat in 1948, Wallgren was nominated by President Truman, a longtime friend and poker-playing pal, to become chairman of the National Security Resources Board.

Cain was infuriated by the nomination. Where, asked Cain, could Communism find a more logical point to penetrate America's vitals, than through the National Security Resources Board? The chairman of the board, Cain said, "should show the ability to stay away from the Communist entanglements. He should be able to recognize the Communists and pro-Communists with whom he must deal and he should be in a position to keep such people from his staffs. The record proves beyond any question . . . that the highest appointive offices in the state (during Wallgren's term as governor) went to Communists and pro-Communists."

Under Wallgren, Cain added, Communists controlled the selection of appointees to state offices and further, Wallgren "aided in the conversion of the Democratic party into

118

a Left-Wing machine controlled directly and indirectly by the Communist party."

When there was a parliamentary move in the Senate to bring the Wallgren confirmation to a vote, Cain staged a one-man filibuster. In March, 1949, the Senate Armed Services Committee, moved by the heat of Cain's attack, tabled the appointment. It was an extraordinary rebuke. Several months later, Wallgren was confirmed as a member of another federal board, the Federal Power Commission. Wallgren had not been a great governor, but he did not deserve the attack, the sting of which lingered until his death in 1963.

Jackson had long before made up his mind to run against Cain in 1952. But he thought it over carefully before announcing his candidacy on May 31, his fortieth birthday. He may well have had some misgivings about his chances. It is difficult to unseat a senator, even such an eccentric as Harry Cain. Then, too, with Eisenhower as the Presidential nominee, there appeared to be a chance that 1952 would be a great Republican year, perhaps even a landslide year.

Salter had been in Seattle since 1950, making all the early arrangements for the Jackson campaign. He was regional director for the Office of Price Administration, but the fact that he was on the federal payroll never distracted Salter from his steady practice of politics. He and Jackson talked it over. They agreed 1952 would be a year of ringing pro-Communism charges. The unpleasant telephone calls to Jackson's mother continued. Now Jackson had a fresh, new, super-liberal target on his voting record. He had voted *no* on an amendment which stripped Alger Hiss of his right to a $61-a-month pension. Anyone who wanted to do something for Alger Hiss had to be a pinko, the Right Wing charged. Jackson regarded the Hiss pension vote in his detached, legalistic way: "It's elementary Anglo-Saxon law. You punish a man for what he does. You don't proceed to punish him beyond the crime." Hiss had been punished for his crime of perjury.

Harry Cain also was vulnerable, though. His popularity was in a steady decline since his 1946 election. Voters remembered unflattering photographs of Cain, wild-eyed, shirt collar open, during another of his filibusters—then it was against rent controls. *Time* magazine designated Cain as one of the Senate's most expendable senators.

The image gulf between Jackson and Cain was vast. Jackson still blushed when reporters asked, "When are you going to get married?" He still spent most of his evenings reading newspapers or documents about his new passion, atomic energy.

Harry Cain, meanwhile, had been involved in a widely-publicized triangle. He set an unusual Senate precedent once by summoning a press conference to announce that his wife was divorcing him. Then came juicy gossip stories about Cain's love affair with a secretary. One story told of an encounter between the two women as they visited Cain at a hospital. Mrs. Cain was quoted as saying, "You may have won the game, but you'll never get the name." The Cains still were married during the campaign.

Joe McCarthy told Harry Cain he would come into Washington to help in his re-election campaign and the Jackson campaign camp was uneasy about the possible impact. It was impossible to guess if the smoldering anti-Communist feelings could be fanned by McCarthy into a political eruption. Jackson had the vivid recollection of the

1950 campaign in Maryland. Senator Millard Tydings, an occasional Sunday-softball-game acquaintance of Jackson, was beaten in a smear campaign abetted by McCarthy.

Jackson attacked Cain hard and early. He seemed almost to have adopted some of the McCarthy style himself: "Cain can talk from now until doomsday, but he cannot escape the fact that he and the Left-Wing senator from Idaho, Glenn Taylor, were the only two senators who voted against a seventy-group air force." Jackson shifted to a home issue. Cain had voted against an appropriation for Grand Coulee Dam. "Imagine, with our state facing a brownout in its defense plant operations . . . with thousands of acres of land thirsting for irrigation, Harry Cain turned his back on his constituents and voted against his state, national security, and the prosperity of the region."

Abruptly Jackson had even some conservatives moving his way, even though Cain charged that Jackson had steadily assisted Communism.

Meanwhile, McCarthyism was on trial in Wisconsin. He had determined opposition in his primary election, but when the September 9 primary election results came in, McCarthy had won an overwhelming vote of confidence: His vote was greater than that of all the other senatorial candidates combined; McCarthy's crusade against Communists and subversive elements was vindicated. Harry Cain was elated that the McCarthy magic was greater than ever. It would be needed against Jackson.

McCarthy arrived in Seattle in the final days of the campaign, feeling especially surly. He was tired and in some pain. He had undergone surgery to correct an abdominal hernia and the incision was still tender. Some friends in Seattle arranged for a bodyguard to protect the senator from foes who would willfully—but seemingly by accident—jam an elbow into his middle. McCarthy's first speech was to be a beauty—at a Republican rally in Scoop Jackson's hometown of Everett. Jackson two years earlier had called McCarthy a tarpot politician and McCarthy, keeper of dossiers, remembered that. Jackson's hometown needed a lecture about their congressman's votes against anti-Communism and his curious support of George Marshall and Alger Hiss, McCarthy reasoned. But McCarthy's airplane was diverted to Portland, so he missed the rally in Everett.

The next day he traveled north to Seattle, contemplating two major speeches. One was listed on his schedule as a press-club banquet. The other was a live telecast on station KING and a major audience was expected.

The press-club dinner was, McCarthy learned, a gridiron affair. Among those in the crowd of about six hundred jammed into a dining room at the Norway Center, many had downed too many cocktails during the prolonged social hour. Furious arguments already were erupting. The forces for McCarthy and Cain were in verbal battle with McCarthy critics. The scene was all the national passions over McCarthyism and anti-Communism compressed into one uninhibited, almost bizarre, comic microcosm.

A raucous mock political convention—lampooning national politics—unfolded. McCarthy glowered at the impropriety of such clowning at a time of such national peril. He asked if he could deliver his speech and leave: Otherwise, he would be late for his scheduled television broadcast.

An uproar of cheers and hoots greeted his introduction. Someone in the divided audience hurled a dinner roll at an "enemy" table. *I didn't come 2400 miles to be a funnyman,* shouted the senator over the din. More noise. More shouts. "Shaddup." "Let him talk." "Go home." "Character assassin." *You can't fight skunks with kid gloves and lace cuffs.* It was no use.

McCarthy's jolting speech on behalf of Harry Cain never was delivered. McCarthy was due at the television appearance and amid the chaos—just before the police were called—he left.

At the nearby television studio, McCarthy ran into still another frustration. He arrived accompanied by local anti-Communists, including Al Canwell, former chairman of the state's Un-American Activities Investigating Committee and the Republican candidate for congressman-at-large in 1952. Station officials told McCarthy that some parts of the script, submitted in advance, had to be deleted.

McCarthy responded angrily: *What are you talking about?* A station attorney pointed out the objectionable passage: "Perhaps the people of Washington State are not aware that Drew Pearson has long had as his leg man one David Karr, alias D. Katz, who worked for the official Communist paper, the *Daily Worker*, and then was rewrite man for the *Communist Party Organizer* and graduated to Pearson's staff. Another member of Pearson's staff was Andrew Older, a man proven to be a Communist by FBI undercover agents. Pearson admitted he knew that Older was a Communist while he was doing Pearson's writing. . . ."

That was potential libel, station officials said. Canwell objected: You're deliberately cutting the heart out of the speech. *A contrived effort to keep McCarthy off the air.*

Under Federal Communications Commission law a station cannot censor a candidate's remarks, McCarthy protested. But McCarthy was a candidate in Wisconsin, not Wash-

ington, Richard Riddell, the station attorney argued. Mc-
Carthy could go on the air, but the controversial section
had to be deleted, Riddell insisted.

Senator Warren G. Magnuson, Washington's Democrat
in the Senate, was at the studio. Unflappable Maggie had
agreed to a Democratic party request that he appear on
the air immediately after the McCarthy speech to rebut
any charges made against Jackson. McCarthy saw him and
exclaimed: *Maggie, they won't let me go on the air.*

Magnuson shrugged, his round Scandinavian face a portrait of mournful, round-eyed consternation. *Hell, Joe, that
means I may not get on either.*

Miffed by the deletion of the Drew Pearson segment of
his speech, McCarthy decided to give no speech at all—not
even his praise of Harry Cain or the allegations of Communist sympathy against Jackson. Threatening to take the
matter up with the F.C.C., McCarthy stormed out of
the studio.

The expectant television audience was denied its view of
Senator McCarthy. It got instead a prerecorded musical
program. It is unlikely that anything McCarthy could have
said or done could have altered the outcome of the Cain-
Jackson race. Scoop Jackson, campaigning hard around the
state, had the homespun-boy look about him. The Jackson
political magic was taking effect.

The top story in the Seattle *Times* the day following
the 1952 election told of the sweeping Republican victory
in the nation and state. The Republican victory news was
so great the story didn't mention until the ninth paragraph
the election of Jackson to the United States Senate.

*The one outstanding Democratic victory in this state
was Congressman Henry M. Jackson's defeat of Senator*

Harry P. Cain. Cain's disfavor with the voters was such that he was unable to win even in the Republican tide.

Scoop Jackson—hard-working politician with the soda-pop reputation, survivor of the Right Wing's fear years, a winner when other Democrats lose, entered the Senate.

6

SHOWDOWN IN THE CAUCUS ROOM

THE DEMOCRATS WERE understandably uncomfortable with their circumstances as the 83rd Congress convened in January 1953. For the first time in twenty years a Republican was preparing to move into the White House and Dwight Eisenhower's landslide victory also had swept the Republicans into narrow control of the Senate.

To be sure, the 1952 elections had not been a complete debacle for the Democrats. Despite losing control of the Senate, they had added a few bright new faces, the kind that gave the party a fresh, young look. In New England a handsome, rich war hero, John F. Kennedy, had bucked Ike's landslide successfully. In the Pacific Northwest an attractive liberal, Scoop Jackson, had survived a last-minute smear campaign and moved into the Senate. In Montana, Mike Mansfield had made it. Missouri sent a new man, Stuart Symington, and Tennessee elected Albert Gore. But they were an elite group, survivors of the great Republican tide that finally ended the Democratic era of New Deals and Fair Deals.

Republican control of the Senate was tenuous—the margin was just 48 to 47—but it was enough to wrest the committee chairmanships away from the Democrats. In 1953 that presented a special problem—not only for the Democratic Party but also for the nation. Elevated to the raw power of the chairmanship of the Senate Committee on Government Operations was Senator Joseph R. McCarthy, who had begun his strange, twisted crusade against Communism three years earlier and now had a new forum.

For the United States the years since the end of World War II had been puzzling, perplexing, and bewildering. A difficult and dangerous new world force had emerged from the ashes of the war, changing the map, subjugating peoples, threatening domination of the whole globe. Half of Europe had disappeared behind an Iron Curtain, China had been lost, a hot war was raging in Korea. Atom secrets had been leaked to Russia and now the Russians had the bomb. The threat of nuclear holocaust hung over the world. And, in the hinterlands of America, people were afraid.

The senator from Wisconsin, Joe McCarthy, appeared on this scene in 1950 when he delivered a speech in Wheeling, West Virginia, waving a file-folder in which he claimed were the names of 205 card-carrying Communists working and subverting in the State Department. McCarthy opted for the easy answer to the new threat: Communists everywhere, in the State Department, in the Information Agency, in the Army, under the bed, subverting, corrupting, spying, selling out America. Over the next three years McCarthy's numbers would change, his charges would vary and almost nothing ever would be proved. But his tactics were consistent. Joe McCarthy was expert at one thing: Exploiting fear and, in this perverted era, there was some truth to the statement that he even held two American Presidents hostage through that exploitation.

As the 83rd Congress was being organized, Minority Leader Lyndon B. Johnson viewed the selection of the

127

Democrats who would sit on the McCarthy committee as his most pressing problem. He made the selections in typical Johnsonian fashion and, on January 12, William S. White described the reasoning in a lead article in *The New York Times*.

"The Senate Democratic hierarchy assigned the party's most aggressive new members today to act as counterweights to Senator Joseph R. McCarthy," White wrote.

". . . To the Senate Committee on Government Operations (parent to the investigating subcommittee) Senator Johnson and his colleagues in the Democratic leadership added three new senators known as strong party fighters and members of the liberal faction—men who will not have to face an election again for six years. These were Senators Henry M. Jackson of Washington, John F. Kennedy of Massachusetts and Stuart Symington of Missouri."

Scoop Jackson did not think Lyndon Johnson was doing him a favor. Jackson had had his fill of battling McCarthyism in his campaign against Harry Cain. And, being an intense and determined man, he had hoped for considerably more substantive committee assignments. Most of all, he had hoped for a seat on the Armed Services Committee. Secondarily, he wanted a place on the Joint Committee on Atomic Energy on which he had served in the House.

The new senator from Washington was convinced that there was a Communist problem. But he and the Commiechasers of the fifties had one basic difference: They were convinced the problem was internal and Jackson was convinced that the threat was external. The Communist threat, in Jackson's eyes, existed in the Kremlin, not in the State Department. Jackson had no use for McCarthy or his crusade. McCarthyism, he said, was "the cheap way out." Still, he had no desire to get into a political meat-grinder—the seemingly inevitable fate of anyone who dared to get in the way of McCarthy's rampage.

As the showdown with Joe McCarthy neared, Scoop Jackson was a very reluctant dragon-killer.

The cramped, fourth-floor office was filled to the ceiling with boxes and files and mementos, just recently transferred across the manicured grounds of the Capitol from the House side to the Senate side. Freshman senators are not given choice quarters, and Scoop Jackson's new office was almost lost in a far corner of the top floor of the Old Senate Office Building.

John Salter and his coterie of secretaries and aides rushed around, jockeying for key desk space, sizing up the location of the nearest lavatories, eyeing their new senatorial neighbors. Wall space was carefully examined as a site for the grinning-politician photo gallery that any man would have after a dozen years in the House—an autographed picture shaking hands with Harry Truman; an arm-around shot with his already well-established Senate colleague, Warren G. Magnuson; a smattering of photos with New Deal and Fair Deal luminaries. There was a handful of plaques and awards, mostly given to him for his liberalism. The new man from the Pacific Northwest had established his credentials well. He was anathema to the conservatives, considered dangerous by the Right Wing.

Amid the hubbub in those heady, first days in the Senate, a fourth-floor neighbor often dropped by, poked his head in the door and asked how things were going. The neighbor was instantly recognizable—thinning dark hair, heavy eyebrows, plump face, jowly chin, easy smile, but a smile that never seemed to spread to the eyes. Joe McCarthy was, on a personal level, a pleasant man. He would joke

129

with Scoop Jackson's secretaries and let them know that he really was just a nice, well-meaning, warm-hearted guy. Sure, he had gone out to Seattle and tried to rough up their boss in the election campaign. But that's politics. Nothing personal in that. . . .

Within weeks after the committee assignments were made, Joe McCarthy once again went for Henry Jackson's vitals. The issue was a Voice of America radio transmitter known as Baker West, located in an isolated corner of Jackson's old congressional district. The site was near the Dungeness Flats, a remote beach in the far northwestern corner of the nation where the frigid Straits of Juan de Fuca divide the United States from Canada. McCarthy concluded that the location had been chosen because of subversives in the information services.

In his last term in the House of Representatives Congressman Jackson—always in search of federal payrolls for his constituents—had fought vigorously to land the political plum in his congressional district. He had argued that his district provided the closest possible site for the transmitter's target area—Siberia and Central China.

McCarthy's approach to Baker West was typical of his style. He found a disgruntled Voice of America engineer named Lewis McKesson and placed him in the witness chair. McKesson testified that the site—even though it had been approved by a distinguished group of scientists from the Massachusetts Institute of Technology—was in a magnetic field that would make it much easier for the Russians to jam the broadcasts.

"Let us assume we have a good Voice of America, a voice that is really the voice of America," McCarthy said suggestively, leaning forward toward the witness for empha-

130

sis. "Assume I do not want it to reach Communist territory. Would not the best way to sabotage that voice be to place your transmitters within that magnetic storm area?"

"I would agree with you one hundred percent," the engineer replied.

No other knowledgeable witnesses were presented and no other substantive testimony was given. But it was a sign of the times, an indicator of the mood of the McCarthy era, that the next day the edgy federal officials who ran the Voice of America closed down Baker West. It never was reopened.

For Jackson, a senator just six weeks and a member of the committee an even shorter time, it was a painful and embarrassing rebuke. He was stung by a swarm of critical editorials, some with nasty implications about this left-leaning newcomer to the Senate. Jackson took McCarthy's lunge at Baker West as a lunge at Jackson and his interpretation probably was correct. But Jackson didn't lunge back. His response, or the apparent lack of it, was the first real tipoff as to the kind of senator the new man from Washington was going to be—methodical almost to the point of becoming tedious, consistent almost to the point of becoming boring, cautious almost to the point of seeming gutless, unemotional almost to the point of seeming uncaring.

Carrying any of those stolid, Nordic characteristics to the negative conclusions would be a serious mistake in evaluating the personality of Henry Jackson. But, at times, the personality traits bothered even Jackson's closest friends.

During his first years in the Senate Jackson lived in a third-floor bedroom of a Georgetown house at 3407 O Street. His landlords were Bob and Frances Low, who were newlyweds at the time and old Jackson friends. Jackson, Low, and Salter had shared the house in their bachelor days. When the Lows were married, Salter quickly moved out to give the newlyweds some privacy. But Jackson, typically, lingered on. Once, Frances' mother gingerly questioned her about the propriety of the arrangement. Frances replied laughingly that anyone who knew Scoop Jackson would know that her reputation wasn't being endangered. "Oh, Frances," Mrs. Low's mother responded, "it isn't *your* reputation I'm worried about. It's Scoop's."

Bob Low was a bright New York lawyer whose job at the State Department involved evaluating McCarthy's charges against department employees. Frances was a former *Time* Capitol Hill correspondent who was working temporarily on Jackson's staff. Like most liberal, New York Jews, the Lows were vehemently anti-McCarthy.

As McCarthy's last great witch-hunt began, a distinct pattern developed among the three Democrats who had taken seats on his investigating subcommittee. The Democrats were led by dour John L. McClellan, a former prosecutor from Arkansas and the subcommittee member who probably had the most to lose, politically, by opposing McCarthy. Next came Stuart Symington, a Missourian who was the most inclined to fight fire with fire. Symington was emotional and occasionally he reacted bombastically to McCarthy's abusive tactics. Then came Henry Jackson, whose subdued and quiet manner attracted the least attention. Jackson had concluded, during McCarthy's extravagant performance in the Baker West incident, that he would not "get into a shouting match with a skunk." He didn't, but Jackson's style caused him some problems with his liberal friends.

At night, after dinner at the house on O Street, Bob and Frances Low worked him over, sometimes roughly. *For*

132

God's sake, Scoop, they would say, *do something. The man has to be stopped*. Jackson answered, defensively, that he *was* doing something, doling out the rope that would allow McCarthy to hang himself. "The worst thing you can do is counter McCarthy with another form of emotion," he told them. "It's like the Cold War itself. It takes patience."

Back home, in Washington State, Jackson was getting heat from another direction. Most of the press, and perhaps even a majority of his constituents, were McCarthy supporters. A major and important exception was the largest and most powerful newspaper in the state, the Seattle *Times*. The *Times* was a solidly Republican, conservative newspaper, but it couldn't abide McCarthyism. Still, almost all the smaller dailies backed McCarthy. At the height of McCarthyism Scoop Jackson's hometown newspaper, the Everett *Herald*, solemnly declared that McCarthy was "essential to the democratic processes that we cherish." Jackson felt the pressures from both sides.

In his early months on the McCarthy committee Jackson steered a cautious course, but there was no doubt where he stood. Two months after he entered the Senate, he told the Women's National Press Club in Washington that he was a "little horrified" by the "pretty close to third-degree" tactics of McCarthy and his young sidekick, Roy Cohn. "More than anything else," Jackson said, "we must safeguard the witness." There would be many ironic twists in Jackson's efforts to safeguard the civil liberties of witnesses taken apart by McCarthy and Cohn. In April McCarthy zeroed in on James Wechsler, the editor of the liberal New York *Post*. Wechsler, who had joined the Young Communist League in his youth, was an easy target and McCarthy mauled him. But Jackson defended the editor, pointing out that he had long since severed his ties with the

League and had been writing anti-Communist articles in the *Post*. Almost two decades later, with Jackson still warning about Communists *in the Kremlin*, Wechsler would decimate his onetime defender, almost accuse him of warmongering because of his tough line on the Russians.

As McCarthy's crusade accelerated in 1953, Jackson edged more and more out of his cautious shell. In late April he joined Senators Herbert Lehman and Mike Mansfield in challenging the Democratic Party to make McCarthyism the issue in the 1954 election campaigns. And, as McCarthy moved into his ludicrous "book burning" episode in May and June, Jackson began to show the first real signs of outrage.

The State Department, already pummeled by McCarthy's charges about subversive employees, caved in easily when the man from Wisconsin darkly announced that America's overseas libraries were filled with Communist-authored and Communist-influenced books. Thousands of books were pulled off the library shelves, and some of them were burned. The European press compared the incident to Hitler's book-burnings in the thirties. Jackson grumbled that books were being removed for the poorest of reasons —math books taken off the shelves because the author had been associated with Communist fronts, technical handbooks because the author had taken the Fifth Amendment. "Good God," Jackson complained, "with that kind of thinking the Gettysburg Address is subversive because, did you know, Lincoln corresponded with Marx."

Still, Jackson played his quiet waiting game. "When he would shout and rave," Jackson said later, "I would always try to come back quietly." In the long run, McCarthy would show himself to be "the fraud he was, intellectually dishonest."

In its July issue the arch-conservative magazine, *American Mercury*, published an article by J. B. Matthews, whom McCarthy had hired a month earlier as the staff director for his committee.

"The largest single group supporting the Communist apparatus in the United States today is composed of Protestant clergymen," Matthews began his article. "Since the beginning of the First Cold War in April, 1948, the Communist Party has placed more and more reliance upon the ranks of the Protestant clergy to provide the party's subversive apparatus with its agents, stooges, front men and fellow-travelers. Clergymen outnumber professors two to one in supporting the Communist-front apparatus of the Kremlin conspiracy. . . ."

Matthews went on to estimate that seven thousand Protestant clergymen were serving the Communist cause in the United States. So much of that kind of talk was floating around in 1953 that, at first, the *American Mercury* article went almost unnoticed. One Right-Wing congressman placed the article in the *Congressional Record*, but even there it attracted little attention. But on July 2, the Washington *Post* published excerpts of the article and the uproar was instantaneous.

Jackson was the first of the committee's three Democrats to read the *Post*'s article and his reaction was anything but unemotional. Frances Low, who had been needling Jackson for his caution, drove to work with him that morning. He was boiling mad. "If this is the way things are going to go," he muttered, "maybe this is a helluva good time to get out." But his highly honed political instincts told him that Joe McCarthy was in potentially deep trouble as a result of the rash charges made by Matthews. Jackson's instincts were that McCarthy was beginning to choke on

135

the rope. Some of McCarthy's strongest support came from the Bible Belt, but within a matter of days the South's most conservative senators would rise on the Senate floor to condemn J. B. Matthews.

When Jackson, still steaming, arrived at his office, he placed an immediate call to McClellan. McClellan called Symington and the three Democrats decided to confront McCarthy to demand the firing of Matthews. McCarthy, rarely at a loss for words, was stunned. He stalled, asking the Democrats for twenty-four hours to think about a course of action. Unified, the Democrats refused. There was nothing to think about, Jackson informed the chairman. Matthews, he said, had black-brushed the entire Protestant church.

With McCarthy stalling for time, the Democrats issued a public statement demanding that Matthews be fired. His article, they said, was a "shocking and unwarranted attack against the American clergy." Jackson added that the charges were "fantastic" and "outrageous." *The New York Times* concluded editorially that McCarthy finally had "overreached himself." The next day, when a Republican member of the subcommittee, Charles E. Potter of Michigan, sided with the Democrats, it appeared that McCarthy could be outvoted on the Matthews question. McCarthy refused to let it come to a vote, contending that he alone had the right to hire and fire.

The Democrats were not mollified. For a few hours they stewed and fretted. Then they announced that they were quitting the subcommittee, complaining that McCarthy had established one-man rule. Neither of the other Democrats on the full committee—Hubert Humphrey of Minnesota or John Kennedy of Massachusetts—was eager to take a position on the subcommittee. For the rest of 1953, as McCarthy's campaign grew wilder and wilder, the McCarthy committee would be without Democrats. It didn't seem to bother the senator from Wisconsin.

"This would appear to be a continuation of the old Democratic policy of either rule or ruin," McCarthy said. "I will accept the resignations. If they don't want to take part in uncovering the graft and corruption of the old Truman-Acheson administration, they are, of course, entitled to refuse."

Later, McCarthy sent the Democrats a sarcastic invitation to rejoin the subcommittee. They all declined.

"Committees dealing with anything so sensitive as people's lives, reputations and livelihoods, by their very nature, must approach their duties in an objective, sane and responsible manner," Jackson wrote in reply to McCarthy. "Since I can find nothing in your letter that indicates any change in subcommittee policies or any desire to afford subcommittee members the authority, right and voice commensurate with their responsibility, I must respectfully decline your invitation.

Three weeks afterward, Robert F. Kennedy, a young assistant counsel to the McCarthy committee for the past seven months, took Scoop Jackson's advice and also quit. Bob Kennedy, brother of a Democratic senator, had joined the McCarthy crusade because that seemed to be where the action was. But the action got out of hand.

Almost twenty years after the collapse of McCarthyism, Jackson still is not certain what motivated the man from Wisconsin. He sees McCarthy as an almost classic split personality.

137

Before the committee would meet he could be the most affable, likable, charming chairman or senator you ever met. But the minute the gavel banged it was the story of Doctor Jekyll and Mister Hyde. You could just see the change come over his face. That voice would rise, just as it did on television and radio, and he would get up to the screaming point in dealing with a witness. "So and so, don't you realize that what you are engaged in here is a subversion of our country, turning it over to the Communists? Don't you realize that?!!"

It's hard to know to this day whether McCarthy really was doing these things because he believed this was the answer or whether he thought it was the way to glory. I have the feeling he took a certain delight in this kind of crusade. I never saw the kind of evidence that he really believed that this was the answer to the problems we faced.

But there are some things in life that really get to you. I watched his tactics. He was attempting to blackmail people. He had a dossier on every member of the committee, on every member of Eisenhower's Cabinet, and even on Eisenhower himself. I was aware that they had sent investigators out to Washington State, that they thought they had something on me in my law practice. They figured they had it on me with Communists—that I'd been associated with Communists.

There was no basis for creating a state of fear in this country. But it was clear he was doing that. Of all the forms of tyranny over the mind of man, fear is the worst. He was using fear to literally repeal the Bill of Rights. . . .

But if McCarthyism was a national tragedy, it also was a personal one for the man who spawned it. As his notoriety grew, McCarthy's heavy drinking intensified. To Jackson, it seemed that he was literally killing himself with liquor throughout his two years as chairman. Once, at a morning executive session of the subcommittee, Jackson arrived early and caught a glimpse of the chairman standing in the bathroom, chug-a-lugging straight whiskey by the glassful. Day after day, McCarthy would show up for committee hearings heavily fortified by alcohol. As his troubles grew, he fell back more and more on the liquor and his charges grew wilder, his accusations more and more irrational. He hinted that he would call former-President Truman to the witness chair. He began talking about subversives in the Army and accused generals of protecting Communists.

Shortly after the Democrats left the committee in disgust, G. David Schine was drafted into the Army. Schine was a young millionaire who had volunteered as an investigator for McCarthy. He was a close friend of Roy Cohn and, earlier in the year, they had gone to Europe together to conduct the investigation that led to McCarthy's attack on the State Department's overseas libraries.

Flushed with power, McCarthy began making private telephone calls to the Pentagon, not too subtly seeking favors for Private Schine. Roy Cohn did the same thing, even less subtly. At the same time McCarthy charged publicly that the Army had allowed the loss of radar secrets to known Communists at Fort Monmouth, New Jersey.

In early 1954, McCarthy, in a fit of rage, ordered Brigadier General Ralph W. Zwicker out of a hearing investigating the Fort Monmouth charges. Later, he called him back to testify on what he called the Army's "coddling" of "Fifth Amendment Communists." For the Secretary of the Army, Robert T. Stevens, McCarthy's reckless action was the last straw. Stevens told Zwicker and other Army officers not to testify before the McCarthy committee and announced that he would testify in their place.

Joe McCarthy had been given all the rope he needed, and he had used it.

Scoop Jackson and the other Democrats returned to the McCarthy committee on February 23, 1954, after receiving the concession that they could hire their own staff assistant. As the showdown between the senator from Wisconsin and the United States Army neared, they hired Bob Kennedy as their minority counsel.

Jackson quickly showed that, if anything, his feelings about the tactics of Joe McCarthy had intensified in his absence from the committee.

The day after the Democrats returned, McCarthy aggressively attacked an attorney for one of the witnesses, telling him that he didn't consider him a "typical Communist lawyer." Jackson bristled and challenged the chairman for implying the lawyer was a Communist but not typical.

"You go ahead, Mr. Jackson, if you like, and protect Communist lawyers coming before this committee," McCarthy snapped back. "You have absented yourself from attending committee meetings. You have no idea how Communist lawyers have been misinforming and misadvising their clients. . . ."

President Eisenhower had been an even more reluctant dragon-killer than Scoop Jackson. His reaction had been quiet wariness. But, by March 1954, he was clearly trying to kill off what he considered a cancer within his own party. He denounced the lack of fair play by some congressional committees and no one had any doubt about which committee he had in mind. Defense Secretary Charles E. Wilson had a candid, terse response to Mc-

Carthy's statement about Commie-coddling by the Army: "Just damned tommyrot."

On March 12 the Army responded with its heavy artillery and it was the beginning of the end of McCarthyism. In a long documented statement McCarthy's aide, Roy Cohn, was accused of threatening to "wreck the Army" unless special privileges were given to his buddy, G. David Schine. The Army charged, and contended that it had proof through monitored telephone calls, that both Cohn and McCarthy had threatened retaliation through the committee if the Army didn't take care of Schine. Cohn reacted by calling the charges "absurd." McCarthy counterattacked, in his usual fashion, by accusing the Army of trying to "blackmail" him into discontinuing his investigation of the Fort Monmouth situation.

Three days later Jackson proposed a joint investigation by the McCarthy committee and a subcommittee of the Senate Armed Services Committee in an effort to determine who was "telling the truth." Asked on television whether he thought someone was lying, Jackson responded, "Well, sure. Someone obviously is not telling the truth." The next day, however, the investigating subcommittee agreed to investigate itself, with McCarthy stepping down and Senator Karl Mundt, a staunch but fair-minded conservative from South Dakota, agreeing to take over as temporary chairman. The Army hired a calm, articulate Boston lawyer, Robert Welch, to handle its defense.

As the pressure heightened, and his drinking intensified, McCarthy became zanier and zanier, almost a burlesque of himself. On the eve of the showdown he left on a national speaking tour which some compared to Woodrow Wilson's quest for public support for the League of Nations. But McCarthy was anything but Wilsonesque. In Mil-

141

waukee he accused the Democrats of "twenty years of treason—twenty years of tragedy." In Oklahoma he threatened to expose Communists in the press, which now was strongly challenging him. In Wisconsin, a Republican newspaper editor began a movement to recall his state's strange senator.

The hearings were begun on April 22 and immediately they became spectacular. For six days the charges and countercharges were flung back and forth. . . . *blackmail . . . Commie-coddling . . . wreck the Army . . . have you no sense of decency?* And Joe McCarthy, under the powerful white lights of early-day television, grew more and more extreme . . . *point of order, Mister Chairman . . . I am above the law. . . .*

On the sixth day, with the accusations getting tumultuously out of hand, Jackson announced to the press that he was looking for a "clean cut" perjury case. Someone, he said once again, is lying. "I am going to try to resolve the confusion about this controversy by asking questions with yes-or-no answers tied directly to the federal perjury statutes."

In the hearing he began with Secretary Stevens. Methodically, Jackson read the federal perjury statute, which established penalties of up to five years in prison and a $2,000 fine for lying on the witness stand.

"There are a number of allegations and statements concerning you, Mr. Stevens," he told the secretary. "If those responsible for making them repeat them under oath before this committee, then someone is guilty of perjury. Now this is a most serious matter, and I know you will consider deeply as I put these questions to you."

Then Jackson began reading the Cohn and McCarthy allegations in full. After each one he asked simply: "Is that statement true or false?" Stevens answered false to each. The same day Jackson questioned Cohn along the same lines and McCarthy sarcastically interrupted him to offer a better line of questioning. Momentarily, Jackson had a flash of anger. He replied sharply: "Since when did I ever suggest to other members of this committee or witnesses what questions they ought to ask?"

The next day the *Christian Science Monitor* concluded that Jackson's questions were "pivotal" in bringing some semblance of rationality to the confusion of the disjointed hearings. Jackson persisted in his unstintingly legalistic questioning throughout the hearings. No perjury charges ever would be filed. But it became clear that someone was lying and, because of the unblinking eye of pubescent television, the public could make the choice as to just who it was.

At the beginning of the Army-McCarthy hearings a Gallup poll showed that fifty percent of the American public approved of the senator from Wisconsin. By the end of the tortuous days on national television that percentage had fallen to thirty-six. But the reverse effect was true for Jackson and his fellow Democrats, Stuart Symington and John McClellan. The gossip columnists referred to Jackson as Senator Jimmie Stewart and pointed out that he was young, on the rise, and an available bachelor. Even the critical Right-Wing columnist, George Sokolsky, commented that he looked like "the eternal collegian, young, fresh, buoyant." For the first time in his career strangers would nod to him on the streets of Washington. The mail came in avalanches, some of it nastily critical but most of it not. He received letters from ten-year-old girls saying he was the "handsomest senator on television" and missives from more mature females suggesting that they, too, were available. The chairman of the Democratic National Committee said Jackson now was in top demand for political appearances during the 1954 election campaigns. The national Teamsters newspaper, admiring his quiet liberalism, said that in the aftermath of the hearings "Senator Henry Jackson . . . is the only political personality that will endure." The first speculation began that Jackson, who had been in the Senate less than eighteen months, might make an attractive Vice-Presidential candidate in 1956.

Jackson's attendance record was the best of any member of the committee. For more than 160 hours in April, May, and June of 1954 his subdued image was projected into living rooms throughout the country. But the new fame took its toll, too. By midafternoon each day Jackson would have a splitting, almost debilitating headache, induced by the punishing glare of the television klieg lights. And at night, after the hearings, he and his staff worked on toward midnight, dissecting the testimony and planning the next day's strategy. At times, late at night, he became snappish and irritable. It was out of character for Jackson, but his staff, understanding, took it quietly.

Over the years, Jackson's relationship with his staff was rare for the calloused atmosphere of Capitol Hill. On stage, he came across as amiable but with personal reserve. The reserve vanished with his staff. The staff was family. The newest, youngest secretaries could go to him for personal advice. He was solicitous about their feelings, inquired about their homesickness, never forgot a birthday. The result was near hero-worship of their boss, "the senator." So the staff, from waspish John Salter on down, sympathized with the senator's occasional irritability as the pressures mounted with the Army-McCarthy hearings raging on and on, seemingly endlessly.

By June 11, the thirty-second day of the showdown in the Caucus Room, Joe McCarthy and Roy Cohn were in deep trouble—floundering in adverse testimony, indicted daily by their own images on television. Their public support was seriously diminished. In the Senate even some of the staunchest conservatives were beginning to turn their backs.

McCarthy was in the witness chair on this spectacular Friday near the end of the hearings. Midway through the day Senator Ralph E. Flanders, a taciturn Yankee Republican from Vermont, dramatically entered the Caucus Room and handed McCarthy a letter containing ominous news: Flanders would make a Senate speech demanding his permanent removal as chairman of the committee. At first, McCarthy was dumbfounded: Quiet Ralph Flanders would do this, depart so far from the unwritten rule of Senate chumminess? Then he replied that someone should "get a net" for his colleague.

At the committee table Scoop Jackson, the interrogator, was questioning McCarthy and systematically demolishing the credibility of his young investigator, G. David Schine. Bob Kennedy hovered at Jackson's shoulder, suggesting occasional questions. In the witness chair, McCarthy fidgeted. At his side, Roy Cohn glowered.

Moments earlier Jackson, questioning McCarthy about Schine's qualifications, had been handed a document written by the young investigator. The document contained Schine's plan for combatting Communism. It was infantile. *Fight Communism with pinups. Fight Communism with*

145

bumper stickers. Work through overseas Elks Clubs. As Jackson continued his cross-examination his questions became teasing, mocking, ridiculing. "Really, senator," Jackson pushed on, "when you look at this document, in all seriousness do you think that this qualified a man to investigate a multimillion-dollar information agency? In all seriousness." *Pinups, bumper stickers, billboards, Elks Clubs. In all seriousness, senator.* And in the great, pillared Caucus Room the spectators began to laugh at the man who had held two Presidents hostage.

After the hearing, as the crowd began to file out, McCarthy came to Jackson and complained, almost good-naturedly, that "you really cut me up." But there was no good nature in Cohn. File-folder under his arm, he went straight for Bob Kennedy and, chin to chin, spat out the threat that he would get that Commie-coddling Scoop Jackson on Monday.

The newspaper reporters milled around, gawking at the near-violence of the showdown between Cohn and Kennedy, and then they rushed to Jackson. The senator's reaction was tense and angry: "This is one senator that's not going to be intimidated by anybody. This is not the first threat Mr. Cohn has made during these hearings." But these were haunting times and the weekend that followed was the worst of Jackson's career.

The senator was tipped off that Cohn had obtained some correspondence between him and an admitted Communist. John Salter's reaction was to go out and buy a case of beer. He plopped it down on Jackson's desk and then he, Kennedy, the senator, and the staff spent the weekend, working late into each night, combing through all the correspondence accumulated in Jackson's fourteen-year career in Congress.

146

Painstakingly, their shirtsleeves rolled up to the elbows, they went through the mail—twelve-year-old letters from longshoremen on the Communist-infiltrated waterfronts of Seattle and Everett; a recent one, scrawled, from a Chinese waiter who wanted to get his aging mother off the Communist mainland and into the United States; an old one in the almost childish Marxist-idealist prose of an aging Wobblie; an aggressive one in the harsh dialectics of Seattle's Communist-bossed Pension League. Soda Pop Jackson—his Jimmie Stewart brow furrowed, his headache throbbing—methodically, frantically searched for a letter that might besmirch his white-knight reputation. Corresponded with Communists? Well, sure. Even Communists write their congressmen. But Roy Cohn had it on him, had something on him with the Communists.

By Sunday night the litter overwhelmed the office, but the senator and his staff had found nothing more incriminating than a letter from the little town of Sequim, up in that far Northwestern corner of the United States where Baker West no longer existed. The letter-writer had been fired from his government job during a security scare. And he had been fired for good reason. Later, he defected to Czechoslovakia. Jackson had forwarded the man's complaint to the Civil Service Commission. . . . *Good God, with that kind of reasoning the Gettysburg Address is subversive because, did you know, Lincoln corresponded with Marx.*

But there really was nothing to find. By Monday Cohn was backing away, denying all, and McCarthy said he did "not intend to go into any senator's background at these hearings." Roy Cohn never brought up the subject again.

On Thursday, June 17, the hearings ended. There had been thirty-six days of an acrimonious political circus, the likes of which the nation never had watched before. Mc-Carthy was in ruin, although it was unclear whether he realized it. The proceedings, under the constant glare of television, provided the fledgling medium's first display of the power it could have to influence public opinion.

As the hearings ended Jackson ruminated about the impact of television: "Anyone who participates in this kind of televised hearing is engaged in an extra-hazardous political adventure. You can't cover up sincerity—or the lack of it. On television a man can't cover up the way he behaves. It's right there for the public to see."

Jackson was referring partly to himself, for he had become a TV personality almost overnight. But the same words applied, negatively, to Joe McCarthy.

And, slightly changed by circumstances, the words would apply in the not-too-distant future to a cruel war in Southeast Asia. Jackson, indirectly, would not fare as well by the televising of great public issues in the coming decade of grief in Vietnam.

On December 2, 1954, the Senate voted to censure Joe McCarthy for his behavior. The margin was 67 to 22, with Henry Jackson voting for censure.

One day, at about the time of the censure vote, Jackson had trouble getting out of his car. Within a week the pain had spread through his back, his legs, and his shoulders, and he was nearly paralyzed.

At Walter Reed General Hospital military doctors diagnosed the senator's ailment as fibromyositis and attributed its cause to Jackson's months of tension during the showdown with McCarthy. Inwardly, the seemingly calm, dispassionate senator from Washington had been tied up in knots. "I was dealing with a fanatic," Jackson confided to the doctors. "I got so mad, just furious, that I always had to restrain myself." Some men get ulcers from that sort of tension. But Jackson was afflicted with fibromyositis, a severe inflammation of the body's muscles. For the next seven months he spent three hours a day, five days a week, in therapy at Walter Reed.

The doctors warned Jackson that an attack of fibromyositis can be an isolated, one-shot problem or it can become chronic and plague a man for life. They warned further that Jackson should find a physical way to work off his tensions or he might be faced with a life of periodic agony.

From that moment on, the appointment book in Jackson's highly efficient office was blocked out for forty-five minutes each day. At 6:15, evening after evening, Jackson had an appointment in the Senate gym. He swam twenty laps in the pool, rode the stationary bicycles, and lifted weights. The appointment came to have such high priority that nothing less than a telephone call from the White House could cancel it. It became such a part of the daily office routine that, in the appointment book, it was listed simply as the senator's "committee of one."

7

THE MAKING OF A
MISSILE GAP

THE SENATE TO which Scoop Jackson came in 1953 was a Senate of genteel but strict traditions, of gentlemanly but unyielding customs. It was a Senate of the Old South and the Inner Club, that half-omnipresent, half-mythical group of insiders whose quiet manipulations appeared to guide even the most minute affairs of what had become the most august legislative body since the days of Rome. It also was a Senate that was, or was about to be, molded by the compelling personality of a free-wheeling and dynamic Texan, Lyndon Baines Johnson.

The Senate of the 1950s tried to tolerate its few rebels— its maverick Wayne Morse, its ego-driven Estes Kefauver and even, up to a point, its unfathomable Joe McCarthy. But, within the institution itself, there really was only one route to success. As in any gentleman's club, flamboyance and unconventional behavior were looked upon with displeasure. The way to get ahead was to work within the system and then draw on all its benefits.

Arriving in the Senate, Scoop Jackson was not the type to enjoy or participate in the boisterous camaraderie of the after-work bourbon-drinking in Lyndon Johnson's chandeliered private office. After work, Jackson worked. Nor would he try to push ahead with back-slapping geniality or sophisticated sociability. Jackson dismissed those common political characteristics in one disdainful word: phony. Even after a dozen years in the maelstrom of politics, Jackson still was reserved, intense, and basically a shy person—at least by political standards.

But Scoop Jackson nevertheless was the almost ideal Senate man. A subdued manner was no handicap in his new surroundings, and Jackson had other assets. This onetime newspaper boy, son of immigrants, not only worked within the system, but he also revered it. It was, after all, a system that had allowed him to rise from humble mill-town origins to the lofty pinnacle of the United States Senate. Years later, when the very system the boy and the man had conquered seemed to be threatened by social upheaval, Jackson would respond by departing the furthest from his life of calculated emotional control. . . .

. . .. *There is no room in America for an extremist of any kind. . . .*

So it was predictable and inevitable that Henry Jackson would work within the Senate's system and, eventually, burrow his way into the inner sanctum of the Club itself.

Liberalism was no particular asset within the Club. But it didn't have to be a liability, either. Unlike most Northerners who entered the Senate in the 1950s, Jackson did not wear his liberalism on his sleeve. Jackson's philosophy was as subdued as his personality. In the great civil-rights disputes of the 1950s, Jackson committed his vote but not his rhetoric. That digested well with the Southerners—and it was the Southerners who doled out the Senate's favors, dispensed the system's rewards. Jackson came to the Senate from the distant Pacific Northwest, an area that was as far from the Old South as the home of any senator. But some of his characteristics were decidedly Southern. He lived by an implacable code of honor, one that was as strong as that of the most courtly Mississippian. Like any good politician, Jackson occasionally could stuff his ideals in his back pocket. Jackson was a pragmatist, a compromiser. To him, politics was the "art of the possible" and the most skilled practitioner made it the "science of the possible." To Jackson, the decisive question about a politician's character was whether he pulled the ideals back out of his pocket and strove for them once again on a better day. But there were some things on which you do not compromise. There is no compromise on a man's word; to Jackson, it is a commitment. There is no compromise on loyalty; to Jackson, it is total.

Loyalty worked two ways with Jackson. He would give it completely. In the 1970s, long after Vietnam had made Lyndon Johnson a devil-symbol ogre to be avoided at all cost by the liberals, Jackson still would make periodic courtesy visits to the ranch on the Pedernales. But he expected loyalty completely, too. "You cross Scoop and it will never be forgotten," one friend said of him. "You could be drowning in one inch of water and Scoop could be up to his neck in life preservers. But you'd drown."

Still, that sort of characteristic was understood, even appreciated, within the Senate Club. And Jackson moved more rapidly within the power structure than most freshman senators. He had not wanted a seat on the McCarthy committee. Nor had he wanted a role in the messy political execution of the senator from Wisconsin. But when Lyndon Johnson asked, Jackson accepted dutifully and without complaint. That is the way things are done—within the system.

The system then doled out its rewards. Jackson was given a seat on the Senate Interior Committee—not his first choice, but nevertheless a good Western committee suited to Jackson's brand of federal liberalism as well as the needs of his constituents. From that power base he involved himself in the crusade for a big, federal dam at Hell's Canyon on the Snake River in Idaho, a crusade that once again enhanced his liberal credentials. He also began enmeshing himself in problems of deep concern in his Far Western state—power development, reclamation, national parks, recreation, mining. Eventually, Jackson would rise to the chairmanship of the Interior Committee and that would extend him immense power over a wide range of interests from preservation of the environment to the rights of Indians.

Within weeks after the end of the Army-McCarthy hearings in June 1954—just eighteen months after Jackson entered the Senate—the system provided another reward. Lyndon Johnson gave Jackson the committee assignment he coveted most, a seat on the Senate Armed Services Committee. And by January 1955, when the Democrats regained control of the Senate, Majority Leader Johnson gave Jackson a place on the Joint Committee on Atomic Energy. No other freshman senator—and few senior ones —had four committee assignments. In the Senate, committees translate into power. So it was clear that Henry M. Jackson, the system player, was going a long way.

There was a twist of fate in the fact that Jackson's role in the McCarthy hearings, a role he would have preferred to avoid, had thrust him almost instantly into national prominence. But it was his role in his last two committees, a role he wanted badly, that would imprint upon Jackson the reputation that would last a lifetime—a reputation as a Cold War liberal and, eventually, perhaps the last of the breed.

Shortly after the fall of Joe McCarthy, Scoop Jackson made a routine social visit to the White House. In the East Room of the President's house the aging portraits of George and Martha Washington smiled benignly down on the crowd of senators, congressmen, and assorted other dignitaries as they moved slowly through a receiving line toward the equally benign smiles of Dwight and Mamie Eisenhower. There were some who saw a resemblance between the two war-hero, father-image Presidents. But Jackson was not thinking such thoughts. He occupied himself in conversation with the congressman in front of him and mentally prepared for the quick, polite, Presidential handshake which protocol dictated for a freshman senator from the minority party.

But when Jackson reached the popular Republican President, a most unlikely event occurred. Eisenhower dropped his formal facade, stepped forward and thrust his arm around Jackson's square shoulders. Profusely, the President thanked the junior senator for his part in bringing about McCarthy's demise. "I wish you were a Republican," Eisenhower told the beaming Democrat. "I could use a man like you."

It is doubtful, however, that Ike would have been inclined to pay that same compliment a few years later. From his new position of power on the Armed Services and Atomic Energy committees Jackson almost immediately became one of Eisenhower's strongest critics in an area in which a war-hero President should have been immune—national defense.

There were some who speculated that Jackson adopted his rigidly tough stance on international Communism to protect his political flanks in the wake of his opposition to McCarthy. It would be difficult for political opponents to make their soft-on-Communism charges stick if Jackson were pushing for the weapons that could atomize the Kremlin. But, even before he came to the Senate, Jackson seemed to have foreseen the grim inevitability of the frantic nuclear arms race of the fifties.

"One of the surest ways to invite the destruction of America is to underestimate the power and expertness of the Russians in the atomic field," he had said in 1950. "If we are to err, I would far rather that we err on the side of too much than too little when it comes to atomic weapons."

It was a theme that Jackson would stick with all the way through the decade as the two Cold War giants, the United States and the Soviet Union, engaged in the fearsome technological contest to obtain the ability to obliterate each other.

For Jackson, it was a time to demand more and more, faster and faster—more Polaris submarines, more B-52 strategic bombers, faster development of the intercontinental ballistic missile. If it would cost billions, then billions should be spent. In the balance, he repeated over and over, was the very survival of the Western world. He flayed the Eisenhower administration for its reluctance to run the race at full speed and attacked Ike's cost-conscious Secretary of Defense, Charles E. Wilson. He warned about nuclear blackmail and became one of the architects of the raging controversy over a so-called missile gap.

Occasionally, Jackson would acknowledge the awfulness of what was happening, admit to the wretched bleakness of a race that could end in the world's doom.

In one of his first actions in the Senate, Jackson introduced a disarmament resolution warning that "the peoples of the earth are plunged into an accelerating arms race that leads to war." The resolution was pushed through the Senate, then died in the House. But periodically, throughout the fifties, Jackson would observe that disarmament was the only *real* answer to the world's dilemma.

"Terrible weapon is being piled on terrible weapon," he bemoaned in 1957. "But a peace of mutual terror cannot last forever. I believe that discussions among nations for a sound and safe system for the control and limitation of armaments should be continuous. The statesmen of the free world must never give up in their search for a security system which rests on more than the threat of mutual destruction."

Still, as the Cold War intensified, Jackson invariably returned to the theme that the United States not only was forced to *run* the desperate race with the Russians but also was forced to *win* it.

Through it all, Jackson rarely found his liberalism questioned. Once in a while some of the superliberals—the Ban the Bomb predecessors of Rennie Davis—would come at him, and it was during this time period that he picked up the nasty Cold War sobriquets that would stay with him throughout his career. They nicknamed him "the senator from Boeing" and "the senator from outer space."

But the Ban the Bomb people were at the leftward fringe and Jackson had far more trouble from the other direction—from the frightened Rightists who called him "pretty-boy pinko" because he stood up to McCarthy and from the dedicated conservatives who were convinced that his support of federal aid to education, federal dams, federal health care, and federal welfare would lead to a god-awful 1984 supergovernment.

Furthermore, Jackson's Cold War views were hardly in

conflict with the Establishment liberalism of the fifties. The great liberal press institutions, *The New York Times* and the *Washington Post*, were inclined to go along with him. They, too, were critical of the cautious Eisenhower administration's slowness in developing nuclear weaponry. The young, pragmatic liberals in the Senate—men like John Kennedy, Mike Mansfield, and Stuart Symington— agreed with Jackson. Mansfield touted him for the Vice-Presidential nomination in 1956. Kennedy almost chose him in 1960.

So Henry M. Jackson's liberalism rarely was in doubt.

Just days after his election to the Senate in November 1952, Jackson flew to Eniwetok to observe the second test of an American hydrogen bomb. While on the desolate Pacific atoll, he renewed his acquaintance with an old friend—a hawk-faced, wiry Navy captain named Hyman G. Rickover. Rickover was Jackson's kind of man—truly expert in his specialty, which was atomic power, but also an impressive generalist, a man who had a good grasp of subjects ranging from education to geopolitics. He also was strong-willed and heavily self-disciplined. Those were characteristics that Jackson saw in himself as well, so their friendship was a natural one.

Single-handedly and single-mindedly, fighting the brass all the way, Rickover had pulled a very reluctant Navy almost into the nuclear age. In Groton, Connecticut, the Navy's first atomic submarine, the *Nautilus*, was nearing completion under Rickover's careful guidance. But now the brash, outspoken Navy captain had a deep problem. In the past year he had been passed over twice for promotion to rear admiral's rank. Under Navy regulations that meant automatic retirement.

For ten days on Eniwetok, Jackson and Rickover mulled over the problem. The situation was a difficult one. Rickover was not a line officer and all but a handful of the Navy's admiralty slots were reserved for line officers. But the single position open to Rickover as an engineering-duty officer was being given to a captain who had been harshly critical of the nuclear program. To Jackson, the Navy's position was indefensible. The nuclear submarine program was moving into its most crucial phases. Rickover, just fifty-three, probably was the world's leading authority on nuclear seapower. Now the Navy was booting him out. Jackson, not yet sworn into the Senate, decided to do something about it when he returned to Washington.

Jackson's first official act as a senator was to call the new chairman of the Senate Armed Services Committee, patrician Leverett Saltonstall of Massachusetts, and ask for a Senate hearing on the Rickover matter. But the more Jackson thought about the Navy's position, the angrier he became. Finally, incensed, he called the Naval chief of personnel, Admiral James L. Holloway. The Navy's position was outrageous, Jackson snorted. "If this is the way the Navy selection system works," he told Holloway, "then we'd better have a new selection system." The Navy selects a man who said the nuclear program wouldn't work, who has opposed it and who is dead wrong. He becomes an admiral. The man who is completely right in what Jackson saw as one of the most important discoveries to improve the Navy and the security of the United States, is tossed out. "What the hell kind of selection system is that?" Jackson asked. If the Navy didn't do something about it and do something fast, the fledgling senator told the admiral, he would go onto the Senate floor and "tell the whole doggoned country about it."

The Senate hearing never was needed. Within two days the Secretary of the Navy, Robert Anderson, called Jackson and told him that Rickover would become an admiral.

It was not the last time that the cocky, abrasive, little nuclear sailor would have trouble with the hidebound Navy hierarchy. Time and again they would attempt to force him into retirement and time and again Jackson would go to his defense in the Senate.

The Navy's lowest cut at Rickover came in mid-1958 after his dreamchild, the *Nautilus*, had triumphantly returned from an historic voyage under the Arctic ice to the North Pole. The nuclear submarine had gone under the ice at Jackson's suggestion and when it returned, its skipper, Commander W. R. (Bill) Anderson, and its crew were heroes. They were called to the White House for a ceremony honoring their feat. But Rear Admiral H. G. Rickover, then needing a promotion to vice-admiral or once again face expulsion, was snubbed and left off the guest list. For the Navy brass, still trying to dump Rickover, it was a major tactical error. Jackson exploded in anger. "We certainly cannot have conformists doing great things," Jackson complained. "It's about time for the services to demonstrate that there is a place for the egghead in uniform." Eleven days later the Secretary of the Navy pledged that Rickover would be promoted once again.

More than a decade later, Rickover, in his seventies by then but still a rebel, remained in the Navy. Tucked away in one corner of Jackson's Senate office was a picture of the *Nautilus* on maneuvers. It was inscribed: "To Senator Henry M. Jackson, with deep appreciation and gratitude for all you have done for the Navy's nuclear power program, for civilian atomic power, and for me. H. G. Rickover, Rear Admiral, U.S. Navy." But far more important to both Rickover and Jackson, the Navy had forty-one modern Polaris nuclear submarines. The submarines were one of the three arms of the powerful nuclear deterrent that Jackson badgered the Eisenhower administration about throughout the fifties.

In his days in the House of Representatives Jackson became almost a faddist about the power of the atom. He had talked, nearly reverently, about a future of atomic cities, atomic farming, and atom-powered vehicles. He developed an interest in irradiation of foods as a substitute for freezing. Visitors to his office occasionally were offered—and sometimes nervously accepted—experimental cans of irradiated bacon. He closely followed developments at the Hanford Works, an atomic installation isolated in a far corner of his state hundreds of miles outside his congressional district.

As a young congressman and member of the Joint Committee on Atomic Energy, he made countless inspection trips throughout the country to the supersensitive, hidden installations that stored America's first, primitive atomic weapons. His curiosity often astounded the military brass. Most congressional VIPs asked a few routine questions. But Jackson, in his systematical way, actually walked down the rows of weapons and counted the big, grim-gray, potbellied bombs. Back in Washington, in the guarded, top-secret rooms of the joint committee, he regularly pored over volume after volume of classified intelligence material.

Jackson concluded early that the United States had an

almost insurmountable lead in nuclear weapons. But then he asked himself a key question. If he were sitting in the Kremlin and wanted to neutralize that lead, what would he do? The answer, as far as Jackson was concerned, was inescapable: He would push for a modern delivery system to overwhelm America's bombers; he would push for development of an intercontinental ballistic missile.

By the time Jackson took his seat on the Senate Armed Services Committee in mid-1954, the United States and the Soviet Union already were well into their race for the ICBM—the deadly missile that could carry an atom bomb from the plateaus of Montana to Moscow's Red Square or vice versa, from the steppes of Kapustin Yar to New York's Times Square. But there were disturbing reports, both in the intelligence information that Jackson read so assiduously and in the press, that the United States was lagging dangerously behind.

Within weeks after he joined the committee Jackson wrote a letter to Defense Secretary Wilson, asking a series of pointed questions about America's missile progress. The Republican defense secretary, not very patient with freshman Democratic senators, brushed Jackson off. It was a serious error.

In this pre-hawk-and-dove era there was almost no one in the government who questioned the need to develop an ICBM. The question was over the need for urgency, for the kind of Manhattan Project crash program that had produced the atom bomb during World War II. Within the Pentagon there was a coterie of dissidents, who thought the Eisenhower administration was proceeding dangerously slowly. These included Trevor Gardner, a driven man who was an assistant secretary of the Air Force in charge of research and development; General Bernie

161

Schriever, who was running the supersecret development project out of a tiny, dilapidated building in Los Angeles; and John von Newmann, a brilliant, Hungarian-born mathematician who had unsnarled many of the 5,000-mile missile's technical problems.

In 1954 and 1955, the dissidents, desperate to get their views through what they called the "kelp beds" of the Pentagon bureaucracy and straight to the President, began surreptitiously turning to Jackson for help. It was a dangerous game, feeding information to an outspoken opposition senator, and Trevor Gardner eventually paid for it with his job. But it worked.

For six months, in a series of clandestine meetings at the back tables of some of Washington's most obscure restaurants, Jackson fitted together bits and pieces of the ICBM story from information fed to him by Gardner's military aide, Lieutenant Colonel Vince Ford. The mood of the meetings was conspiratorial, with both the skinny lieutenant colonel and the freshman senator constantly peering over each other's shoulders. Under Pentagon etiquette, Ford had no business leaking information to politicians, especially opposition politicians. It was, he told Jackson, "a pretty sporty game for a raggedy-ass lieutenant colonel to be hobnobbing with a senator." His career was in the balance, but Ford had concluded that the fate of the nation might be, too.

The covert operations between Jackson and the Pentagon rebels culminated early one spring morning in 1955, with Ford and an Air Force major named Beryl Boatman nervously lugging two briefcases into the darkened, almost seedy old dining room of Washington's quiet Fairfax Hotel. There were only a few early-bird customers eating breakfast as Ford carefully selected an out-of-the-way table in the far corner of the room. In a moment Jackson arrived and strode toward the table. Ford fidgeted as they went through the ham-and-egg formalities of a breakfast meeting. Then, in hushed tones, he began to review the problem. Both the United States and the Soviet Union now had the technological know-how to build a sophisticated intercontinental missile, one that could reach the shores of either nation in a matter of minutes. Intelligence sources indicated that the Russians were proceeding on a crash program. If the Russians got there first, they would have the ability to destroy the United States. But, more realistically, the Soviet Union would have the power to blackmail the United States diplomatically, the power to force the United States into making major concessions around the world. Trevor Gardner, who believed all this, too, was getting nowhere at the Pentagon. "If we continue to try to go through the system," Ford solemnly told Jackson, "we won't come within a country mile of making it in time." Gardner and his small group of allies wanted to make an end run around Defense Secretary Wilson and the Pentagon bureaucracy, Ford said. They wanted to brief President Eisenhower directly. And they wanted Jackson to do the running for them.

Jackson listened quietly as Ford and Boatman reached into their briefcases for the documents that they were certain would convince the President. The senator scanned through them in silence, as Ford made his final pitch: Would Jackson be willing to use this information to make a direct appeal to the President? Much of the information supplemented data Jackson had accumulated in missile hearings earlier in the year. Without hesitation, Jackson agreed.

Incredulous that Eisenhower never had been briefed

about the ICBM program, Jackson and the chairman of the Joint Committee on Atomic Energy, Senator Clinton P. Anderson of New Mexico, compiled a top-secret report for the President. Much of the report still has not been declassified. But the senators pleaded with the President to seek a briefing for himself and the National Security Council. Within two weeks Gardner, Schriever, von Newmann, and Ford were called to the White House. Shortly thereafter the wraps began to come off ICBM development— but still not fast enough for the Cold Warrior from Washington State.

In January 1956, Jackson made a major Senate speech warning that the Russians were ahead of the United States in development of an intermediate-range ballistic missile —a 1,500-mile missile which could be used to intimidate most of Europe and Asia. In the speech Jackson introduced a new phrase into the language of the Cold War, a phrase that he would use over and over in the next fifteen years. He warned that Russian superiority would enable the Kremlin to engage in "nuclear blackmail"—a diplomacy of nuclear threats. He graphically described what might happen, if the Russians could deploy the missiles before the Americans:

"I invite you to put yourself in the place of a government leader of France or West Germany or England or Pakistan or Japan. Any of these nations could be devastated by a 1,500-mile missile launched from Communist-controlled bases.

"Imagine that Soviet Defense Minister Zhukov has just invited the military attaches of the world to meet at a missile site near Moscow. Imagine Marshal Zhukov then explaining that he is about to press a button which will fire this world's first 1,500-mile ballistic missile. Marshal Zhukov might say that this demonstration missile carried only a TNT warhead. But he would undoubtedly add that a hydrogen warhead could be substituted. Standing in a concrete blockhouse for protection, the military attaches would see the missile launched. Some 1,500 miles away— perhaps in the wastes of Soviet Central Asia—another group of free-world observers would be assembled. Mere minutes later they would witness the crashing explosion of the missile at the end of its journey.

"Picture what might happen next. In the wall of the concrete blockhouse would be a huge map, outlining in vivid red the range of the Soviet missile. This range would embrace all of Western Europe, all of North Africa and the Middle East, most of south and Southeast Asia, the Philippines, Formosa, Okinawa, Korea and Japan.

"The demonstration might end amidst assurances of Moscow's peaceful intentions and many Soviet smiles. A few days later Premier Bulganin might invite the foreign ministers of the NATO powers to a conference in Moscow. While proposing no formal agenda, Bulganin might indicate that the Soviets would advocate dissolving NATO and establishing a new type of defense community. Bulganin would be thinking of a defense arrangement that would not interfere with the Soviet objective—world domination.

"Caught in this bind, our most redoubtable supporters might falter. It is well-nigh certain that crucial allies would be forced into neutralism, or even into tacit cooperation with Moscow."

Jackson's speech came at the beginning of a Presidential-election year and it caused a major uproar. The liberal, but internationalist, *New York Times* printed the text in full.

Defense Secretary Wilson, still smarting over Jackson's ICBM end run, grumbled testily about Jackson's sources: "I don't think his information is any better than mine."

But three months later the Soviet chairman, Nikita Khrushchev, visited England and complained that the Britons were reluctant to trade with the Soviet Union. "I am quite sure that we will have a guided missile with a hydrogen bomb that can fall anywhere in the world," the sabre-rattling Russian leader said ominously. "In spite of that, you do not want to trade with us."

After that, Jackson's attacks on the Eisenhower defense policies accelerated. Time and again, he criticized the defense secretary and the President for going too slow, for allowing Russia to get ahead. *More bombers*, he chanted. *More submarines, more missiles*. Charles Wilson, far from a mild-mannered man, reacted strongly. It was an election year, he told the press, and the Democratic charges were "phony."

During a Senate hearing in July of 1956 Jackson cornered Wilson and asked him if he didn't think he owed Congress an apology for that remark.

"I do not," the defense secretary replied in a loud, firm voice. "It would not be out of order for certain senators to apologize to me."

Jackson bristled and asked if Wilson had any particular senators in mind.

"You are one of them," Wilson responded.

At first, the spectators at the hearing gasped. Then they started to laugh and Jackson, taken aback for a moment, started to laugh, too. But he didn't think it was *that* funny.

On August 27, 1957, the Soviet Union announced through its Tass News Agency that it had successfully fired the first intercontinental ballistic missile a "huge distance" and that the results showed that the Russians now could "direct rockets into any part of the world." The United States had attempted one test of its 5,000-mile Atlas missile. But the big ICBM had risen a mile over Cape Canaveral, rolled over in mid-air and tumbled into the sea.

On October 4, 1957, the Soviet Union announced that it had launched the first man-made earth satellite, a 184-pound scientific package which brought a new word into international language: Sputnik. President Eisenhower called a press conference to play down the military impact of the satellite launching. But Senator Henry M. Jackson said the defense implications were "enormous" and called the first week in October 1957 "a week of shame, of danger, for America."

America, that great technological giant that had led the world into a new industrial revolution, lay stunned in the wake of Sputnik. The early fifties had been years of American condescension toward the Russians. A few isolated voices, like that of Jackson, had warned of Russian scientific prowess. But the general American attitude was supercilious—an attitude of contemptuous jokes about fat mamushkas pushing brooms in Moscow streets, of peasant girls grinning through stainless-steel teeth, of dim-witted commissars fouling up quotas on collective farms.

But with millions of Americans gazing upward into space for a glimpse of the little beeping Russian star, all that changed. To a generation weaned on Buck Rogers the incredible thought occurred that the first words from the moon might be spoken in Russian. To others it became abundantly clear that, indeed, as Nikita Khrushchev had warned, the Russians did have the ability to launch death from Kapustin Yar to Times Square. The Senate began an acrimonious investigation of the American scientific and political lapse. The White House ordered a crash program to catch up. For months the American effort was spectacular—but for its failures. Shimmering rockets exploded and tumbled off their launching pads—huge American phallic symbols gone limp. American humor turned defensive. *Well, their German scientists are better than our German scientists.* Then it turned sour. *The kids around the Cape are learning to count younger, but it has its disadvantages—"10-9-8-7-6-5-4-3-2-1 . . . shit!"*

By December of 1957—four months after the launching of the first Russian ICBM—the United States had successfully tested its 5,000-mile Atlas. By February of 1958—four months after Sputnik—the Americans successfully placed a grapefruit-sized Explorer satellite into orbit around the earth.

The Americans were not far behind. But they were behind. Once it had been relatively easy—and somewhat believable—for the Republicans to chant *politics* at their antagonistic defense-policy critics, Jackson and Symington. It was not so easy—nor so believable—now. Jackson had warned Eisenhower about Soviet ICBM progress as early as 1955—and he had been right. He had gone to Russia in 1956, returning with dire warnings about the Soviet drive to overtake the United States—and he had been right. Jackson's credibility was high. Some called him a prophet.

The *Bulletin of the Atomic Scientists* heaped praise on him. "Perhaps no civilian in public life in the United States is better informed on the facts of missile development or more deeply concerned about their meaning for the future of this nation," the *Bulletin* said at the time of Sputnik. And Jackson became a young hero-image—anti-McCarthy, anti-Kremlin—within a Democratic Party that was tired of the casual meandering of the Eisenhower administration.

With both the world's super powers possessing intercontinental missiles, the concern in the Pentagon and the Kremlin turned to deployment of the ICBMs. The missiles themselves were no serious threat until they were operational—buried in their concrete death-wombs in the plains of America and the steppes of Russia. In early 1958, some American experts were predicting that the Russian ICBMs would be operational by the middle of the year—eighteen months ahead of the United States. The experts were wrong, but Jackson, believing them, reasoned that the only way to fill the gap was by building more B-52 bombers. This, he said, was one of the "things we need to do immediately to stay alive." Jackson's comments were one of the first rumbling forewarnings of the heated charges with which the Democrats, led by Scoop Jackson, would flail the Republicans in the 1960 Presidential campaign. The issue would be over a missile gap.

In the late 1950s, American spying techniques still were relatively primitive and unreliable. In the coming decade the spy-satellite descendants of Sputnik and Explorer would change all that. They would produce photographs so perfect that the CIA could entertain curious senators with details as fine as the Cyrillic lettering of the Top Secret warning signs at the doors to Russian defense plants. But that still lay in the future as the CIA attempted to assess Soviet missile progress in the last years of the Eisenhower administration. CIA sources were varied—some photographs from occasional, risky overflights by needle-nosed U-2 spy planes; electronic monitoring from bases in Turkey, Pakistan, and other outposts along the Soviet frontier; eye-witness accounts from agents and defectors; fuzzy pictures of the gaping holes in which the missiles would be planted, of the railroad cars that transported them, and of the plants in which they were built.

From this mishmash of information the CIA analysts extrapolated the Soviet Union's ability to deploy their ICBMs. The conclusions were grim ones, placing the Russians far ahead of the Americans. From time to time Allen Dulles, the suave, pipe-smoking head of the American spy network, would trek to Capitol Hill to brief the deadly serious members of the House and Senate Armed Services Committees. Dulles, brother of the Republican Secretary of State, scrupulously avoided the growing political controversy over an alleged missile gap. But he made no bones about the CIA's extrapolations of the intelligence information: The running figures showed that the Russians were on a crash program and that they were substantially ahead in deployment of the Cold War's newest terror weapons.

Scoop Jackson listened quietly through the CIA director's briefings. Few questions were necessary. But he was not quiet in public. His criticism of the Eisenhower administration grew increasingly bold.

In late 1957, he said the blame for American defense lapses "lies directly with the President." In 1958, he warned that the administration's defense policies were causing the United States to "lose our lead in critical item after critical item." By 1959, he was warning that the United States trailed the Soviet Union three to one in ICBMs and that Eisenhower was risking national security in his efforts to avoid being called a "military President."

By early 1960, with the Presidential campaign nearing, Jackson's missile-gap charges reached full bloom.

"I say we can't afford the risks the administration is taking," the senator wrote in February of the election year. "The overall deterrent capability they are talking about is a short-term one at best. The time is nearing when our deterrent forces will be vulnerable to enemy attack. In the period just ahead the very real danger is that the Russians will have such a numerical missile superiority, with sufficient accuracy, that by surprise attack they would be able to liquidate our fixed missile bases and knock off our planes before they could get off the ground."

Jackson's doomsday warnings were not universally appreciated. The Republicans accused him of contributing "to an unfounded sense of fear and panic." Conservative newspapers in his home state attacked him. "Our senator is rapidly becoming the most pessimistic before- or after-dinner speaker in the land," the Tacoma *News-Tribune* editorialized. "His opinion is at odds with very many public officials in as good a position to appraise our needs as he. He may not be troubled by an ulcer, but if he isn't careful about the timing of his speeches, a good many diners are going to have ulcers."

But Jackson had been right before and the Democrats trumpeted his charges. John F. Kennedy, an old friend now preparing to reach for the Democratic Presidential nomination, began placing Jackson's hard-line speeches and articles in the *Congressional Record*. More and more often Kennedy would come to Jackson for advice on campaign strategy involving defense issues. And Jackson's advice was pointedly repetitious: *missile gap, missile gap, missile gap*. The Russians, he told Kennedy, would use their advantage to engage in nuclear blackmail. There were dark times ahead, dark times indeed. John Kennedy, picking up the cue, began lashing the Eisenhower-Nixon administration with charges about a missile gap.

Unseen by the prying eyes of the CIA, the Russians were running into deep difficulties with their infant missile program. At Kapustin Yar a series of crucial misfirings went undetected by American spies. Within the secret Russian missile plants, production schedules broke down under technical pressures. At hidden missile sites deep inside Asia the Russians began having construction problems on the heavily fortified silos in which their ICBMs would be buried.

Unknown to Jackson, Kennedy, Symington, and the other aggressive Democrats, the missile gap was not a missile gap at all. It was a fiction, albeit a helpful political fiction that would aid Kennedy in his razor-thin victory over Richard M. Nixon in 1960.

Years later, as Scoop Jackson prepared for a Presidential campaign of his own with remarkably similar warnings about nuclear blackmail and Soviet missile advances, Jackson would concede that he had been wrong in 1960. It was one of the rare moments of error in a career of almost uncannily accurate predictions about the intentions and capabilities of America's Cold War adversary.

Jackson, as a politician, is not one to stretch what he sees as the truth. So, in the 1970s, he was defensive in looking back on the missile-gap controversy.

"All we did," the senator would say, "was rely on the information given to us by the Eisenhower administration. They were very careful not to deny their own intelligence information. Their position was that we could overcome

172

the missiles with the number of bombers we had. Whatever gap there was, it was their gap, because it was based on Eisenhower's own presentation through his man, Mr. Dulles. We simply relied on their chief intelligence spokesman, who said there was a gap."

CAMELOT

GEORGETOWN AND ITS residents responded to the pleasant warmth of a spring Sunday—a day for strolling, for dropping in on friends, or for the easy fellowship of an impromptu game of softball.

The people—government officials, young attorneys, politicians, writers, a retired admiral with a poodle on a leash, Capitol Hill secretaries—began appearing on the sidewalks around noon, after the time of the Sunday paper, church, and brunch. Their pace was leisurely. Some stopped to talk at a street corner where the herringbone pattern of bricks swelled over the root of an old tree shading the street.

Georgetowners savored the quiet graciousness of their village-within-a-city; the inviting doorways, the shutter-framed windows, brick walls, ivy, and the courtyards, where spring gardens were splashed with the colors of azaleas and geraniums.

There was never any need to issue invitations for the afternoon softball game at the playfield on Thirty-Fourth and Volta Place. It was ritual. Among such young men as Mike Mansfield, John Kennedy, Scoop Jackson, their friends, and the children who lived nearby, it was understood the game could commence sometime after noon, or whenever some players and a bat and ball arrived.

Jackson lived on the third floor of the Bob Lows' house at 3401 O Street Northwest. Some of the friends assembled there first. After late-morning coffee, they emerged from the house and together walked up Thirty-Fourth. Jackson, with his bouncy stride, led the way.

The children and teen-agers, mixed black and white, already had begun to arrive. Impatient for the game to begin, they romped on the bleacher seats behind the backstop or around the grassy, tree-bordered softball diamond.

As the players gathered, there was noisy debate among the youngsters over who would be the team captains. A 14-year-old blonde girl who lived across the street, an enthusiastic and skilled athlete, became one captain. The other was a younger boy. Solemnly they made their choices. Sometimes senators were late picks. Bobby Kennedy was an early choice: Thin, wiry, he was a nervously intense, if sometimes abrasive, competitor.

Bobby energized the game with his ferocious spirit of all-out. There was no allowance for sex or age. His high-pitched shouts echoed across the diamond exhorting senators, women, and children with equal vigor. *Ethel, dammit, hang onto it,* he shouted.

A secretary near second base, in her first day within the softball fraternity and unaccustomed to Bobby, blanched. How, she wondered, could a marriage endure outbursts like that? But Ethel Kennedy, with a grin, ignored the ferocity of the shout. She retrieved the ball which had spun away from her grasp at shortstop and, with athletic grace, tossed the ball to the pitcher.

There was one ground rule in the game: John Kennedy was entitled to a substitute runner when he came to bat. He moved with the slow stiffness of a man suffering severe back pain.

Despite his sore back he was a keen competitor, too. The

bachelor girls talked about how very handsome he was—tall, young, suntanned, a mixture of chestnut and sun-bleached gold hair flopped boyishly on his brow. He concentrated on the pitch. The swing of the bat was level and smooth. The hit bounded toward second base and the nine-year-old substitute runner bolted from his starting position beside home plate. A swarm of infielders pursued the roller and, amid rising screams of excitement, the throw and the little runner converged at first base.

Secretaries in Jackson's office had a standing invitation to the Sunday game: "If you don't come, you're fired," the senator said with a grin. They admired their good-looking boss and some had fleeting romantic ideas about him. But they knew he was absorbed in his Senate work and disinterested in dating, so the Sunday softball games were the secretaries' opportunity for exercise and amusement. They sustained an occasional broken fingernail, but the softball had been pounded into a merciful mushiness, and its impact was not stinging.

Scoop, where on earth did you get those boots? Jackson lifted one foot to examine the dusty boot admiringly. They had been given to him out in the Pacific during a congressional inspection trip late in World War II. "The soles are a special material so they wouldn't get cut up on the coral," he explained. "You'd be surprised how light they are. I can really run in 'em."

Jackson, a frugal man, utilitarian, never discarded anything merely because of style. In a softball crowd wearing sports garb, he was the rustic. He chatted about how the exercise helped slim off twelve pounds, and the waist of his brown cotton trousers, wrapped in bunches beneath the belt, was proof.

Dorothy Fosdick could have sworn there were cleats on Jackson's boots because the footfalls, as he galloped fero-

176

ciously toward second base where she stood, sounded ominous. She moved away from the basepath.

Everyone, except Bobby, engaged in the easy banter. *Easy out, easy out*, someone said when Mike Mansfield came to bat. The thin, quiet Montanan grinned.

No wonder you can't get a bill out of committee. You can't even get to first base.

Some Georgetowners slowed their walk, then stopped to watch. A few came to sit for a while on the grass behind third base, then they drifted into the game. They joined the group of other left-fielders which included the boyish six-footer who, in the ordered Cape Cod dishevelment of walking shorts and canvas shoes, seemed much too young to be the senator from Massachusetts. He challenged two small boys standing in the outfield with him: When the next hit comes this way, which of you can get to it first? He grinned when, as the ball approached, they ran, tripped, rolled, and wrestled for it.

There was an ebb and flow of people. After a couple of innings, the passersby left the game to resume their walk. Some of the youngsters headed toward the swimming pool beyond the metal fence in right field.

Bobby had brought his football. He decreed when it was time to begin the game of touch football. The senators and their coterie moved to the open grass of outer left field.

The action was faster and rougher. John Kennedy, avoiding body contact, played a loose safety-man position. Salter, an aggressive competitor, though less noisy than Bobby, popped Bob with a quick block when, with squeals and shouts, the ball was centered. Bobby went out for a pass. It hit his shoulder and bounced to the ground. The others suppressed mirth as he wheeled and shouted angrily to the quarterback: *Ethel, why can't you get it to me?*

In mid-afternoon, they walked away from the playfield,

toward beer, Cokes, and conversation—often about heady political dreams—in Georgetown living rooms.

John Kennedy soon afterward underwent hazardous surgery to correct his back ailment.

And, on October 28, 1959, John Salter, Jackson's administrative assistant, went to the Hyannisport home of Bob Kennedy where a group of sixteen men mapped out a Presidential campaign for 1960.

CHAPTER 8

ALMOST, ALMOST . . .

IT WAS THE morning of the last day of the Democratic National Convention of 1960 and even the Los Angeles smog, that hazy precursor of the crud that almost all Americans would be breathing by the end of the decade, failed to smudge the illusion that a new era was dawning in American politics. The hoopla, the sugary oratory, and the child-like razzmatazz of a thunderous political convention were all but over now. The headlines in the morning Los Angeles *Times* told the story emphatically.

KENNEDY WINS!
Symington, Jackson Boosted as Running Mates

Suddenly the center of the universe seemed to be Suite 9333 of the elephantine, stuffy, old Biltmore Hotel. Inside the suite John Fitzgerald Kennedy, already a symbol of the new era, sat flanked by shirt-sleeved aides. Kennedy, who had won the Democratic Presidential nomination on the first ballot the night before, now had one major decision to make before embarking on his campaign for the White House. The election was almost certain to be close and so his decision—the choice of his Vice-Presidential running mate—was a crucial one. Speculation was rampant. Some were certain it would be Stuart Symington, who had made his own futile bid for the Presidential nomination. Others were certain it would be Scoop Jackson, who was the personal favorite of the standard-bearer's brother and confidant, Bob Kennedy.

One by one the big men of the Democratic Party paraded into the suite to give their advice and, in some cases, make their demands. First came the leaders of the big-city machines—Lawrence and Green of Pennsylvania, Wagner and DeSapio and Prendergast of New York, Daley of Chicago. Then came the labor moguls—Goldberg, Reuther. Occasionally one of the Southern strong men would arrive, but they still were somewhat wary. A liberal, Catholic, New Englander would not be helpful to them in the fall elections. So they hovered around the command post, two floors below, of the man whom John Kennedy had beaten in a bitter battle for the nomination, Lyndon Baines Johnson.

The men who came to Suite 9333 were forced to run a traditional obstacle course. The scene in the hallway outside the Kennedy suite was one of near pandemonium. A small army of antagonistic reporters pushed and shoved for vantage points to get at the party chieftains as they entered and then emerged from the rooms in which the day's biggest news was being made. The great, gawking cameras of television—one for each of the three networks and others for the local stations—blocked passageways. Their sinewy snake-cables tangled in the feet of the milling reporters, curiosity seekers, and occasional VIPs. Their lights blinded and boiled the mob. Newspaper reporters cursed their instant-truth competitors. Television cameramen cursed the bobbing heads that blocked and blinded their camera eyes. By late morning the mob exuded a sweat-stench and it seemed odd that the hallway should stink outside the rooms of a Presidential nominee.

It is typical of scenes like the one outside Suite 9333 that, despite the momentous events taking place inside, little news is produced. The exchanges between the press and the newsmakers are a game, a ritual. The reporters' questions are sharp, antagonistic; the party pros' replies muted, evasive. *Symington, the Missourian, would help in the crucial border states. Jackson, the Washingtonian, would help in the West. Gore, the Tennessean, might pick up a few Southern states. And then there was Freeman. How about Lyndon Johnson? No. He had said a dozen times that he wouldn't take it and Nance Garner, a Roosevelt Vice-President, had given him the terse advice that the job "isn't worth a pitcher of warm spit."*

Shortly before noon on this day, July 14, 1960, a solid, square-shouldered man, grinning from ear to ear, pushed through the swirling scene in the ninth-floor hallway of the Biltmore Hotel. Scoop Jackson was forty-eight years old, but a spartan life had maintained a boyishness about him, and a casual observer would have guessed he was perhaps a decade younger. His face was not quite handsome but when he grinned, the effect was magnetic. The face transformed into a perfect pattern of warm curves and he looked like everyone's friend.

Some of the pushy, sweating reporters read special significance into the fact that Scoop Jackson now was maneuvering through their midst. He was the only one of the several Vice-Presidential possibilities who had been called to the Kennedy command center. And just the day before, Bob Kennedy had made it clear publicly that the Washington Democrat, his old pal from the McCarthy days, was his personal preference. But there were other reasons, too. The morning's *Times* had not been filled only with news of John Kennedy's spectacular convention victory. There was other news, much of it ominous, from other parts of the country and world. In New York the United Nations had announced that it was sending troops into the war-torn Congo. In Moscow the Russians were sabre-rattling after having shot down an American RB-47 reconnaissance plane. At Cape Canaveral the new nuclear navy was preparing to marry an atomic missile to a Polaris submarine for the first time. It would not hurt to have a Cold Warrior, a man who had warned repeatedly about overseas threats, on the Democratic Presidential ticket in 1960.

The press of this era liked Scoop Jackson. He made news. But, more than that, he was unlike most of the eastern pols who had marched in and out of Suite 9333 throughout the morning. Jackson was affable, friendly, folksy, candid. A pointed question would get a straight answer.

Briefly, as he pushed through the crowd, Jackson smilingly arbitrated a jostling dispute between a hot-tempered reporter and a testy television cameraman. When he reached the door, he turned to answer the handful of inevitable questions.

"Senator, would you like to be Vice-President?" came the first query.

"Yes, I would," Jackson replied in his typical candor. Then he went on to say that "in all sincerity" he believed that he would help the Kennedy ticket.

Would he outline his qualifications, his strong points, to the Presidential nominee?

"That shouldn't be necessary," Jackson responded.

"Senator Kennedy and I are old friends. He knows me and he knows my record."

With that Scoop Jackson turned to enter Suite 9333 to talk with John Kennedy.

By 1960, Henry M. Jackson had developed a distinctive political style that eventually would become almost a prototype for other successful politicians in his far, northwestern state. Politically, the state of Washington is extremely loosely structured. A blanket-primary system enables Republicans to cross over and vote for Democrats and, of course, vice versa. The result is that the political parties are seriously weakened. Occasionally a politician will put together a fairly strong personal organization. But there are no machines, not even in the metropolitan area of Seattle. A big-city eastern politician, visiting Jackson's home state, would be horrified by the absolute lack of party control.

Also, Washington is diverse—often with widely conflicting political interests from region to region. It is, in some ways, as diverse as the nation itself. The eastern part of the state is conservative and generally Republican—a desert plateau of wheatlands and cattle ranches and reclaimed sagebrush prairies that have been turned into gleaming-green farms through irrigation. In the middle of the state the jaggedly beautiful Cascade Mountains bull upward into a natural, north-south barrier—the Alpine slopes dropping eastward into pine forests and grazing meadows, westward into the sweeping stands of majestic Douglas Fir that first attracted the Rockefeller money into Scoop Jackson's hometown. The bulk of the population—and thereby the political power, too—resides in the west. There, tough little logging towns dot the mountainsides and picturesque fishing villages enhance the shoreline of Puget Sound. But the western half of the state is dominated by a sprawling metropolitan area that stretches roughly from Tacoma, thirty miles south of Seattle, to Everett, twenty-eight miles north of the state's urban center. Seattle still is touched by some traces of a romantic past—a waterfront that once launched the gold-seekers to Alaska, a Skid Road that still harbors society's rejects, a colorful water-side outdoor market, a harbor teeming with battered fishing boats. But the Seattle of the 1960s already was developing most of the grim characteristics of modern America's jungle cities—suburban expansion that left behind an urban center of blight, smog, a seething ghetto, crime, and dope problems. And Seattle's economy was almost totally dominated by the sprawling empire of that maker of airplanes and missiles, The Boeing Company. Boeing almost made Seattle a company town.

To serve the interests of such a diverse, politically fractionated state, Jackson inevitably developed a something-for-everyone political style. The federal favors that he appeared to deliver ranged from the almost comically minute to the massively impressive. He arranged for the Army to serve asparagus in its mess halls to help the farmers in the Yakima Valley. And he announced the award of $100 million bomber contracts for Boeing. He and his colleague, Senator Warren G. Magnuson, became almost classic pork-barrel politicians.

But there was another, more significant, side to Jackson's political style. He developed what came to be known as the cult of the personality—a highly personalized style that was almost nonpartisan. He delivered government goodies to Republicans as easily as to Democrats. He seemed as at ease at a Chamber of Commerce luncheon as he did at a millworkers' meeting. During a campaign he was smiling, affable, and he ignored no one. Gradually, he drew together a Jackson personality cult that included almost all the Democrats, most of the independents, and a fair share of the Republicans in his state. "Sometimes," Jackson has said, "the best politics is no politics." So, where Magnuson might be the favorite at a highly partisan Democratic convention, just the opposite was true in the streets of Washington's towns and cities.

Jackson's recall of names and events became almost legendary. As his law professors had concluded years earlier, he was not exceptionally intelligent. But he seemed to forget nothing. He would call a shopkeeper, whom he hadn't seen for years, by his first name. He would thank a housewife for a ride to the airport six years earlier. Jackson, to be sure, had his memory aids. On the campaign trail he often had with him three bulky, black, looseleaf books filled with the names and other relevant information about hundreds of little-known people he would be likely to meet. A sample sheet from his 1970 campaign read this way:

KUBOTA, Takeshi (Dear Tak)
1817 55th South
Seattle, Washington

PA 2-6868

Business:
Kubota Gardening Co.
9727 Renton Avenue South
Seattle, Washington

Wife: Kiyo
Children:

Affiliations:

On Christmas Card list
1963 (fund-raising) dinner—1 (ticket purchased)
Helped: January 11, 1964—luncheon for Helen
          April 15, 1965—Arranged dinner meeting of
          Jackson Street Community Council and gave
          gift to Anna Marie

Armed with that kind of information Jackson would be certain to thank Tak Kubota for the thoughtful present he had given to the senator's young daughter. And Tak Kubota would be just as certain to smile broadly and spread the word around Seattle's Japanese community that Scoop Jackson was one helluva guy.

Like any good politician, Jackson avoided unnecessary confrontations. When trouble brewed, the senator's administrative assistant, John Salter, did the dirty work. And it is doubtful that Capitol Hill had a staff man as well-suited to handling that task. Salter's tongue was as sharp as his mind. When necessary, Salter's abusive words could figuratively flay an antagonist. The result was that Salter offended many, while Jackson offended few. It was an ideal political combination. Once, just before he left Jackson to go into the public-relations business, Salter bumped into Senator Howard Cannon in the halls of the Senate Office Building. Cannon was immensely pleased with himself, because he just had won re-election by a landslide in sparsely-populated Nevada. "How many votes make a landslide in Nevada?" Salter asked Cannon. "Ten thousand," Cannon replied proudly. "Hell, I wouldn't be any good for you," Salter said. "I *offend* that many voters in an election campaign." Perhaps he did, but Jackson could merely shrug his shoulders at the workings of his hatchet-man. Every politician occasionally needs some dirty work done and, with Salter around, Jackson could go right on smiling.

The election of 1958, as Jackson sought a second term in the Senate, set a pattern that would last through most of the rest of his career. The Seattle *Argus*, a perceptive little weekly for the downtown professionals, was the first to notice that something very strange was going on around the state's junior Democratic senator. "The handwriting on the wall is being accepted by some, with interesting side effects," the *Argus* wrote in predicting that 1958 would be a bad year for the Republicans. "Senator Jackson, for example, is more and more seen in the company of some of the state's leading businessmen to whom a few years ago he was strictly persona non grata." His Democratic support intact, Jackson began coveting the Republican vote. In later years, Jackson's personality-cult coalition would become so strong as to make him virtually unbeatable in Washington State.

There was another pattern developing in 1958, too. In the Democratic primary he was opposed by a Leftist who accused him of everything from "fear mongering" to "sowing the seeds of cancer in our little children" through his support of atomic testing. In the general election he was opposed by a Rightist who accused him of "socialistic spending" and being soft on Communism. For Jackson, the centrist, it was an ideal situation. He railed at the extremists, Right and Left, and assumed control of everyone in the middle. He won re-election by 300,000 votes, a record.

With his reputation embellished by a landslide victory, Jackson returned to Washington to immerse himself in the subject that fascinated him most—national defense.

187

In 1959 he formed the Subcommittee on National Policy Machinery, a subcommittee that studiously examined the shortcomings of the government's policy-making procedures. The panel became known as Jackson's "egghead" committee. It sought few headlines and received few. But, eventually, the subcommittee would produce remarkable results—including an almost minute-by-minute schedule for John Kennedy's Presidential transition period and the plan with which Kennedy completely reorganized the sluggish National Security Council.

To run the egghead committee, Jackson lined up some impressive Cold War talent—ranging from Richard Neustadt, a former Truman adviser, to Dorothy Fosdick, the hard-headed, warm-hearted daughter of the theologian, Emerson Fosdick. Years later, Neustadt, by then the director of the Kennedy Institute at Harvard, became a Vietnam dove and shied away from Jackson's hard-line Cold War stance. But Dorothy Fosdick, still a tough-minded Cold Warrior, remained with Jackson and, in the 1970s, continued to write Jackson's aggressive speeches about nuclear blackmail.

If Cold War rhetoric was somewhat out of vogue in the 1970s, it nevertheless was a central issue in the late 1950s. John Kennedy began borrowing from the subcommittee's findings for his own campaign ideas, words that urged the country to get moving again, rhetoric that warned about a missile gap. And, with John Salter sitting in on Kennedy's Presidential strategy sessions, there was not much doubt about where Scoop Jackson stood as the 1960 Democratic National Convention neared.

As Scoop Jackson pushed past the reporters and through the door into Suite 9333, he didn't know exactly what to expect. There is an old political maxim that says you do not run for the Vice-Presidency. He had broken that rule—but only reluctantly. For months his staff had been pushing him but, as his former press secretary, Russ Holt, later recalled, "He would grin his boyish grin and put you off." Unknown to Jackson, Holt and Salter were slipping speculative stories into the press in the hope that Jackson's own clippings might convince him.

But it wasn't until the eve of the convention that Jackson made up his mind. It was then that Bob Kennedy told him flatly that he was his first choice for the position—if his brother, John, won the Presidential nomination. He asked Jackson to speak on behalf of his brother in caucuses of some of the large delegations—particularly Illinois, Ohio, Pennsylvania, and New York. In the process, Bob said, Jackson might pick up some Vice-Presidential support for himself. Jackson agreed, and methodically began making the rounds. Simultaneously, Salter, Holt, and a handful of other Jackson boosters opened a headquarters in Suite 5W17 in the Statler Hilton Hotel and began pushing green-and-white "Scoop Jackson for Vice-President" buttons. The Jackson command post was a slapdash, three-room suite. On the door there was an electric "hamburger" sign promoting Jackson's candidacy. But, slapdash or not, it was real.

Gradually, in the first days of the convention, Jackson appeared to be making positive headway. Mayor Bob Wagner of New York came out for him. Governor Pat Brown of California indicated his support. So did Senator Mike Mansfield of Montana, Senator Frank Moss of Utah, and Representative Stuart Udall of Arizona. The Alaska and Hawaii delegations strongly backed Jackson, because he had been a leader in the fight for statehood for both those former territories.

But Scoop Jackson had another problem, a problem that

would haunt him almost all the way through his career. Bob Kennedy was a feisty, aggressive, driven man. He and his brother, too, expected results. They expected Jackson to deliver the Washington State delegation to Kennedy. "Scoop is my personal choice and Jack likes Scoop," Bob told Salter. "But you've got to give us some pegs to hang our hats on. Go, go, go! Deliver your delegation!" But Bob was asking the impossible—Scoop Jackson could have more luck switching votes in New York than he could within his own stubborn delegation.

The Washington delegation had little clout at the convention, having only twenty-seven votes out of the 761 needed to nominate a Presidential candidate. But, influential or not, the Washington delegates were stubborn—and hopelessly divided between the four major candidates, Kennedy, Johnson, Symington, and Adlai Stevenson. Of the major politicians within the delegation, only Jackson was committed to Kennedy. Jackson's senatorial colleague, Warren G. Magnuson, was sworn to Lyndon Johnson. Governor Albert D. Rosellini, a Catholic, who was up for re-election in 1960, was fearful that the religious issue would pull him down, too. Rosellini fought to remain uncommitted. Among the rest of the less-known delegates, the religious issue reverberated threateningly. Many of them were from the conservative, farmland plateaus of Eastern Washington and they didn't want, as the phrase went, the Pope's emissary in the White House.

On July 13, the day of the Presidential balloting, there were two caucuses of the Washington delegation. The delegation might not have much influence, but it received very special attention on the most crucial day of the convention. First Lyndon Johnson came calling, and then Bob Kennedy came to make a pitch for his brother.

The last few weeks of the battle for the Democratic nomination had been vitriolic, with Johnson bitterly attacking Kennedy. His eleventh-hour talk before the Washington delegation was no exception. A few of the delegates grumbled angrily as the big Texan, a man who exuded power, hacked away first at Kennedy's religion, then at his health, and finally at his father's alleged pro-Nazism. The speech was a little too raw to change any votes from Washington, where the game of politics is played less virulently. But it still alarmed the Jackson and Kennedy forces, so alarmed them that they put in a quick call to Bob Kennedy.

Kennedy rushed from the Biltmore to the Statler and, in his nasal New England twang, laid it on the line for the Washington delegates: John Kennedy would win on the first ballot, but he wanted their votes. Then Bob Kennedy said publicly what he had been saying privately: Scoop Jackson was his personal choice for the Vice-Presidential nomination. No guarantees, no promises. But Scoop Jackson was his personal choice.

The Kennedy forces, in their vigorous search for delegates, had made almost a ritual out of hinting that a local favorite son might be John Kennedy's running mate. Once, just before the convention, Johnson visited Seattle. He was asked if Scoop Jackson would make an acceptable running mate for him. "Well now, Son," the hulking Senate Majority Leader replied, "I don't believe it's a wise practice for a fellow to go campaigning around this country promising the Vice-Presidency. You know, there's a certain colleague of mine who's already got eleven Vice-Presidents!"

But Bob Kennedy's statement was public, was not an outright promise and had to be taken as real. Magnuson, as a favor to Jackson, switched to Kennedy. So, eventually, did Rosellini, giving Kennedy just over half the Washington delegation. But not another member budged—not even as a favor to their popular, powerful senator.

That night, during the alphabetical balloting in the vast, littered Sports Arena, the clerk called *Washington* just before ten o'clock. At that point, Kennedy had 697½ votes. Needing only sixty-four more to gain the nomination, he was a virtual shoo-in. Luke Graham, the portly chairman of the Washington delegation and a close political ally of Jackson, stood at the microphone and fidgeted briefly. The political thing to do would have been to cast the entire twenty-seven votes for the inevitable nominee. But Graham swallowed and then did what he had been instructed to do: *Mr. Chairman, the State of Washington casts 14½ votes for John F. Kennedy . . . 6½ votes for Adlai Stevenson . . . 3 votes for Stuart Symington . . . 2½ votes for Lyndon B. Johnson . . . and one-half vote for Albert D. Rosellini.*

Three states later, Wyoming pushed John Kennedy over the top by giving him all fifteen of its votes.

What followed then was almost total confusion. A battery of Jackson aides—Salter, Holt, Sterling Munro, Mike Cafferty, Archie Baker—had established themselves in an eight-foot-by-eight-foot, unfinished-plywood cubicle which served as a Jackson command center near the convention floor. Even before the balloting, Bob Kennedy had called Salter and told him the plan for selecting the Vice-Presidential nominee: Jackson was to choose three "seconds" to present his case to Kennedy and eight or ten party leaders who would help make the choice. Salter leaned back against a plywood wall and frowned; it seemed a little too complicated, too unwieldy. But, systematically, Salter and the others settled on three names: Mike Mansfield, because he had supported Johnson and was a Jackson friend; Mayor

192

Robert Wagner of New York, to exhibit Jackson's strength in the East, and Stuart Udall, who had been Kennedy's Western campaign coordinator.

Toward the end of the balloting Holt found Mansfield, a professorial figure, leaning against a back wall of the convention hall, one knee up, gloomily watching his candidate lose. Holt put the question to him: Would he speak to Kennedy and the party leaders on behalf of Jackson? Mansfield averred briefly that he was a Johnson man. That's why we want you, Holt said. Then Mansfield agreed. Others rounded up Wagner and Udall and soon the three seconds had elbowed in among the Jackson aides in the plywood cubicle, awaiting word from the Kennedys. Outside the cubicle the sweepers were cleaning up the litter —fallen Johnson posters, broken Symington standards, crushed Kennedy straw hats, green-and-white Jackson buttons, ruptured balloons, and tons of confetti. The phone rang after an hour and a half of waiting. Salter leapt at it to hear the news: But Bobby told him the signals had changed. Now they wanted just one "second" for a meeting early the next morning.

But, by morning, the signals had changed once again. Salter received a call at seven A.M., after an hour's sleep. The Presidential nominee wanted to see him, not a second. Bleary-eyed, Salter floundered around the room looking for a set of cufflinks for the only shirt he had left after a week in Los Angeles. He grasped a pair of cheap, campaign cufflinks off his dresser and ran out the door toward his meeting with John Kennedy.

The meeting was in Kennedy's bedroom, with the Presidential nominee, his brother, Bob, and Salter sitting almost knee to knee. The talk was about the Vice-Presidency and it revolved mostly around Jackson and Symington. Salter, the partisan, portrayed Jackson as steady, a good man to have behind you. Symington, Salter said, was excitable. "He'd just blow, Jack. I don't know that you'd want to have him with his finger on the button in case anything happened to you."

Salter is a volatile man and, as he made his point, he waved his hand under John Kennedy's nose. It was then that he noticed that the cufflinks were inscribed with the initials L.B.J. He stopped gesturing.

A few hours later, inside Suite 9333, Scoop Jackson's ear-to-ear grin faded to solemnity. John Kennedy rose from a sofa, smiled, and shook Jackson's hand. Almost immediately he told Jackson that no final decision had been reached on the Vice-Presidential nomination. But then Kennedy related the news that deflated the hopes of Scoop Jackson: It no longer was a choice between two men, Jackson and Symington. Sam Rayburn, the powerful Texan and Speaker of the House of Representatives, had been in to see him. Rayburn had made it brutally clear that Kennedy could not win the election without carrying Texas and a handful of Southern states. He also had made it clear that he could not carry those states without Lyndon Johnson on the ticket. An hour earlier, Kennedy told Jackson, he had gone down to the seventh-floor suite of the Majority Leader. They had talked carefully, around the edges of the subject of the Vice-Presidency, and no formal offer had been made. But Lyndon Johnson had not seemed unreceptive.

Scoop Jackson listened and nodded. He was a pragmatic man and he knew that John Kennedy was, too. It was not too difficult to foresee what was going to happen.

The talk continued for fifteen minutes and then Jackson

rose to leave. Kennedy asked him to wait in his Statler suite for a telephone call later in the day. "Whatever the decision," the Presidential nominee said, "you'll be the first to know." Jackson smiled wanly, but as he emerged from Suite 9333 into the mob of reporters, the ear-to-ear grin was firmly back in place. He was buoyant, almost jaunty. But he answered fewer questions on the way out than he had on the way in.

Jackson returned to the Statler at 1:30 P.M. and was forced to run the obstacle course once again. By now, in the minds of the press, Jackson was the leading candidate for the nomination. Almost 250 reporters and a half-dozen television cameras were jammed into the hallway outside Suite 5W17. Jackson looked tired and he walked slowly, reluctantly, toward another showdown with the press.

The questions caromed off the sturdy Norwegian and his replies were mostly unresponsive. It was not like Jackson. The reporters knew him for his candor. "Honestly, gentlemen, I can't tell you any more than I have," he finally said and then strode inside his room to await the telephone call.

The minutes seemed to drag, turtle-slow, and the gloom was pervasive. Still, there was that one, outside chance. . . .

At 2:30 P.M. the telephone rang. Everyone in the room jumped. Salter grabbed the phone and handed it to Jackson. Jackson said, "Yes?" and then chuckled mirthlessly. The call was from a teenager, trying to dial his girl friend from the lobby.

Moments later, the phone rang again. Once again Salter answered and handed the phone to Jackson. Everyone's shoulders slumped simultaneously as they listened to just one end of the telephone conversation. "Yes, Jack. I under-

stand, Jack. You're perfectly right, Jack. Of course I understand, Jack. No, Jack. Under no circumstances, Jack. . . ."

Toward the end of the conversation Salter, even more
pragmatic than his boss, rushed to the telephone, thrust
his hand over the speaker and told Jackson: "I don't know
what you're saying no to, but for God's sake, say maybe."

A minute later Jackson cradled the telephone and told
his disheartened troops the startling news that the Vice-
Presidential nomination had been offered to and accepted
by Lyndon Johnson, a man who had said a dozen times he
would never take the post. Jackson, as a consolation prize,
had been offered the chairmanship of the Democratic National Committee during the election campaign. Jackson
had asked for time to make up his mind. Then he walked
out of the room and told the milling reporters that Senator
Kennedy would make an announcement at four o'clock.
Jackson had been authorized to make the same announcement at the same time.

At precisely four o'clock, in the Sierra Room of the Stat-
ler-Hilton, Jackson addressed the press: "Is everybody in?
Good. Senator Kennedy called me to advise me that, after
careful consideration, he had decided to place in nomination the name of Senator Lyndon Johnson for the good of
the ticket."

The reporters gasped. In the back of the room Russ Holt
and several Jackson secretaries had tears running down
their faces.

"No one should enter politics unless he is a good sport,"
Jackson continued, a brave smile planted on his broad face.
"I will do whatever Senators Kennedy and Johnson want
me to do. I will do everything a good sport should do."

The toughened reporters, some of them with gleaming
eyes, too, stuck their pencils in their mouths, tucked their

notebooks under their arms, and applauded the plucky senator from Washington. It was a rare gesture from an especially cynical press corps.

In the Sierra Room there were three television monitors, one for each network. Briefly Jackson was on all three, breaking the news to the nation. John Kennedy had been less precise than his methodical friend. Then, at exactly three minutes past four, Jackson's face disappeared from the monitors. The screens faded to blankness and then the stolid, Nordic features of Henry M. Jackson were replaced by the handsome, Irish face of John Fitzgerald Kennedy.

Later that day Jackson reluctantly agreed to become Kennedy's national chairman, the first Protestant chairman of the Democratic Party in thirty-two years. It was an odd position for Jackson—and one that, in all probability, he should have refused. The personality-cult, cater-to-the-Republicans, almost nonpartisan style he had developed so successfully in his own state was in sharp conflict with the role of a party chairman. The chairman is the most partisan of individuals. To the chairman, there is no such thing as a good Republican. But Jackson disavowed that role immediately. "I don't go for the idea that we're all right and the Republicans are all wrong," he said in one of his first public statements in his new position.

The first hint that Jackson would have trouble in his new job came just two weeks after his appointment. He traveled to Hyannisport for a long conference with the Presidential nominee. After the meeting, Jackson told the press that he and Kennedy had "a complete understanding —I am to handle the entire campaign. It will be no hydra-headed monster." Jackson said he would work with Bob Kennedy who would handle "the minute details."

It is unclear whether Jackson really meant those words or whether they were merely a political defense mechanism. But it is not unclear who was really going to run the campaign: Bob Kennedy and the group of J.F.K.'s Boston pols who became known as the Irish Mafia were in total control. The press began speculating within days of his appointment that Jackson would be no more than a figurehead chairman, an articulate Protestant to balance Kennedy's Catholicism. And the press was right.

Jackson installed Salter and another longtime associate, Clarence D. (Dan) Martin, as deputy chairmen. Martin, a big, easygoing man, fitted in well. But Salter was as cocky and abrasive as the antagonistic Irish Mafia themselves. Salter and J.F.K.'s aides were cut from the same cloth. But they had different leaders and their conflicts were bitter and regular. "Bob Kennedy was running the campaign," one Kennedy partisan said later. "Apparently John thought Scoop was running it."

A second sign of trouble for Jackson came shortly after Labor Day in the opening stages of Kennedy's formal campaign. The Kennedy forces scheduled a major visit to Seattle, with a motorcade through the downtown streets and a speech in the largest hall in town. Jackson and Brock Adams, a young Kennedy organizer, argued futilely that it was a terrible time to make the visit. Seattle is a city of outdoorsmen and a summer's-end political visit invited disaster. But Kennedy came anyway.

The Kennedy motorcade wended its way from Boeing Field through starkly empty streets toward downtown Seattle. Block after block of total silence greeted the Presidential nominee and someone recalled Woodrow Wilson's visit to Seattle four decades earlier. The Wobblies had

198

stood in silence, arms crossed, block after block, as President Wilson's countenance turned ashen.

Downtown, a boisterous crowd of 5,000 waited for Kennedy, but even that was a smaller group than had greeted Stevenson in 1956. And that night, despite frantic efforts to bus in spectators, only the floor of the 5,000-seat Civic Auditorium was filled for Kennedy's speech. The balconies were partly empty.

The Kennedy people were miffed at the poor turnout in their national chairman's home state. It was early in the campaign and an image of success was important. Later, Kennedy would bring the word "charisma" into the political lexicon. But, after the dismal Seattle visit, many of the national reporters began to question Kennedy's ability to turn on crowds. It was a bad start—both for Kennedy and for Jackson.

But just days later, Jackson got in his innings. The religious issue boiled to the surface when Norman Vincent Peale, the preacher, joined in signing a statement questioning whether Kennedy would take orders from the Vatican. Jackson, the Protestant, sharply attacked Peale for "employing religious hate and prejudice." Jackson then observed, in good political fashion, that he was a thirty-second degree Mason and a Presbyterian, but he wasn't worried about Vatican influence on a Catholic President of the United States.

From then on, Jackson's attacks became more aggressive and he began to sound more like a party chairman. He began a series of frontal assaults on Kennedy's opponent, Richard M. Nixon. Nixon, Jackson said in New York, is dropping his "mask of respectability" by "imputing disloyalty and lack of patriotism" to Kennedy and the Democrats. In Washington, at the National Press Club, Jackson accused Nixon of demagoguery. "With defeat staring him in the face," he charged in Boston, "Mr. Nixon is shedding his mask and showing the true Nixon—the same old Nixon of the smear and the slur."

Back home in Washington State, however, the campaign was not going so well. Al Rosellini, the Catholic Democratic Governor, had control of whatever Democratic organization there was in the state. Rosellini, fearing the religious issue, was running away from Kennedy. Three weeks before election day Salter walked into the state Democratic headquarters in Seattle and found that not a single Kennedy poster was in sight. Salter exploded in anger. But the regular Democrats stuck with Rosellini, the man who would pass out political favors in Washington State after election day. And they ignored their Presidential standard-bearer.

On any Presidential election night the returns pile up in an inexorable pattern of East to West—first from New England, then from the rest of the East, then from the crucial midwestern states, and finally from the far western bastions of California, Oregon, and Washington.

The election of 1960 was razor-thin close. But, even before the tide of the returns began flowing out of the Far West, it became apparent that John Kennedy was the almost inevitable victor. And so the broad face and solid torso of Scoop Jackson was on the television screen once again, proclaiming victory for the Democrats. His arms were upstretched in the universal sign of victory. A huge grin split his face and he was almost giddy. A viewer speculated that maybe he was a little tipsy. But not Scoop Jackson, surely not Soda Pop Jackson. Giddy, maybe, on the heady wine of victory, but not on anything else.

Moments later the figures began to arrive from the West and it became clear that Richard M. Nixon had carried Washington State. In the Kennedy compound at Hyannisport the new President-elect turned to his aide, Ted Sorensen, and grumbled a little about losing his national chairman's state.

CHAPTER 9

A VOICE IN THE SENATE

WITH A SURGE of excitement, the crowd pushed against a restraining rope as the President's gleaming plane touched down on the runway. Military policemen reached with white-gloved hands to grip and tighten the rope to keep the milling people off the airport apron.

The inevitable spontaneous cheer went up as President Kennedy stepped off the plane, suntanned, squint-smiling into the brightness of the early autumn day in 1963. Emerging from the plane behind one Presidential shoulder was Scoop Jackson. It was to be only a brief touch-down at Larson Air Force Base in eastern Washington. The Presidential party was to board a nearby helicopter immediately for a quick hop to the dedication ceremony of a nuclear plant at Hanford.

The President was behind schedule, but Kennedy couldn't resist the lure of the waving, applauding people about one hundred feet away. They had come to catch a glimpse of him and, impetuously, with his athletic stride, he hurried toward the people. Secret Service men scrambled into their pattern of protection while Jackson and Senator Warren G. Magnuson hurried to catch up with the President.

The crowd surged anew against the ropes as the President approached and began shaking hands. Then, grinning, he moved along the rope, one arm thrust outward like a wand to touch the forest of bobbing hands.

"Oh, Daddy!" squealed a saucer-eyed blonde girl of eleven. "President Kennedy shook my hand!"

Jackson glowed in the excitement. His political instincts told him that, despite what had happened in 1960, this buoyant, magnetic young President would carry Washington State in 1964. Jackson had a race of his own that year and he looked forward to campaigning with a popular President and friend.

At last the Presidential party turned and hurried toward the waiting helicopter, its rotors turning slowly. The craft rose and headed southeast. Swiftly, the jet-assisted Presidential helicopter moved over green farmlands that pushed verdantly up a high-plateau hillside. And then, on the far side of a dividing ridge, the farmlands turned abruptly back to the burned sand and sagebrush that had been native to this country since the last Ice Age. It was a dramatic example of what federal irrigation had done for arid and bleak eastern Washington.

Shouting over the engine noise, Jackson described to the President the plans for bringing more irrigation into the desolate land of the Columbia Basin down below.

Momentous events had streamed through the lives of the two men during the past three years. While the young President coped with a series of crises, he had generated a new kind of pragmatic idealism that would alter the nation and the world for years. Meanwhile, Jackson had developed into a senator with more influence. He had become a committee chairman and a man whose words on national security and defense held significance.

Theirs was an easy, implicit friendship. And they had a

mutual political understanding which made it unnecessary to talk about some of the things that were being written— articles such as the one in the Newark *Star Ledger* about the "curious split-level political relationship between Jackson and the President."

Jackson, the article said, "is the leading Democratic critic of the administration policies in the sensitive national-defense and security field . . . at the same time Jackson holds the two-year record of the highest percentage of favorable votes (90 percent) cast by a Democrat in the Senate for the Kennedy program. . . . Although he is the former national party chairman, Jackson has virtually no direct voice to either the President or his brother, Attorney-General Robert F. Kennedy."

It was, like most of the stories about their relationship, exaggeration. But the stories persisted. Throughout the brief years of the Kennedy Presidency, the rumor mills said that JFK and his national chairman had had a parting of the ways—and a major one. As with most Washington rumors, there was a mixture of truth and pure gossip in the story of a Kennedy-Jackson split.

After John Kennedy's election victory in 1960, Jackson was eager to shed the figurehead role as chairman of the Democratic National Committee. In almost the same breath with which he congratulated Kennedy on his election, Jackson said he wanted to leave the chairmanship quickly. Kennedy thanked him and said he wanted John Bailey of Connecticut to be his successor. Jackson agreed to contact Bailey. "You're the man he wants," Jackson told the new chairman-designate in a telephone conversation. "Get down here and take over."

But as Jackson prepared to move out of the national committee headquarters, his close friend and onetime administrative assistant, John Salter, was being passed over as jobs were handed out by the new administration. Jackson thought Salter, who had been involved in the earliest Kennedy strategy sessions, was entitled to at least an assistant secretaryship in one of the departments. Salter's unrealistic choice was to become the top White House congressional liaison man. But that job went to Larry O'Brien. Jackson's other deputy at the national committee, Clarence D. (Dan) Martin Jr., a more amiable person than Salter, easily got his new job in the Kennedy Administration. He became an assistant secretary of commerce.

Jackson talked with the President-elect about a job for Salter. Kennedy, obviously preoccupied with his massive responsibilities, promised something would be done. "But," Jackson explained later, "you know when you're President you've got all those guys down below. Jack Kennedy had trouble—most Presidents do—in getting an order carried out."

The "guys down below" included some of the Irish Mafia with whom Salter had feuded during the campaign. Salter became bitterly certain they were blocking his job aspirations.

At last Jackson testily persisted with Robert Kennedy, who took care of the problem. In March, Salter became deputy director of the International Cooperation Administration, the forerunner of the Agency for International Development. A foreign aid congressional liaison job with a $19,000 salary—tops for its day—it still did not satisfy Salter: It lacked political excitement. Two years later he was back on Jackson's Senate payroll.

Jackson had a share of the historic action of Kennedy's entry into the White House. Beginning in 1959, his

Subcommittee on Government Machinery of the Senate Government Operations Committee made a methodical examination of the way the President reached his decisions on Cold War strategy. A special target of the study was the structure and function of the National Security Council.

Jackson's committee aroused scant public interest, but its meticulous work fascinated political scientists. An early report of the subcommittee criticized the "supercabinet officers and superstaffs" which had evolved during the Eisenhower Administration. The subcommittee recommended an overhaul of the procedures of the N.S.C. which, Jackson said, had become overstructured, overstaffed, and hampered by complicated procedures.

"During the Eisenhower Administration," Jackson said, "there was a tendency to hand to the President a *fait accompli* on national-security decisions. Eisenhower had the army tradition in which the commanding officer would be given a plan. All he had to do was initial it. This might have been fine for a military operation, but what concerned me was the failure to provide an opportunity for the President to look at his options; to see and hear those debated.

"The President must make the major decisions. In order to make the right decisions the President really needs to have articulated the options available to him." In reaching national security decisions, particularly, the President should hear the most skilled advocates debate the alternatives. Instead of the Eisenhower concept of a "grand council of wise men," Jackson urged a return to the traditional executive roles, with the Secretary of State serving as the President's principal adviser, working closely with the Secretary of Defense. Below those men, he said, there would be fewer committees, fewer people, but of higher quality.

The suggestions became Kennedy's blueprint for national-security decision-making. A lean, quick, effective procedure would be needed. Grave international crises would cascade upon the White House: the Cuban missile crisis, requiring instant decisions of vast potential consequence, lay just ahead.

Under other circumstances Robert McNamara and Henry Jackson might have been great friends. McNamara had all those characteristics which Jackson admires in a man—the corporate-executive countenance, the assurance of a superb technician, and uncanny organizational skill. He was tough, persuasive, and stubborn. In his testimony to congressional committees McNamara was dazzling in his ability to recall facts instantly from his computer-bank memory. Those were, in fact, many of the same characteristics possessed by Jackson.

During the campaign Kennedy had asked once, conversationally, if Jackson were interested in a cabinet job. Jackson shrugged. He said he had no inclination to move into the executive branch. Still, he was flattered and a little expectant. The talk did not center on any specific job, and Kennedy made no specific offer. The President-elect was considering Jackson for the Defense job after the election. But, seeking a new face and a new name, Kennedy chose McNamara instead.

Almost any Defense secretary would have difficulty measuring up to Jackson's yardstick and, for all his skill at overwhelming admirals and generals, and awing lawmakers, McNamara stumbled early and often in Jackson's view. McNamara had been in office only a few weeks when he calmly shot down the missile-gap issue. There was no missile gap, he said candidly in a briefing for reporters. It was a disturbing utterance to Jackson and Senator Stuart Symington who had so eagerly developed the campaign issue through earlier months.

McNamara, however, worried little about political nerve endings. The administration later sought to recover by explaining that the missile gap was an imprecise issue, founded on ambiguities of intelligence during the Eisenhower Administration: Later the intelligence reports about Russian missile strength were more reliable. Still, it was an embarrassing, irking incident, the first of a series of events which inhibited Jackson more than a decade later from finding words of praise for McNamara. . . .

. . ."McNamara," Jackson says, "went into the job with a management concept which he thought could be utilized not only in the manufacture and production of weapons systems, but also could be used to reduce international problems and tensions to some kind of mathematical formula. There always could be a planned solution in McNamara's view. His problem was dealing with the highly inexact problems that were not susceptible to management planning. . . ."

Jackson worried during the early stages of the Kennedy Administration about its responsiveness to the Russian threat. Within days after he moved into the White House, Kennedy summoned Jackson to talk about the pulsing crisis over nuclear-testing. The Soviet Union and the United States had a tenuous voluntary moratorium on testing in the atmosphere. But Jackson told the President there was no doubt in his mind that the Russians would break the moratorium. He urged that the United States have a plan in readiness to promptly renew nuclear testing if the

Russians started testing again. To fail to do so, Jackson warned, would allow the Soviet Union, through a series of quick, well-planned tests, to make major gains in nuclear knowledge.

As they talked, though, the President's attention strayed. "He just wouldn't listen," Jackson said to a reporter months later. Kennedy soon turned the conversation to Vietnam. Apprehensively, he talked about Southeast Asian nations perched like dominoes in the path of Communist aggression.

Efforts to negotiate a nuclear test-ban treaty were jolted when the Soviet Union in late summer of 1961 announced it was about to resume testing. It was one of the Kremlin's toughest, loudest, sabre-rattling pronouncements. The Soviets criticized the aggressive policy of the NATO military bloc; warned that Soviet scientists were ready to begin testing superpowerful nuclear bombs of immense magnitude; and boasted that Soviet rocketry had reached such a stage of perfection that they could deliver a nuclear bomb to any point in the world.

It was a depressing development for a world tired after a decade of nuclear fear. Jackson seethed. His warnings had gone unheeded. The United States was not prepared to resume testing at once. Russia would enjoy major gains from its well-planned test series.

Although he was in his late forties, Jackson still looked youthful. He defended against an aggressive waistline through diet and a daily regimen of exercise and swimming in the Senate gym. Jackson's continuing bachelorhood still inspired an occasional mention in the press. But politics and government ruled his life and, if he dated a woman, weeks often elapsed before she received another telephone call.

His most frequent companion through the late 1950s was Helen Langer, niece of the late senator from North Dakota, William Langer. Friends sensed their relationship was leading toward marriage. But their most conspicuous appearance together—at the Kennedy inaugural ball—was their last.

In 1955 when Salter married Bettye Bates, an employe of the Senate office, the Associated Press report departed from the usual drab AP lead paragraph: "Washington, AP —Cupid finally made a dent in the office of Senator Jackson, Democrat, Washington." Salter, the story added, "is the first of five men in the Jackson office, including Jackson, to be married. . . ."

His bachelor life style would have provoked, within most women, a surge of maternal instinct or, more likely, profound despair. When Martin went to work for the national committee during the 1960 campaign, Jackson invited him to move into the Jackson apartment at 2500 Q Street. It was a more fashionable address than the Capitol Hill apartment where Jackson and Salter began Washington life nineteen years earlier. But its atmosphere of bachelor disarray was the same, if on a more grand scale. Jackson padded around in tattered pajamas during evening hours, oblivious to the litter of newspapers and magazines which surrounded him. Martin was puzzled by the diet. "All he had to feed me was bran flakes and canned orange juice. He had a radio—the guts were falling out of it—and some awfully hard furniture." Martin has a deep fondness for Jackson, as do almost all of Jackson's close friends. But the primitive environment of the Jackson apartment was a cultural shock: Martin, a wealthy Southern Californian, was accustomed to elegant surroundings. When Senator Warren G. Magnuson offered Martin the use of his considerably more comfortable Shoreham Hotel suite, Martin made excuses and moved out of the Jackson apartment. "Besides," Martin said, "Jackson snored louder 'n hell."

Jackson and Helen Hardin met in an elevator the day the new Congress convened in January, 1961. Senator Clinton Anderson of New Mexico, a close friend of Jackson's, introduced them. She was his new blonde receptionist from Albuquerque and Anderson was escorting her to the gallery to watch the senators' swearing-in ceremony. The strikingly beautiful woman noticed that, as Jackson murmured a greeting, he seemed terribly nervous for a veteran senator.

A few days later he telephoned to invite her to tea in the Senate dining room. Tea dates led to weekend days of bicycling in Washington's rustic Rock Creek Park. Jackson was forty-nine. She was twenty-eight, a tall, almost regal beauty with a proper background. The daughter of the president of the American Gypsum Co., she had attended Hockaday School in Dallas, Vassar, then Scripps College in California, and later earned a master's degree in contemporary literature at Columbia University. She had been married briefly to a young doctor, but that marriage ended in an early divorce.

In November, 1961, when Washington newsmen got word that invitations were being issued in Albuquerque for a Henry Jackson-Helen Hardin wedding, they swarmed to the senator for confirmation. In his easy, accommodating way with the press, Jackson gave them a direct confirmation. It was an easy mistake for a longtime bachelor to make. But it was a social error. The groom just *doesn't* announce the wedding.

It was a small wedding ceremony in the Central Methodist Church in Albuquerque December 16, 1961. An invitation had gone to the President and First Lady. They responded with an ornately framed portrait of themselves. Jackson's old friend, Bob Kennedy, now Attorney-General of the United States, had been asked personally to attend the ceremony. But he didn't come either, and the bride-groom was disappointed by the lack of Kennedy attention, even though he understood they were buried in responsi-bilities.

When the newlyweds arrived in Hawaii for their honey-moon, Jackson told a reporter he intended to avoid official duties. But, as Helen Jackson soon discovered, that didn't fit the Jackson life style. A little more than a week later, he interrupted the honeymoon to attend a naval briefing at Pearl Harbor. The subject, he told newsmen, was "the increasing Communist submarine threat in the Pacific."

Initially shy and aloof, the senator's wife in time mastered the political-wife style. Interviewed after their honey-moon by Seattle newsmen, she cooed, "Some of Scoop's political friends have told me it must be true love, because I come from a state which has so few electoral votes."

Especially because he was a supporter of the administra-tion, Jackson's speech to the National Press Club in March, 1962, caused a major stir. He delivered some startling views about what the liberal establishment was calling the world's best hope for peace—the United Nations. The speech also came at a time when the UN was in financial distress. The Soviet bloc had refused to pay its obligations and armed UN actions in the Congo had been unexpect-edly costly. So President Kennedy now was asking Con-gress to authorize purchase of up to $100 million in UN bonds. In that delicate political atmosphere, Jackson spoke some tough words about the beleaguered world organiza-tion.

Conduct of UN affairs, Jackson said,

absorbs a disproportionate amount of the energy of our highest officials. The President and the Secretary of State must ration their worry time—and the hours spent on the UN cannot be spent on other matters. All too often, furthermore, the energies devoted to the UN must be spent on defensive actions—trying to defeat this or that ill-advised resolution—rather than on more constructive programs.

The Cold War may destroy the United Nations if that organization becomes one of its main battle-grounds, but the United Nations cannot put an end to the Cold War. . . . The truth is, though we have not often spoken it in recent years, that the best hope for peace with justice does not lie in the United Nations. Indeed the truth is almost exactly the reverse. The best hope for the United Nations lies in the maintenance of peace. In our deeply divided world, peace depends on the power and unity of the Atlantic Community and on the skill of our direct diplomacy.

There is a tendency—to which the press itself is not immune—to believe that the UN makes more history than it really does. . . . If the UN were used less for drum-beating on every nerve-tingling issue, and if its energies were quietly devoted to manageable problems, there might be fewer headlines from the UN, but more contributions to the building of a peaceful world.

Jackson was indirectly critical of the attention given to UN Ambassador Adlai Stevenson by the media and the world. The prestige attached to the ambassadorship by Eisenhower "and continued by this administration seems unfortunate: The ambassador is not a second Secretary of State."

213

Because the speech was delivered only days before the scheduled Senate vote on the UN bonds, Jackson's remarks caused a furor. Reporters judged it as a serious attack on the world organization and an effort to put the bond issue in political jeopardy. Ambassador Stevenson was angered, as was Senator Hubert H. Humphrey. Eleanor Roosevelt, in her syndicated column, registered "shock and disappointment." Such talk, she said, disturbs the smaller UN nations and could produce the same cynicism that destroyed the League of Nations. But some Senate Democrats privately complimented Jackson for, as one of them put it, "telling a much-needed truth."

Still, truth or not, the aggressive UN speech reinforced the growing speculation that Scoop Jackson was a lone rider in the New Frontier. Shortly thereafter, other events would point further to Jackson's independence from the administration that he had helped elect.

The Nuclear Test Ban Treaty was perhaps the most significant aspiration of President Kennedy and 1963 polls showed there was a swelling public mood to put an end to nuclear testing in the atmosphere and ease the tensions of the Cold War. Emotions were rising. So Jackson, in his typical form, stubbornly held out against, as he described it, the "euphoria" of what might prove to be a dangerously misleading feeling of *detente* with the persistent and tough Russians.

Great Britain and the United States had submitted a draft test-ban treaty in April, 1961, but in September the Russian test series blasted hopes for that year. The final explosion, in October, was one of fifty to sixty megatons and described as a terror weapon. Through 1962, there were intermittent efforts to resume talks, but both the

United States and the Soviet Union resumed atmospheric testing. The year ended with the Soviets and the Western powers offering conflicting proposals for supervision and detection of tests.

By April 1963, a mood of agreement began to appear. A "hotline" communication system, linking Washington and Moscow, was agreed upon and the pundits began talking about an era of Soviet-American *detente*. In June, President Kennedy announced that the United States, Britain, and Russia would begin high-level talks aimed at an early agreement on nuclear testing. In the meantime, the United States ceased atmospheric testing.

After American, British, and Russian negotiators agreed to and initialed a limited nuclear-test-ban treaty July 25, President Kennedy went on national television to proclaim it "a victory for mankind." He said it "will not resolve all conflicts or cause the Communists to forego their ambitions or eliminate the dangers of war." But President Kennedy then added that "it is an important first step—a step toward peace—a step toward reason—a step away from war."

The treaty was submitted to the Senate for ratification. Republican leaders regarded it warily. So did—conspicuously—Jackson. He said the Soviet Union had entered into the agreement with the cynical intention of "a planned abrogation."

Kennedy, pleading for action, warned that "if we don't get it now, I would think generally perhaps the genie is out of the bottle and we will not ever get him back in again." Jackson responded with a speech of rebuke: "There is no need for passionate action with that kind of thinking. . . . we will keep trying to achieve a system for controlling and limiting arms. But it is a disservice to conjure up visions of catastrophe unless success is achieved in five or ten or twenty years.

"It does not advance the cause of peace to propound the dogma that every disarmament conference is the last best hope of mankind."

Liberals were outraged: The best hope for easing nuclear tensions now was at hand. And Jackson was suggesting that somehow action could be postponed for as long as twenty years.

There was a suggestion in his approach to the issue that Jackson ultimately would vote for ratification, but the White House was fretful. Its liaison men considered his vote a crucial one.

There is no need for passionate action. Jackson repeated the phrase often. It was his predictable response when any issue arose on a wave of emotionalism. He would be the devil's advocate, particularly when the waves of passion moved toward an accommodation with the Russians.

"There is a widespread assumption that we can win our way with the Russians with a policy of inoffensiveness," Jackson wrote in a *New York Times Magazine* article in August. "This is a fallacy held by many good and decent people who let their hearts prevail over their heads. We have all heard arguments that amount to nothing more than 'if we trust the Communists, they will trust us.' We are told that the United States should take unilateral initiatives to reduce our strength to set a 'good example' and quiet Soviet suspicions. It is not convincing to say that we won't know whether this policy will work until we try. There are some experiments that are best left undone."

He quoted the theologian and philosopher, Reinhold Niebuhr: "If the democratic nations fail, their failure must be partly attributed to the faulty strategy of idealists who have too many illusions when they face realists who have too little conscience." The only realistic bargaining hope, when dealing with expansionist states, he said, is to "maintain the strength to make bargaining attractive to them."

Mao had not been invited to participate in the Geneva talks, Jackson noted, and De Gaulle refused. Both China and France, he reasoned, would go ahead with nuclear programs, regardless of the treaty. So there would be no guarantee that the treaty would bring an assurance that the earth's atmosphere would be free of nuclear contamination.

As he became a target of liberal criticism, Jackson suddenly was being showered with praise by conservative foes of the treaty. They speculated hopefully about a coalition of the forces of Jackson, Richard Russell, and Barry Goldwater—perhaps potent enough to block ratification.

The liberal New York *Post* editorialized, "The enemies of the treaty have begun to fight. Their ranks are not restricted to the right-wing Republicans or Chinese Communists. Senator Jackson, who has steadily emerged in recent years as a leading echo of the rigid military minds in the Pentagon, served notice over the weekend that he saw nothing but peril in the prospective accord. His speech was a call to arms for the anti-treaty forces."

In early August Jackson led a push to secure some safeguards. He wanted the assurances that the United States would go ahead with underground testing and maintain nuclear laboratories. The United States, Jackson insisted, should maintain a standby plan to be able to resume atmospheric testing at once, if the Russians violated the treaty.

Jackson sensed that the treaty would be ratified by the

Senate—and perhaps that it should be. Polls indicated there was strong public support for it, which made Jackson all the more determined to take the hard line, arguing with cold reason that ran against the warm stream of hopeful emotions which, he thought, pushed the pendulum of national opinion too far from reality. But the Administration desperately wanted ratification and, hopefully, ratification by a big vote. Jackson's safeguards were accepted—both by the eager White House and the reluctant Joint Chiefs of Staff.

As the showdown vote approached, Senator Everett Dirksen, the Republican leader, said he would vote yes. Dirksen's bloc virtually assured the needed two-thirds majority and ratification became certain. Still the Administration fretted about Jackson who still was making obstinate sounds. As the historic debate moved toward its climax, Jackson began his speech to the tense Senate and its packed gallery. One by one, he described the safeguards which had been assured. The Administration had promised it would keep up its capability. And he pointed out a pledge of the Preparedness Investigating Subcommittee: It would become a watchdog to be certain that the nation keeps up its research and technology, to be able to resume atmospheric testing quickly if the Russians violate the treaty.

In his legalistic way Jackson made his case. Then he began his summing up: The treaty did not mean that the Russians had changed, he warned. Nor did he see the treaty as any weakening of the American will to maintain nuclear superiority. "Whether this country maintains its superiority, which is the means by which we have kept the peace, will depend on our will and determination to do so. Even if there were unrestricted nuclear testing, should we come to the conclusion that somehow we could cut back, we would

218

then invite a thermonuclear war, because we would lose our military superiority.

"The overriding challenge—the American people now face and will face in the years to come is 'Can we maintain a strong posture in a long, drawn-out conflict?' The Chinese and Russian Communists question whether we can do it. We have been doing it for seventeen years. This . . . causes me the greatest concern. It has in the past. It is my great concern now. And it will be in the years that lie ahead. . . ."

He reminded everyone that the administration had agreed to his safeguards and added, with a flourish, "I believe that the Senate may prudently give its advice and consent to ratification."

Jackson's support helped swing enough votes to give the President the overwhelming vote he wanted, 80-19.

His eventual vote for the treaty was less noticed nationally than was his widely publicized insistence on an American toughness. Jackson began to receive praise from conservatives and from worried Right Wing people around the nation, such as the letter from Florida which contained a newspaper clipping describing his wariness. Scrawled across the top of the newsprint was the message: *"Don't let them sell us down the river. We need mature thinking!! Keep it up. . . ."*

Throughout the debate the Russian press focused often on Goldwater and Jackson. A Radio Moscow commentator, Vladyslav Kozyakov asked, "Who are these most reactionary and war-minded of America's leaders? . . . A nuclear test ban is . . . opposed by the bloc of white-supremist and war-hungry senators led by Barry Goldwater, Arizona Republican, and Henry Jackson, Washington Democrat. Senator Goldwater is known as the champion of

an immediate preventative thermonuclear war. Jackson . . .
is the main spokesman of the diehards in the Pentagon."

Each year, usually in the fall, around the anniversary of
the great debate over the Nuclear Test Ban Treaty, Jackson rises in the Senate and delivers a quiet speech which
seldom makes news. He reports that a subcommittee representative has inspected the nuclear research work at Los
Alamos, New Mexico, Livermore, California, and the other
federal laboratories. He describes how the safeguards are
working—particularly how quickly the United States
could resume testing if the Soviet Union breaks the treaty:

Since the adoption of the Limited Test Ban Treaty
in 1963, staff members of the Joint Committee on Atomic
Energy and the Preparedness Investigating Subcommittee
have continually monitored the safeguard program to
insure that the safeguards are implemented in accordance
with the presidential commitment. Each year since 1963
I have presented a report to the Senate assessing the safeguard program. This is the sixth annual report and, as on
the five previous occasions, I am able to report that, on
the whole, our implementation of the treaty safeguards for the period since the last report has been
satisfactory.

It is his own dogged follow-up on an issue forgotten by
most Americans.

Because of his criticisms of the UN, which seemed to be
opposition to the administration, and because of his hold-
out on the test-ban treaty, political writers speculated about
the "split" between Jackson and the Kennedys. Perhaps,
they speculated, he was miffed at being shelved during the

Presidential campaign. Then it grew worse when the President and his brother ignored the Jackson wedding and failed to include the Jacksons in the New Frontier social whirl.

There were, no doubt, personal hurts, especially the Kennedys' lack of personal attention at the Jackson wedding.

Jackson sat in his office one day in 1963 while a writer asked questions about his relationship with the President. In the White House, the newsman said, "They're thinking of turning your picture to the wall."

Leaning back in his chair, his feet propped on a wastebasket, Jackson gestured toward a picture on his office wall—a black-and-white photo of the Georgetown softball days. A determined Scoop Jackson, in T-shirt and baggy pants, is swinging at a ball. Kennedy crouches behind the plate as catcher, and behind him, theatrically waving one arm, is Mike Mansfield. "I have no thought of turning that picture to the wall," Jackson mused.

In a private conversation, the President once told Jackson that his UN speech had been a good one. "He said it was something that should have been said and in the end, made a contribution to the UN," Jackson said. It is important to him that history not stand with a Kennedy-Jackson split. The President, his brother, and Jackson were all instinctive politicians who understood each other. If there were some personal hurts, they were inevitable for the times: The President was engrossed in the awesome responsibilities of his job, Bobby was preoccupied in his cabinet job, Jackson assumed new burdens as chairman of the Senate Interior Committee and he was increasingly absorbed in defense and national security matters.

His constant wariness of the Russians became intensified by Soviet provocations. Jackson's outspoken views on de-

221

fense became tougher because the United States seemed to be moving out of its period of Cold War watchfulness. Those views would qualify him to be known as—when the word swooped full-winged into the national vocabulary—a hawk.

Profound personal changes had come into Jackson's life. A daughter, Anna Marie, was born in 1963. His life still was politics and government, but in the evenings he tip-toed awkwardly into a blue-and-white nursery to see his daughter. The bachelor days of newspaper litter, hard fur-niture, bran flakes, and canned orange juice were sup-planted by a quietly gracious life of rosy-beige carpeting, silk draperies, expensive upholstered chairs, and sofas, pre-sided over by his wife.

He was at lunch in the Senate dining room when the tele-phone call came from his office saying that John Kennedy had been shot.

It was a day of tears on Capitol Hill and elsewhere. Senator Magnuson wept openly. He and other senators closed their offices and sent their secretaries home. Helen Jackson was in Albuquerque, so Jackson didn't want to go home. His staff remained at work, unsuccessfully trying to occupy their minds with routine matters. Jackson took tele-phone calls from newsmen who asked for his reaction. "Incredible. I'm stunned," he said.

There was the inevitable question that lurked phantom-like around the edge of the tragedy: What if there had not been the last-minute decision to choose Lyndon John-son, instead of Henry Jackson, as John Kennedy's vice-presidential candidate?

"It didn't run through my mind at all that I might have been sworn in that day," he said much later. "I was so upset about what had happened that the only time it ever came up was when somebody would come to me and say, 'Well, you might have been sworn in today.' "

There was a tomblike atmosphere in the Old Senate Office Building. Halls were almost deserted, with only an occasional staff worker leaving the building—a secretary, carrying her coat, dabbing at tears. In his office Jackson's disciplined mind turned to minutiae. He decided to go to the payroll office in the Capitol to straighten out a trivial error in his paycheck. In an elevator he encountered Bill Fulbright. Fulbright's face was a pale mask. "A woman in Dallas said now we can return to constitutional government," Jackson said. "Good God." Fulbright only stared at the elevator door.

CHAPTER 10

A DEMOCRAT'S DILEMMA

BUMPING THROUGH THE storm's turbulence, the jetliner was nearing Hawaii as shirt-sleeved Henry Jackson solemnly read a newsmagazine. It carried Lyndon Johnson's final Presidential Thanksgiving message in italics: *Americans, looking back on the tumultuous events of 1968, may be more inclined to ask God's mercy and guidance than to offer Him thanks for His blessings.*

Not eloquent, *Time* said of the message. Yet in tone and temper, it probably came close to expressing the mood of Americans in a year many of them would rather forget. The assassinations. Protests. Riots. Division. Anger over the war. Shouts for new priorities. . . .

Jackson turned the page to another article.

President-elect Richard Nixon, the story said, now faced the awesome task of bringing Americans together. He was under the pressure of time to announce the names of the men who would serve in his cabinet. But Nixon was making a cautious search.

Jackson folded the magazine, removed his brown-rimmed glasses, turned, and smiled reassuringly toward his sister, Gertrude. Well, he said, we'll get some sunshine and warmth in Hawaii. Gert nodded. But as she peered through the rain-sprayed window of the airplane, the approaching island wasn't a sun-sparkled emerald. It was a sodden, mottled blue-gray scene. Dark clouds clung to Diamond Head. Honolulu still was being soaked by rain in the aftermath of the Thanksgiving storm which had battered Hawaii.

Others in their group lounging in the first-class seats—the senator's wife and his hometown friends, Judge and Mrs. Phil Sheridan—held the same tense hope for Hawaiian sunshine. They chatted with forced exuberance. Everyone wanted the vacation week to be an especially golden one for Gert. Emaciating and in pain, she was dying of cancer.

The bizarre events which had lashed America during 1968 left Jackson bewildered, like other politicians, and tightlipped. Besides the demonstrations, the riots, the anger, he had been struck by a deeply personal blow when he received the news about Gert just before the Democratic Convention in Chicago. He had hurried to Seattle to be there when his sister underwent surgery in Providence Hospital. Her condition worsened each day. She fought valiantly. She burst into tears only rarely. "Oh, I'm not getting any better. But I'll keep trying," she said.

His tall spinster sister, now seventy, was the most important person in Jackson's personal-political life. She was his second mother, personal confidant, and adviser. Gert had squeezed enough money out of her teacher paychecks to help him finish law school. During his political campaigns, she drove into the countryside to distribute his campaign signs and cards and to talk about her brother's hard work and integrity. Never married, she stayed in the family home at Everett. From there she pridefully watched her brother's rise in politics.

In 1960, when Jackson almost became John Kennedy's Vice-Presidential candidate, there were a few forecasts that he might have a rendezvous with the Democratic Presidential nomination in 1968. Kennedy, one writer said, would have had two terms in office by then. Jackson, young, diligent, and likable, would have developed a national reputation and a broader political base. But the sixties brought upheavals. Most political projections miscarried.

In 1968 Jackson was almost a political dropout. He had commiserated fleetingly with a hurt, confused Hubert Humphrey in the middle of his heartbreak campaign. Staggering under the multiple burdens of Johnson, Vietnam, and Chicago, Humphrey came to the Pacific Northwest in late September. On September 28, he was the main speaker at the dedication of John Day Dam, one of the last of the great Columbia River dams that Jackson and his colleague, Warren G. Magnuson, had spent a career fighting for. Jackson and Magnuson went there for the ceremony. The three senators slipped away from the crowds for a few minutes, to hold a brief conference in a stark clapboard construction shack at the project. Humphrey was desperate. What, he asked, could he do to turn this nightmarish thing around? Jackson had some dispassionate advice: "Why don't you just be yourself?" Humphrey later said it was valuable, timely advice.

The be-yourself method did not work instantly for Humphrey. During a speech that evening at the Seattle Center Arena he was buffeted by the worst heckling of the campaign. The auditorium was filled, mostly by Humphrey loyalists. There were hundreds of others outside, unable to get in. But from the balcony, war protestors, equipped with a bullhorn, shouted down the candidate. They refused to let Humphrey deliver his speech. "I charge you with war crimes," the bullhorn voice echoed through the arena. Humphrey sputtered. The turmoil grew. Humphrey blew his cool. "Oh, shut up," the frustrated Presidential candidate shouted. Fighting erupted in the crowd and a mini-riot broke out as police moved in to drag the demonstrators out of the auditorium. The Chicago virulence had tumultuously spread to Seattle, as it had throughout the land.

Jackson missed Humphrey's Seattle agony. He had a previous commitment that evening. He was delivering a quiet speech to a realtor's group in Wenatchee, discussing power and reclamation in eastern Washington.

Totally frustrated, Humphrey spent that night and the next day in his room in Seattle's Olympic Hotel, working on his next speech, the one to be delivered in Salt Lake City. In the speech he pledged that, as President, he would halt the bombing of North Vietnam and begin a concerted quest for peace. Humphrey's campaign turned upward after that, but not quite fast enough and not quite high enough.

Flaps down, the airliner carrying the Jackson party glided through the warm rain, touched the ground, rolled its course along the runway, then turned and fanned waves on the rain-made lakes of the apron as it moved to the Honolulu terminal. Jackson is a VIP to the armed services everywhere, so he often is accorded a modest military reception. A young lieutenant waited to greet him at Honolulu as Jackson walked slowly with his sister and the others through the crowd of deplaning passengers. The lieutenant delivered a message: President-elect Nixon was trying to reach the senator by telephone.

Two military cars were waiting to take the Jackson party

to Fort deRussy on Waikiki Beach. Jackson was exhilarated, fascinated by the thought of a message from Nixon. He sensed what it was about: There had been many hints the President-elect, who was talking about getting some Democrats into his cabinet, would ask Jackson to be his Secretary of Defense. One day in September Jackson was stopped in a Senate corridor by Roger Mudd, the television newsman. Confidentially, Mudd said, Nixon had mentioned Jackson would be his top choice for the cabinet post should Nixon win the election. Jackson grinned and shrugged off the suggestion. Following the Nixon victory, Jackson was in Europe, attending a NATO parliamentarians' conference at Brussels, when a NATO nation friend told him in hushed tones that his government had been asked if Jackson would be an acceptable defense secretary. His nation's response, the man said, was decidedly affirmative. Jackson, a bulldog-tough advocate of NATO strength, is popular in West European defense circles.

A few days later Jackson was at a routine political ceremony—dedicating a swimming pool at the Seattle suburb of Mountlake Terrace—when there was a telephone call for him. It was Bryce Harlow, Nixon's chief talent scout. Harlow asked if Jackson would be willing to talk with the President-elect if Nixon were to telephone him. Jackson agreed.

The army cars carrying the Jacksons and Sheridans passed slowly through the gates of Fort deRussy and at last stopped near the beachside guest cottage reserved for VIPs—old Quarters 27. Fort deRussy remains an array of slightly seedy World War II military buildings in a refuge of sand and palms—still holding out against the encroaching concrete and high rises which have overrun the rest of

Waikiki. As they climbed out of the cars, Jackson, a compulsive tour guide, gestured toward the sweep of beach and told his sister and the Sheridans the history of the military post. "This really is the most beautiful piece of property anywhere in the world," he said. Real estate developers steadily pressure the federal government to sell the land. But, he added, "as long as I'm on the Armed Services Committee, I'm going to see to it that this is saved for the GIs."

GIs who have passed through deRussy in recent years have been tragic-hero figures in a continuous, heart-tugging drama. The post is a rest-and-recreation center for men in the Vietnam combat zone. The soldier arrives at deRussy to embrace his weeping young wife who has flown from their home state to this long-awaited reunion. Their hours together are precious. They sit on the beach in the sun. And on an occasional evening out, they hold hands in a pseudo-Polynesian cocktail lounge at one of the posh Waikiki hotels, surrounded by martini-drinking, jet-set vacationers whose chatter collides with the saccharine sound of a Hawaiian band. Then the boy and his wife have their tearful, fearful farewell. She flies back to the mainland. He is whisked in ten hours back to the hellish jungles of Nam. Next day the scene begins anew, with new young couples and new tears.

Telephones in the VIP cottage were dead. The storm had raised havoc in the islands. Military brass offered their hand-wringing apologies to the senator. One officer told him there was a telephone available at a nearby military-police headquarters, so Jackson went there. Noncoms and officers waited in an outer room to give Jackson privacy in the drab army office where he placed the call to the President-elect.

Nixon confirmed all the speculation: He wanted Jackson to be his Secretary of Defense. Jackson was his first choice. He had offered the post to no one else.

Jackson was delighted, flattered. He asked, "Could I have about three days to consider it?" Nixon agreed. Jackson outlined some other requests, too. He worried about the effect there would be on his party if he vacated his Senate seat. Dan Evans, governor of Washington, was a Republican and he probably would appoint a Republican to serve out the remainder of Jackson's term, which ran through 1970. Would the President-elect, Jackson asked, seek an arrangement with Evans, whereby the governor would appoint a Democrat? A Democrat who would agree not to run for the full term in 1970? Nixon agreed to seek such an arrangement with Evans. Nixon liked Jackson's defense views and it was implicit that Jackson would have full reign over the Pentagon. The conversation was on Sunday. The senator agreed to telephone Nixon with a final decision the following Wednesday.

The rest of that Sunday was spent sightseeing, a day arranged for Gertrude's enjoyment. Mrs. Sheridan, a nurse, was qualified to administer drugs to ease Gertrude's pain. Yet she was suffering through the day. Pillows were fluffed in the back seat of one of the army cars to make the ride as comfortable as possible for her. When they stopped to do some shopping, Jackson bought his sister a green flower-print mumu which she wore daily thereafter. In the meantime technicians scurried to repair the line damage and make two telephones operable in the cottage.

Always an early riser, Jackson was awake by four A.M. Monday. He went to the telephone in the dinette of the cottage, closed a door so as not to disturb the others and began making pre-dawn telephone calls to the East Coast, where it already was midmorning.

He had transoceanic conversations with many friends and political colleagues—Mike Mansfield, Ted Kennedy, Richard Russell, John Stennis, Secretary of Defense Clark Clifford, and others. Their reactions to his job offer were mixed. Some were openly dubious about the notion of a Democratic senator joining the Nixon cabinet. It was a renegade suggestion.

When Jackson described the offer to his longtime friend Dan Martin in Los Angeles, Martin quipped, "What are you doing out there, boozing it up?" Accept the job if you want it, Martin went on. "It's a nice prestigious way to wind up a career in public life. But I'd have a lot of second thoughts about giving up a seat in the United States Senate. Secretaries of Defense come and go."

It was pragmatic advice, Jackson knew. He inevitably reached the same conclusion almost every time he thought it through. But he was a compulsive fact-gatherer, so the telephoning continued. One call went to Lyndon Johnson, who was preparing for his departure from the White House. Johnson, too, was cool to the idea. During their conversation, Gertrude was nearby and Jackson, looking toward her, spoke into the telephone, "You remember my sister, Gertrude, Mr. President. She was a teacher who retired not long ago and you sent her a letter at that time. Let me put her on here so you can say hello." Gertrude took the receiver from her brother and, for several minutes, she and the President—two ex-schoolteachers—chatted.

There were compound political paradoxes in the cabinet offer. It had been just eight years since Jackson, the Democratic national chairman, traveled across the nation, delivering speeches on behalf of John Kennedy. When things seemed to be going badly at the last minute of that campaign, Jackson pinned his Masonic button onto his lapel and went on a personal mission to try to stem the silent, tugging tide of anti-Catholicism which seemed to be moving voters. In Oklahoma City he talked with a wavering Democrat. "Why can't you support Kennedy?" Jackson asked. "I dunno. I just can't," came the reply. Jackson said he was a Presbyterian, a Mason, and he would feel very comfortable with Kennedy as President. And consider the alternative: *Nixon.*

After the 1960 Kennedy victory, Jackson seemingly was ignored. He read later that he had been, until the last minute, under consideration by Kennedy for appointment as Secretary of Defense, but no one talked with him about it. The job went to Robert McNamara and, in the following years, Jackson often despaired over many of the policies—the stubborn, pinstripe-corporate-executive way the Defense Department was being run, oblivious of the counsel of the most knowledgeable military men.

Jackson had been sharply critical of the defense secretary in the previous decade, too. Charles Wilson, secretary in the Eisenhower-Nixon administration, was making risky cuts in the defense budget, but at the same time seemed conspicuously helpful to General Motors, where Wilson had served as president. During Wilson's first eighteen months in office General Motors' defense contracts climbed by $1.7 billion, while contracts to other firms declined $359 million, Jackson charged. Wilson snapped in reply that Jackson was serving as "the Democrats' mouthpiece to spout off statements that only prove he doesn't know what he's talking about."

There was further irony in the memory that Jackson had been one of the architects of the missile-gap issue which had been a factor in defeating Nixon in 1960.

Nixon and Jackson had a personal acquaintance which dated back to their years together in the House of Representatives. They had occasional games of paddleball in the House gymnasium, but they differed dramatically on domestic political issues. Nixon catapulted into prominence as a Communist-hunting young congressman on the House Un-American Activities Committee during the period when Jackson was opposing that committee, disdaining those witch-hunts, fighting against the men who were whipping up fears of subversion within the United States. But events through the years brought Nixon and Jackson closer together on foreign policy and national-security matters.

Jackson avoided speechmaking during the turbulence of 1968. But once, during the fall, he took a verbal shot at the radical Students for a Democratic Society, charging that it was "definitely engaged in subversive activities." The SDS aim was to destroy the institutions of the nation, the senator said, adding, "They may be getting help from outside the United States." Not even the political super-liberals were embracing the hell-raising SDS. But the Jackson statement still was a somewhat strange one for a man who had so openly fought McCarthyism when it made such sounds about subversives.

One almost could hear the cries of the doves reacting to the choice of Jackson as Secretary of Defense: *This* was Nixon's plan for ending the war in Vietnam? Turning the Pentagon over to *Jackson?*

Through each week of the Vietnam combat, Jackson, the man so loyally supporting L.B.J., was being escalated to ever higher places on the doves' hate chart. No one seemed to pay much attention to Jackson's own near-dovish words, murmured quietly, offhandedly. When Johnson halted the bombing of North Vietnam, Jackson praised the decision: It could, he said, be an important step toward peace. He repeated a suggestion he had made before: "I hope that the second step will be a ceasefire so that meaningful negotiations can get under way." But such words were inaudible to his critics because of his noisy sword-rattling during a year in which such sounds were obscene. While Bobby Kennedy was mounting has last, desperate campaign in the California Presidential primary election, Jackson was standing stolidly in the Senate, lecturing his colleagues on the need for an antiballistic-missile system.

It was a crucial year for the ABM. For years the Jacksons, Russells, and others of the military committees on Capitol Hill advocated—in vain—the start of a system to protect the United States' nuclear deterrent against missile attack. McNamara and the White House opposed it. But the Soviet Union had long since begun building its own ABM system, the Tallin system, a defensive system which mainly protected Moscow from bomber attacks. Johnson at last recommended an ABM start. The proposal debated on Capitol Hill in 1968 involved the Sentinel System. It was a $5.5 billion program —a thin, minimal-protection shield to guard against an impetuous missile attack by China, the enigmatic, unpredictable adolescent among nuclear nations.

ABM verbal battles flurried through the year. Critics railed against it. The "thin" system, they said, was the ultimate hypocrisy . . . a boondoggle . . . the phony, inefficient come-on which would suck future budget makers into a full-blown system, so that in time a rocket would be planted in every American neighborhood. Worse, they said, such a provocative act would kill all hope for disarmament talks.

The Senate in June debated a move to delay the project a year. Jackson was commanding the defenses of the ABM, as floor manager for the bill. The Soviet Union has its own ABM system, he said. An American start could be the lever to pry the obstinate Russians into disarmament talks. As always, Jackson pointed out, the Soviet Union thinks of peace only when the United States shows its muscle. The Senate voted 52-34 against a one-year delay of the ABM. Three days later the Soviet Union agreed to disarmament talks.

In the explosive parade of news events through 1968, Czechoslovakia earned a low-retention score with most Americans. But Jackson particularly fretted about developments in Europe. When the Czech Communists drifted toward nationalism, there was a swift, awesome Soviet response. While Americans agonized over the gradual accumulation of American troops in Vietnam, a massive army of Warsaw Pact troops had overrun Czechoslovakia.

Jackson summed it up with one of his pedantic phrases: "The Soviet leopard has not changed its spots."

The NATO meeting in Brussels had a somber mood to it. The Soviet military push was an obvious overkill of the Czech activity. The real purpose of the swift maneuver, Jackson analyzed, was to push Soviet military influence into a new forward position to intimidate Western Germany. Soviet and NATO forces now, for the first time, were dangerously nose-to-nose.

Addressing the North Atlantic Assembly, Jackson described the Soviet move in Pentagonese: It was "a vivid demonstration of Soviet capability for rapid selective mobilization for efficient movement of large combat and support forces over extensive distances and the establishment and testing of effective lines of communication in support of military operations from the Russian homeland."

The need for a strong, willing NATO was never greater, he said. Unless other NATO nations assumed a full share of the money and manpower burden there would be political pressures within the United States to cut U.S. military strength in Europe, he predicted to his NATO colleagues.

Those grim-humor signs being sold around the University of Washington said "Henry Jackson suffers from a military-industrial complex." The kids who were peddling them had been grade-schoolers when Eisenhower coined the phrase, "military-industrial complex." Endowed and burdened with the responsibility of free-world leadership, the United States had the obligation, Eisenhower said, to keep "a permanent armaments industry of vast proportions." That element in American life could easily become a powerful domestic political pressure group. "In the councils of government, we must guard against the acquisition of unwarranted influence, whether sought or unsought, by the military-industrial complex," Eisenhower said.

The phrase stuck in the vocabulary. Then it took on a costly, flesh-and-blood, corporate-report, big-budget, steel-and-warhead believability to more and more Americans. The defense budget was about $47.5 billion when Eisenhower made his statement. By 1968 it was almost $80 billion.

When the emotional attacks were made on the ABM, Jackson said it was "the opening shot in a campaign to gut our key defense programs and to ransack the Defense Department. . . . We should make no mistake about it." He supported programs for the poor, the aged, the minorities, the underprivileged, Jackson said. "But our serious concern for domestic problems is no excuse for any of us to lose our perspective as to what comes first. . . . What

236

comes first in this tumultuous and dangerous world is the maintenance of the American nuclear deterrent."

Jackson was a natural candidate to be cast as high priest of the military-industrial-complex cult. He knew and understood the Pentagon, its programs, and its people as well as any other man on Capitol Hill. He also had some highly conspicuous constituents doing defense business. The Boeing Company was based in Seattle. A string of shipyards were busily at work around Puget Sound doing military work. There was the big Puget Sound Naval Shipyard at Bremerton, as well as Fort Lewis, other military installations and a growing young electronics industry.

"You hear the phrase military-industrial complex from people who are frustrated," he said, "people who just don't have an answer, really, to the problems . . . It's the devil theory of history." *Military-industrial complex* . . . Repeated enough times, it can become an easy frame of reference, into which—as was Communism during McCarthyism's fear days—all of one's social-political frustrations could be angrily stored. It is, said Jackson, an echo of the *merchants of death* tag placed on the munitions corporations during an earlier period of deep armaments-weariness in American history.

He could hardly be classed as a military-industrial power broker, Jackson felt, despite the military presence in his home state. Boeing, although sixth-ranked among the nation's corporations in terms of dollar volume of defense contracts made fifty-four percent of all its sales to the Defense Department during the 1960s, and far less than that by the end of the decade. Lockheed's sales for defense, meanwhile, were at eighty-nine percent of the firm's total. Washington State ranked a modest nineteenth in military contract awards among all states in 1968. Connecticut, with a lesser population, did more than three times the volume of business enjoyed by Jackson's home state.

Often the Congress sliced defense budget requests, Jackson said, and he joined in those cuts. But there is no scorecard available to compare his budget reduction votes with his efforts to boost the defense budget.

He bristled at the criticisms. Why must the decisions on behalf of national defense be such lonely, criticized ones? "You just don't get any brownie points for worrying about national defense," Jackson complained.

Jackson had been involved in a rugged question-and-answer session on the Columbia Broadcasting System's "Face the Nation" television show July 14, in the midst of that frayed-temper summer. Questions had been fired at him by Martin Agronsky and Steve Rowan of CBS News and Chalmers Roberts of the Washington *Post*.

Nixon told him that, while leafing through the transcript of that broadcast, he had been impressed by the way Jackson handled himself.

The newsmen had questioned Jackson about Vietnam and the desirability of a voluntary withdrawal of American troops as a good-faith gesture. "I certainly do not agree with a unilateral de-escalation approach," Jackson said. "If it can be verified that they are carrying out their part, then I think we could engage in certain types of withdrawal." Jackson repeated his proposal of a cease-fire as a first step in talks.

The newsmen pushed forward in their questioning. The talks, under way for months, are getting nowhere. Isn't it time to try something new?

Jackson: "Only the naive had any idea in mind that this would be a relatively fast process. Obviously, the protracted conflict also involves the protracted conference. The Communists think that we do not have the staying power. And I believe that we have the staying power. I believe we must demonstrate it. We must do everything we can in good faith to try to reach an agreement. . . ."

The newsmen focused on the ABM controversy and the arms race. Agronsky recalled President Johnson's pledge that the United States would seek de-escalation. How, then, will the start of a U.S. ABM system bring de-escalation?

Jackson: "Well, Mr. Agronsky, if I may say so, I think you are giving a one-sided version of this controversy. Who was the first nation to develop an ICBM? The Soviet Union. Who was the first nation to develop an ABM? The Soviet Union. Who was the first nation to develop a fractional orbital bombardment system? The Soviet Union . . . They are feverishly deploying intercontinental ballistic missiles at a rate and a pace that will give them more missiles by next year than we have, and they will be missiles with a greater destructive power than we have. Now let me make this very clear. . . ."

Agronsky: "Senator . . ."

Jackson: "Let me just finish this point . . ."

Agronsky: "Yes, go ahead . . ."

Jackson: ". . . I believe that we should follow two consistent courses of action with the Soviets. I think we should keep talking with them and we should try to work together in those areas where our interests converge and at the same time maintain . . ."

Agronsky: "Compete with them."

Jackson: ". . . maintain a strong balance of forces in concert with our allies . . ."

Agronsky: "Okay, they take the same approach and where are we, back in the same old rat race."

Jackson: "No, no, no. That is not . . ."

Agronsky: "They have got to stay ahead of us and we have to stay ahead of them."

Jackson: "I don't think that you can spell out—I don't need to get into the argument about superiority—but I don't think you can just spell it out in quantitative terms. There are qualitative terms that are involved in this . . . What we need is a strategic force capable of maintaining and protecting the American deterrent. I don't think that one can just add up a column of figures."

Rowan: ". . . The experts have said that . . . the technology doesn't exist to put up a defensive system that will stop the rapidly advancing offensive capability of both sides. Now, just because there is no point in their building a defensive system, should we go ahead and build a defensive system which also has no point, which is, as Secretary McNamara said, highly penetrable?"

Jackson: "I don't agree with that at all. It does have a capability—definite capability against the Chinese nuclear ICBM situation in the seventies. That is number one. Number two, it will complicate a Soviet attack . . . It will save in the event of an attack—if they should decide that they are going to move against us—at least twenty million American lives. . . ."

Agronsky: "Well, nobody can prove that, Senator."

Rowan: "If it comes to that, Senator, that stage in the game, then the deterrent of both sides has failed and the ball game is over."

Jackson: "I know, but bear in mind that if the Soviets continue to do what they are doing—and you gentlemen don't seem to get into that question—the rapid pace at which—last year, for example, they doubled the number of ICBMs on launch. And at the rate they are going they will have more by next year than we will have."

Agronsky: "Senator, may I ask you a simple question. You have heard of overkill. You know what that means."

Jackson: "Oh, I understand what that means."

Agronsky: "How many times do we have to take out Moscow or do they have to take out New York? If you can take it out with one, do you need 150, 200, or 1,000?"

Jackson: "Well, Mr. Agronsky, the overkill argument is simply oversimplification."

Agronsky: "Well, everything . . ."

Jackson: "Well, let me ask you something that we don't know. Maybe you know the answer . . . We don't know how many missiles we would have left after the Soviets launched a first strike against the United States. They are building some highly sophisticated missiles, with a tremendous number of megatons in their warheads. We are assuming here that they should have the same number of missiles that we have and that that is a fair way to settle it. Now, what we have to take into consideration is what kind of a retaliatory force would we have left after a first strike. Now, we don't know. And I would like to be sure that my nation has a good margin for error."

Wednesday was the day he had promised to telephone Nixon.

His conditions had been met. John Ehrlichman, a top Nixon adviser and former Seattle attorney, telephoned Governor Evans to discuss the subject of Jackson's possible successor. Evans was agreeable. "I'll do anything I can to help the President organize his cabinet," Evans said. He agreed that he would, if Jackson resigned from the Senate, appoint a Democrat to the vacant seat—a Democrat who would not seek re-election. Evans had in mind John Cherberg, the state's Democratic lieutenant governor, a veteran, though nondescript politician. Jackson's request

241

that the appointee not be a candidate in 1970 suggested that he wanted to keep a personal option—to return to the Senate if things did not go well with the Nixon Administration.

At Nixon's request, a military jet was standing by in Hawaii. Should Jackson decide to say yes, he would be flown to Palm Springs, to meet with Nixon, who was going there to a conference of governors.

Jackson decided on a morning walk along the beach. Other Hawaii visitors might don the bright floral clothing of the islands but Jackson was dressed in a quiet blue sport shirt and cotton pants—native enough for his taste. He walked, watching the long, slow breakers roll over the coral reefs toward the beach, engaged in one of the rare contemplative moments in a life which he compulsively filled with activity. He strolled along a concrete walk for a while, then along the sand in the direction of the Hawaiian Village Hotel, then turned and walked back toward Diamond Head. . . .

. . . I had pretty well made up my mind the night before, the Democrat said.

From the very beginning I just had very deep reservations about the thing. I was convinced that, if this were 1940 and we were in a true national emergency, and if I were a Knox or a Stimson, I should do it as a matter of national unity during a difficult period.

But it was not a period of great peril for the nation. President Nixon would have trouble with the Senate, no doubt, and not even the presence of a respected member of the Democratic Senate Club in his Cabinet would ameliorate that. In fact Jackson could well become the lightning rod for the criticism which inevitably would come

242

rumbling out of Congress. To close out a political career under the attacks of members of his own party would be a dismal finale to a political career which had begun twenty-eight years earlier with a young man idealistically marching off to the grand political cause of the New Deal. . . .

Jackson retraced his steps back along the beach. A few R and R Vietnam soldiers were on the beach. A young couple wrestled a playpen into place as a toddler played in the sand. Jackson entered the cottage and placed his telephone call to the President. The answer was an appreciative, respectful "no." The conversation was amiable. Nixon invited him to a meeting to be held within the next few days at his Pierre Hotel headquarters in New York. Jackson accepted. At that meeting he would learn that he might have had his choice: Secretary of State or Secretary of Defense. The conversation ended, as Jackson told Nixon the offer was the highest honor he had ever had.

He hung up the receiver. His pretty wife couldn't restrain herself. "What do you mean the highest honor of your life?" she said. "The highest honor in your life is when I said 'I do.' " The others laughed. Jackson grinned.

The new Congress had barely begun when Jackson was summoned to the White House to discuss intelligence and defense issues with the President and Henry Kissinger. Nixon took abundant notes on a yellow legal pad as Jackson discussed the need for the ABM. Nixon asked probing questions. Jackson was surprised at the President's quick grasp of facts and ideas. It was the beginning of a period of general agreement between Nixon and Jackson on national-security issues. Soon thereafter, Jackson, as chairman of the Senate Interior Committee, began hearings on the confirmation of Walter J. Hickel, Nixon's controversial appointee as Secretary of the Interior. They turned out to be grueling, tough days for Hickel—a harbinger of Jackson's general disagreements with Nixon over domestic issues.

The new Congress was barely a month old when, on February 4, Jackson was summoned home to Everett for Gertrude's funeral.

Through her years as a teacher, Gertrude gave shoes, clothing, and sometimes money to needy children at Garfield School. Her interest and help followed some of her students through their high-school and college years. She did it secretly. Since he was elected to the Senate, her brother, too, unobtrusively helped needy students. He turned over to that purpose all the fees he received for public appearances. After the funeral he set up in their hometown a needy-student scholarship fund, supported by his honoraria, in Gertrude's memory.

CHAPTER 11

THE SENATOR FROM BOEING

THE GREAT GRAY mockup model of a supersonic transport, one wing off and its guts filled with intricate veins of electrical wiring, sits like a dried-out carcass of a huge insect in the south end of Seattle. The SST is dead, killed by a fickle Congress, and now its sleek body is covered with a fine layer of dust.

The shell of the SST stretches 298 feet from a droop nose to a soaring tail. To some that shell once represented the greatness of America, a bold new stride forward in ever-advancing technology. To others it represented the very foolishness of the nation, a mindless, needless frill that would empty America's pocketbook and blemish the world's environment. But no matter now. The SST is dead and much of what it represented is, too. The shell sits in a cavernous building near the end of East Marginal Way in a sprawling complex of Boeing plants whose uninspiring architecture can only be described as aerospace-stark.

The building that houses the remains of the SST is known as the Boeing Developmental Center. It is dimly lit now and the dust covers not only the carcass of the big airplane. It is spread finely over acres of floor space and over the helter-skelter array of parts, forms, tools, pallets, boxes, and now-useless alloys of exotic metals. There is pathos in the presence of the dust. Once this building was nearly as clean as the operating room of a hospital. In the development of a modern new airplane the tolerances are so precise that dust is an enemy. In all of the vastness of the building there are just two engineers and, to them, it seemed almost sacrilegious as they smudged the dust to take inventory.

By the time the Congress finally meted out the death sentence for the SST in March of 1971, the airplane had become a symbol of many things. It was symbolic of the clash between industrial development and the environment. It was symbolic of the decline of the old Senate power structure—the Inner Club. And it became symbolic of the deep economic depression into which Seattle, the largest city in Scoop Jackson's state, had fallen as the decade of the seventies began.

Like most symbols, however, the SST told only part of the Seattle story. At the time of its demise the airplane represented perhaps seven thousand jobs. But Boeing employment in Seattle already had skidded from a high of 103,000 in mid-1968 to 45,000 at the time Congress killed the SST. It dropped to 35,000 by the end of 1971. At the height of the Boeing boom in the sixties the box-like aerospace plants spread carnivorously through the suburbs and farmlands around Seattle. During the bust many of the new plants and some of the old ones were buttoned up tight and their sprawling parking lots became concrete deserts.

What had happened to Boeing was misunderstood by many. The congressional gouging of the defense budget had not hurt the company that much. During World War II Boeing had built the bombers that demolished Germany and Japan. During the Cold War Boeing had produced the Minuteman intercontinental ballistic missile and the B-52

246

strategic bomber. But by the late sixties Boeing's defense work was minimal. By then the company had become largely a commercial enterprise—the world's largest manufacturer of jet-liners. When the market for jet-liners dried up in the recession of the late sixties, Boeing nose-dived—and nose-dived badly.

Boeing was to Seattle what the auto industry is to Detroit or steel is to Pittsburgh. When the aerospace company took 68,000 jobs out of Seattle in less than three-and-a-half years, the city and its people staggered. In Seattle there was no recession; there was a depression. Unemployment soared near the levels of the thirties. But it was a strange sort of depression. It struck the upper-middle class even more conspicuously than the poor. Engineers who had been earning $20,000 a year now were buying their groceries with food stamps. Scientists with doctorates were selling encyclopedias door-to-door. Some men, young men in their forties with no hope left, walked into the bathroom and blew their brains out. Others bundled up their families in the middle of the night and disappeared—leaving behind their $30,000 homes, their mortgages, their furniture, their boats, and their bright dreams of the future.

The depression was far from universal. Those who still held jobs were earning record salaries and living better than ever before. But almost everyone in Seattle had a neighbor or friend who had been jobless for six, twelve, even eighteen months. The contrast between the affluence of those who held jobs and the hopelessness of those who didn't made the situation all the more pathetic.

The demise of the SST seemed to symbolize all that had gone wrong in Seattle. On the Senate floor men like Jackson and Magnuson talked about human suffering in the city, about preserving jobs, about preserving the aerospace

247

industry, about building a great airplane as America had built great airplanes before. But they were countered by men like Proxmire and Percy, whose arguments ranged from the possible—that the SST would be an economic disaster—to the almost ludicrously improbable—that it might cause skin cancer. In Seattle, where the men already were out of work, it all seemed a playlet acted out on a distant stage.

As Congress debated the fate of the airplane, a few stiff-upper-lip Seattleites pasted stickers to their car bumpers: SST—Seattle Stands Tall. Then, when Congress finally killed the program, two wry real-estate salesmen erected a bitter-comic billboard:

Will The Last Person to Leave Seattle Please Turn Off the Lights?

No one is certain exactly how or when Henry M. Jackson picked up the nickname, "the senator from Boeing." But its usage goes back to the height of the Cold War at about the time in the mid-fifties when Jackson first warned that the Russians might engage in what he called nuclear blackmail. One thing is certain: The person who first applied that unflattering sobriquet did not like the methodical senator from Washington State. "It was an attempt to say that I was tied up with the munitions makers, the merchants of death, and all that business," Jackson says, somewhat bitterly, because the nickname has been used by his detractors almost ever since.

At first, the nickname seemed unfair. Most of the weapons systems which Jackson crowed loudest about in the fifties were built by other defense contractors. Only the B-52 bomber, the mainstay of the Strategic Air Command, was built by Boeing. But even the B-52 was manufactured in Wichita, Kansas, not in Seattle.

Fair or not, the nickname was used against him in his first campaign for re-election to the Senate in 1958. And it stuck. It was somewhat paradoxical that he was called the senator from Boeing in that particular campaign. The hottest issue on the ballot that year was not Scoop Jackson's re-election but a controversial right-to-work proposal, which would have made labor-union membership voluntary. The unions, believing that their very existence was at stake, fought the proposal bitterly. So did Jackson, whose support of organized labor has been total. The chief advocate of the anti-union proposal was William M. Allen, the almost legendary, arch-conservative president of The Boeing Company.

Allen, in some ways, was almost a reincarnation of old Bill Butler, the last of the *laissez faire* capitalists in Scoop Jackson's home town. Unlike Butler, Allen became neither bitter nor a recluse late in life. But like Butler, his conservatism ran so deep that it almost became anarchistic. Bill Allen, like Bill Butler, didn't want the government messing around with anything—which was fascinating because, by its very nature, Boeing had to deal often with the government.

Even after Allen went into semi-retirement as board chairman, the imprint of his personality was left indelibly on The Boeing Co. He was unfailingly conservative. So was Boeing. He demanded excellence. Boeing built excellent airplanes. He was almost hopelessly naive politically. So was Boeing. There is a story, perhaps partly apocryphal, that illustrates the last point. Shortly after Boeing opened a plant near New Orleans, the company gave a large cocktail party and hired some off-duty state troopers to direct traffic. After the party the troopers not too subtly made the point that, in Louisiana, it was traditional to give them the leftover liquor. *Hell no*, responded the Boeing officials, *you got paid*. In Louisiana there is a state law that says the speed limit is twenty-five miles an hour on all unmarked roads. The next morning the speed-limit signs were mysteriously gone on the super highway leading to the Boeing plant and the state troopers were methodically detaining and fining Boeing employees on their way to work. But Bill Allen would have been proud of his underlings, for they had done the *right* thing.

At first glance it seems unlikely that Allen, the anti-government conservative, and Scoop Jackson, the big-government liberal, should become friends. But both were driven men, heavily self-disciplined and consumed by their work. Both were what the psychologists would call over-achievers. Gradually, after their showdown on the right-to-work proposal, the two grew closer together. When Jackson and his bride returned from their honeymoon in early 1962, Bill Allen gave a lavish party for them at his home in Seattle's exclusive Highlands. During that party Allen made a brief speech praising Scoop Jackson. Then, just before toasting the bride and groom, Allen reportedly made this disclaimer: "I don't want to mislead anybody. I'm a Republican and I don't vote for Democrats." But, as time wore on, the arch-conservative president of The Boeing Co. even would find it within himself to vote for the federalist liberal who became known, to his detractors, as the senator from Boeing.

There are many implications to the senator-from-Boeing nickname, but the most obvious one is that Jackson, through his power in the Senate, produced a bevy of juicy federal contracts for the largest employer in his state. But that isn't true. Boeing is conspicuous for the military contracts it lost rather than the ones it gained during Jackson's tenure in the Senate. During the eight years of the Kennedy-Johnson Administration, a time when Jackson's influence should have been at its peak, Boeing failed to win a single major military contract. Instead, the company *lost* the bitter battle to build the TFX warplane and *lost* the keen competition to construct the huge C-5A troop-carrying plane. And Boeing had contracts—such as the billion-dollar Dynasoar space-glider program—canceled in midstream. So, even from a meat-and-potatoes standpoint, Jackson did not merit his unkind nickname.

But it was Jackson's role in two major political failures —the TFX and the SST—that glued the Boeing tag to him forever.

The TFX affair was the worst kind of political brawl. It was internecine, with Democrat attacking Democrat. At its height in 1963 the charges and countercharges were brutal, often going at a man's honor. At one point Defense Secretary Robert S. McNamara broke down and cried in the witness chair, burbling that his 12-year-old son was questioning his honesty.

The TFX, later known as the F-111, was a fighter-bomber originally meant for use by both the Air Force and the Navy. The contract was valued at a minimum of $6.5 billion, one of the largest in American history and therefore an extremely succulent economic and political plum. Throughout 1962 Boeing and the General Dynamics Corp. competed vigorously for the award. Four times the Boeing and General Dynamics proposals were judged by a mili-

251

tary selection board. Four times the board concluded that Boeing could build a better plane cheaper than General Dynamics. After the fourth go-around, however, McNamara overruled the selection board and awarded the huge contract to General Dynamics. Some observers of the Pentagon noted that General Dynamics was in deep financial trouble at the time and that the TFX award may have been a rescue contract. Others observed, more cynically, that General Dynamics planned to build the warplane in Texas, which happened to be the home of the Vice-President of the United States and was crucial in the re-election plans of the Kennedy Administration.

Jackson was campaigning in the little Cascade foothills town of Sedro-Woolley when he got the news of the contract decision. He was outraged. First he called the deputy secretary of defense, Roswell Gilpatric, who assured him that the selection had been proper. Unsatisfied, Jackson called Bill Allen and asked him if Boeing would cooperate in an investigation. Allen said the company would. Then Jackson called Senator John L. McClellan, chairman of the Senate permanent investigations subcommittee. It was the same subcommittee that Joe McCarthy had used in his witch-hunts a decade earlier and the same subcommittee that eventually sat in judgment of the senator from Wisconsin. Jackson could not have known that the investigation he sought from McClellan would become almost as bitter and tumultuous as the Army-McCarthy hearings themselves.

Almost everyone in Washington thought the hearings would be perfunctory. It was, after all, a Democratic-controlled committee investigating a decision by a Democratic administration. Also, President Kennedy, in his senatorial days, had served on the committee. Robert Kennedy, until he became Attorney-General, had been the committee's chief counsel. Scoop Jackson, the man who had started it all, had been John Kennedy's national chairman less than three years earlier. So no one in politically attuned Washington expected more than a few days' headlines and then a quiet end to the investigation.

McNamara, in potentially deep trouble over the controversial contract award, hoped for even less than that. Just before the TFX hearings began, he called on Jackson and asked the senator to stop the investigation. Jackson refused and McNamara left the senator's office a very disturbed man.

Almost immediately the hearings became acrimonious, with the subcommittee hearing overwhelming testimony that McNamara had made the wrong decision. The Defense Department, at first taken aback, then began returning salvo for salvo, using anonymous spokesmen to attack the motives of the subcommittee members. Most of the shots were aimed directly at Jackson, who, because of his ties to Boeing, was vulnerable. One Pentagon spokesman charged that Jackson had "mousetrapped" the Defense Department into thinking the hearings would be brief and superficial—just enough to "get him off the hook with his constituents." Another charged that it was impossible to get a fair shake from the subcommittee because certain senators had "state self-interest in where the contract goes."

In gossipy Washington it does not take too much effort to discover the identity of an "anonymous spokesman." And within days the subcommittee had called Gilpatric and Arthur Sylvester, the Defense Department's press secretary, to explain their charges. Gilpatric was apologetic but Sylvester, a man who earlier had defended the government's right to lie, was stubbornly persistent.

"A contract has been let and an effort is being made by the disgruntled losers to knock the contract down," Sylvester insisted to the subcommittee.

Jackson, bristling, demanded that Sylvester "back that statement up."

Sylvester, retreating somewhat, replied that he had not meant to suggest that the investigation "stems from the Boeing Company."

"You said that it is an effort on the part of the disgruntled loser," Jackson persisted. "I think that this all brings out something. You are a little careless with words. This is where you get in trouble, Mr. Sylvester. This isn't the first time."

The TFX investigation, messy and unpleasant as it was, stretched on for ten long months in 1963, besmirching the last year of the Kennedy Administration. By the end of it —just two days before the assassination of John Kennedy —Democrats were grumbling that Scoop Jackson, their former national chairman, had a strange way of showing his party loyalty. After Kennedy's death, it would be seven years before the investigation would reopen. By then, time had all but proven Jackson's charges. The Navy version of the TFX had long since been canceled. The Air Force version had been used briefly in Vietnam and then grounded. Costs had soared and quality had plummeted.

But the TFX investigation had pasted that nasty nametag, the senator from Boeing, considerably more securely on Henry M. Jackson.

At the height of the TFX controversy the Washington State Chamber of Commerce held its annual congressional night, a tedious stag affair at a downtown Washington hotel. It usually was highlighted by a rather painful congressional recitation of off-color jokes.

The party in 1963 was an exception. William M. Allen, the president of The Boeing Company, was there, because he had been testifying in the TFX investigation. Allen sat at the long white table between two Republican congressmen. Jackson sat at the front, which might be called the head table. When the time came for the congressmen to rise and tell their jokes, Jack Westland, one of the Republicans next to Bill Allen, decided to discard his usual routine. Instead, he made a crack about Jackson being at the head table and then added, grinning, that he was sure that Jackson would prefer to be "down here in Mr. Allen's lap."

It was just about exactly the time that the anonymous Pentagon spokesmen were saying almost the same thing. Jackson is not one for dirty jokes, but he didn't appreciate the Republican congressman's departure from the routine.

In the 1964 elections Jackson was opposed by a conservative Republican named Lloyd Andrews. Andrews ran with the rather strange campaign theme that Jackson was not doing *enough* for Boeing. He blamed the senator for the loss of the TFX contract: "He was in a position to stop the TFX contract from going to Texas, but he bowed to his political master."

It was apparent long before election day that 1964 was going to be a landslide year for the Democrats. Accordingly, Jackson was in about as much trouble as Joe Namath in a chorus line.

But Jackson, who makes a habit of running scared in any election year, was angered by this reversal of the-senator-from-Boeing charge. In early September, after hearing Andrews' charges for months, Jackson met his Republican opponent on a campaign platform and issued a terse warning: "You are going to hear from Bill Allen."

Ten days later, just before the primary election, the

Seattle *Times* published a most unusual letter to the editor.

"The Boeing Company does not enter partisan politics," the letter began. "However, incorrect statements and conclusions which involve The Boeing Company are being circulated by Lloyd Andrews, the Republican candidate for the United States Senate, which, in good conscience, should not go unchallenged.

". . . In my opinion, it is entirely improper to criticize Senator Jackson because the TFX contract was not awarded to Boeing. The loss of TFX was a major blow to Boeing, but certainly Henry Jackson cannot properly be held responsible. . . ."

The letter was signed, William M. Allen, president of The Boeing Company. In November Jackson beat Andrews by 538,812 votes, a record for the state of Washington.

On April 21, 1967, Henry MacLeod, the managing editor of the Seattle *Times*, was invited to the White House along with the rest of the nation's editors who were in Washington for their annual convention.

Going through the receiving line, MacLeod, like Henry Jackson more than a decade earlier, expected no more than a routine Presidential handshake. But he was in for a surprise.

"Seattle? Did you say you were from Seattle?" the President asked as MacLeod started to move on. Lyndon Johnson reached out and pulled the editor back by the arm.

"We're going to have some big news for you out there soon," the President said.

"Oh, yes, about the SST," MacLeod responded.

"Scoop and Maggie have been talking to me about it," the President continued. "Well, you know, I'm going to need some help from the newspapers on this one. Some people are going to accuse me of taking money from the poor and giving it to the jet set. I need your help when they start in on me."

On a spate of rumors Boeing stock shot up 4½ points that day to an all-time high of ninety-three. A week later President Johnson announced his decision that the government would help Boeing build its SST, an 1,800-mile-an-hour airplane that would whisk people from New York to Paris in two-and-a-half hours.

Five months later, in October, the Senate began what became a yearly ritual: With charges that President Johnson was taking money from the poor and giving it to the jet set. Senator William Proxmire, a Democrat gadfly from Wisconsin, tried to block funds for the SST. That year and for several years afterward Proxmire, an outsider to the Senate Establishment, ran into the combined strength of the two insiders from Washington State, Club members Henry M. Jackson and Warren G. Magnuson.

During the debate in 1967 Senator J. William Fulbright, who delights in riling Scoop Jackson about his ties to Boeing and the so-called military-industrial complex, rose on the Senate floor to oppose appropriations for the SST. Fulbright, in his rambling fashion, questioned the need for extra speed. He had just flown home from Arkansas in a Boeing 747, he said, and didn't see the need to go any faster.

Jackson, a stickler for accuracy, interrupted to correct Fulbright. He must have flown in a 727, Jackson said, because Boeing's 747 jumbo-jet wasn't flying yet.

Fulbright, sensing opportunity, responded that there are so many different airplanes flying these days that "only someone who is close to Boeing" could tell the difference.

Jackson, standing just six feet away, blanched and angrily

responded, "Now just what does the senator mean by that?"

Innocently, Fulbright replied that he simply meant Boeing was the largest employer in Jackson's home state. "I didn't know the senator was sensitive about it," Fulbright cooed. Then he added that the SST was a creation of the military-industrial complex.

Once again Jackson blanched and this time he turned angrily toward Senator Robert F. Kennedy, who was sitting nearby. Jackson asked Kennedy if he thought his brother, the late President, had been influenced by the military-industrial complex when he began SST research in 1963.

"Oh, no," Kennedy hastily responded, even though he, too, opposed the airplane project.

Then Fulbright, smiling broadly, made a half-try at smoothing things over. "I don't criticize either senator from Washington State," he said. "I only envy them their influence. I wish I could do half as well."

Jackson and Magnuson then mustered their strength and defeated the attempt to kill the SST, 55 to 31. Proxmire persistently tried again and failed badly in 1968. And he tried again in December of 1969, observing wryly at the end of the debate that there were only two persuasive reasons for supporting the SST. One, he said, was Henry Jackson. The other was Warren Magnuson. The Club members showed their muscle once again: Proxmire's attempt to ground their airplane was overwhelmed, 58 to 22.

How times change. . . .

It is almost exactly a year later—December of 1970— and the intervening year could be called the year of the environment. It was a year of strong emotions, a year in which citizen lobbyists rose and made themselves heard.

It is evening, two days before the Senate's annual show-down on the SST, and an aide emerges from a strategy meeting in Senator Magnuson's office. The aide acknowledges the obvious: "It's beyond any trading now. All we can do is make a straight plea for help. We're dying."

Out behind the staff man traipsed the big guns of the SST: Jackson, Magnuson, the White House man, the Boeing lobbyist. Their faces were long and tired. The latest Senate head count showed forty-two senators for the SST, forty-nine against it and just eight undecided. A year ago the count had been 58 to 22 in favor of the airplane. But now, after a year of citizen lobbying, senators were riveted into their negative positions. No one was budging. It was very nearly hopeless. In the background Magnuson was dictating a defeat statement to his press agent . . . "the death knell for American superiority in aviation . . . $1 billion lost. . . ."

The phone rang and it was the undersecretary of transportation. Tired and irritable, Magnuson asked what the hell he could say to him. "Tell him," someone said, "that if he's a religious man he had better start praying. We've tried everything else." And indeed they had, in one of the most awesome displays of the personal power of two long-time senators that Capitol Hill had seen in years.

But this year it all would be to no avail. In the past the subtle trades, the quiet calls on friendship, the unstated threats of retaliation by the two powerful committee chairmen from Washington had meshed to push the controversial SST through the Senate. But not this year. This year the old power structure of the Senate, the quiet strength of the Inner Club, was fractured.

In many ways the nearing showdown on the SST was a question of muscle versus emotion, of the old politics versus the new. In this case emotion and the new politics would win.

A citizens' lobby had stormed Capitol Hill. The Sierra Club had sent in its legions of passionate environmentalists. An obscure scientist had warned that the SST might alter the upper atmosphere and cause an increase in skin cancer. Others had warned that the sonic boom might wipe out the insects that feed the fish that feed the people and on and on and on. . . .

Often it was whacky, disjointed. But on Capitol Hill, at times, it *did* seem like a citizens' uprising. It was oddly poetic: The little guy against the vested interests, the little guy out to save the world.

To be sure, Jackson and Magnuson had pushed their power to the hilt. They had blocked one of Senator Hatfield's pet projects—and held it hostage until he agreed to duck the vote, rather than oppose the SST. They had convinced Senators Church and Montoya, both opponents of the project, to stay out of town an extra day and miss the vote. They got Senator Russell out of his sick bed to vote for the airplane. They called Senator McClellan back from a relative's funeral.

But, by the morning of the showdown, Jackson and Magnuson still were trailing by at least six votes. The only hope then was to get some of the anti-SST senators to duck the vote, to take a walk. The senators met once again in Magnuson's office and began to call their list of potential walks—Bayh, Hartke, McGee, Williams of New Jersey, McIntyre, Kennedy, Burdick, Mondale.

"Hello, Leader," Jackson said in his most convivial voice as he got Senator Williams on the line. But Williams wouldn't budge. Jackson was less convivial when he reached Senator Mondale. Weeks earlier, Mondale had all but promised Jackson that he would take a walk on the SST, if Jackson needed the help. Now Jackson was trying to call in his chips. Mondale backed away. The pressures were too great, he said. He would have to vote against the SST. To Jackson, Mondale's words were almost sacrilege. In the Senate, in the Club, a man's word is his bond. Pointedly, Jackson observed that Mondale's pet bill—creating the Voyageurs National Park in northern Minnesota—was awaiting action by Jackson's own Interior Committee. Still, Mondale wouldn't budge. Jackson slammed down the telephone in disgust and anger.

One by one, Magnuson and Jackson went through their list. But the answer was the same each time: The pressures were too great to duck this vote. There had been too much publicity, too many letters. Jackson emerged from Magnuson's office in a black mood, grumbling "Down the tube."

The citizens' lobby had beaten two of the Senate's most powerful men. The SST was dead in the Senate. The debate went on for three hours, occasionally passionate but meaningless by then. "Speeches are fine, but it's what you do off the floor that counts," the arch-foe of the SST, William Proxmire, said later. He knew that well. Until this day, he had been beaten off the floor in showdown after showdown with Jackson and Magnuson.

Then came the yeas and nays on a vote that would unveil one of the oddest philosophical coalitions the Senate had ever seen. The first vote against the SST came from Senator Allen, an Alabama Democrat and possibly the most conservative man on the floor, the only man in the Senate who had endorsed George Wallace's reach for the Presidency. The second vote came from Senator Brooke, a liberal Republican from Massachusetts. The third from Senator Burdick, a farm-belt liberal. The fourth from Harry Byrd, Jr., a Virginia conservative.

Up above the Senate floor the gallery was filled with environmentalists and conservationists, those citizen lobbyists who had warned that the SST would pollute the air and dangerously alter man's environment. From the well of the Senate came the droning voice warning, as it always warned, that the galleries were not to make any show of emotion over the outcome of the vote. The tally was 52 to 41 against the SST, and the galleries took it quietly, filing out silently. They already had shown their emotions and it had worked.

Down on the floor Scoop Jackson was showing his, too —a rare moment. He marched across the floor and stood chin to chin with Stuart Symington, who had flip-flopped back and forth on the SST. This time Symington had voted to kill the program. Jackson's words couldn't be heard from the gallery, but his chin was working vigorously and he did not look happy.

A month later, as the new Congress organized in early 1971, Ted Kennedy found himself in a heated battle to retain his leadership post as majority whip of the Senate. He was challenged by Senator Robert C. Byrd, a tough and plucky Democrat from West Virginia.

Ten years earlier Scoop Jackson had been John Kennedy's national chairman. Six years earlier he had introduced Bob Kennedy to the Democratic National Convention. Four years earlier he had seconded the nomination of Ted Kennedy when he first ran for—and won—the whip's post in the Senate. He still was a member of the John F. Kennedy Foundation's board of directors.

But Scoop Jackson voted for Bobby Byrd, who success-fully wrested the whip's post away from Ted Kennedy. Byrd had voted for the SST; Kennedy hadn't.

The SST died a lingering death. Even after the dramatic showdown in the Senate, a series of compromises kept the project alive for more than three months. Desperately, the White House, the two senators from Washington, the la-bor lobbyists, the Boeing lobbyists fought to keep the proj-ect alive. Nearly $1 billion had been invested in the SST. The Russians, the British, and the French were flying their own SSTs.

For Jackson, the first three months of 1971 were especi-ally trying ones. He had poked his toe into the maelstrom of Presidential politics. All of the other Democratic Presi-dential candidates had opposed the SST. But, then, all the others disagreed with Jackson on a dozen issues—ranging from the Cold War to the hot war in Vietnam.

What seemed to bother Jackson the most was the emo-tionalism of the opposition to the SST. He flailed out at the "environmental extremists" he thought were spreading scare stories about possible ecological damage. He rebuked the speculation that the jet-liner might cause skin cancer or alter weather patterns so severely that the polar icecaps would melt. If the same sort of logic had prevailed in earlier days, he said over and over, we wouldn't have the automo-bile or the railway or the airplane. But it was a sign of the times that the reply to that argument often was: *Maybe we'd be better off.*

Throughout the three months the Boeing lobby operated out of Jackson's Senate office. That did nothing to put down the-senator-from-Boeing talk. Nor did the fact that Boeing's chief lobbyist was John Salter, Jackson's longtime administrative assistant who had left the senator's office in 1964. Salter took his Boeing telephone calls in Jackson's office—and even some of the SST's supporters winced over that.

Then on March 24 the final rites were held. Once again, the showdown was in the Senate. And once again the activity off the Senate floor had been hectic. President Nixon, gamely trying to salvage the project, called several wavering Republicans down to the White House to talk. Organized labor, worried about the fifty thousand jobs at stake, worked on some of the Democrats, including Hubert Humphrey. But Humphrey said *no* and so did almost all the Republicans who made the trip to the White House.

At about eleven o'clock in the morning, five hours before the final vote, Jackson scurried down the hallway of the Old Senate Office Building to Magnuson's office for one last strategy session. Briefly these two symbols of power in the old Senate Establishment talked of a compromise, of a fallback position. That's the way things are done. *Compromise.* Compromise is the essence of politics, the essence of the Senate Club. But there was to be no compromise on this day.

The debate in the Senate rumbled on toward an inevitable four o'clock deadline. And then suddenly it was four o'clock, and all time had expired. The even voice of Spiro Agnew, President of the Senate, once again was warning the galleries, filled with those citizen-lobbyists, that no show of emotion would be tolerated.

"Mister Aiken . . ."

"No."

"Mister Allen . . ."

"No."

"Mister Allott . . . "

"Yes."

"Mister Anderson . . . "

Clinton Anderson of New Mexico, possibly Scoop Jackson's best friend in the Senate, the man who had introduced Jackson to Helen Hardin, a man who had moved over so that Jackson could become chairman of the Interior Committee, an old man now, doddering.

"No."

So it went through the alphabet of one hundred eminent Americans, jury for the people and jury for the future.

As the roll reached Edward M. Kennedy of Massachusetts the vote was tied, 25 to 25. Almost a decade earlier Kennedy's brother in the White House had begun the long fight for an SST. But the world had changed so much. Technology, the tool, had become technology, the enemy —or so the popular passion went. Three months earlier Ted Kennedy had switched on the SST and some said he lost his Senate leadership post as a result.

"Mister Kennedy . . ."

"No."

Then it was all over—fifty-one nays, forty-six yeas, and the SST was dead.

Moments later Senator Proxmire climbed up the stairs, two steps at a time, toward the television studio one floor above the Senate chamber. The vote was a victory for the people, Proxmire said. Then Jackson arrived, no smile on his face, calling the vote symbolic of a dangerous anti-technological revolution.

"I bleed for the guys hitting the bricks all over the country," Jackson said.

In the game of Presidential politics that Jackson was just beginning to play in early 1971, his support of the controversial SST was unpopular. It ran against the public tide. But what else, the critics asked, could be expected of the senator from Boeing?

Still, as with most of the other issues that had helped inlay the senator-from-Boeing tag, the SST almost surely would have had Jackson's support even if it had been built, say, in Texas. With the SST in Texas, some other members of the Washington State delegation might have wavered. But not Scoop Jackson. Perhaps he had earned his unkind nickname. But he believed in the SST—and neither a budding Presidential campaign nor harsh criticism would change that.

Almost religiously, Scoop Jackson believed in technology. He believed that it could and should be meshed with the world's environment. He believed in saving both the planet and the payrolls—and that was the heart of his strong feelings, and once-again controversial position, on the great issue of the environment.

12

THE PLANET AND THE PAYROLLS

AN ELEVATOR DOOR opens and Senator Henry M. Jackson steps out instantly, talking, as though the elevator had pre-served him in mid-stride and mid-sentence during the mo-ments of ascent from the basement of the New Senate Office Building. He walks rapidly down the third-floor corridor talking staccato-style to two aides. Bill Van Ness and Jerry Verkler, who hurry along beside him, carrying file-folders of papers. The conference-while-walking ends as Jackson enters a private doorway, ducks through a small conference room, quicksteps up one small, marble stair, and enters his special province of political power—the wood-paneled hearing room of the Senate Interior Com-mittee.

His arrival is accorded the reverence owing an ecclesi-arch of the Senate—the committee chairman. There is a discernable stir among the government officials, the wit-nesses, the lobbyists, the environmentalists, and other spec-tators who half-fill the room. He nods and smiles toward fellow senators—Gordon Allott of Colorado, Len Jordan and Frank Church of Idaho, and the others sitting at their places along the curved judicial bench in the front of the room. Committee staff men solicitously swarm around him, arranging the chairman's papers. He pushes his glasses in place and studies the witness list.

It is one of the quietly powerful committees on Capitol Hill. Its jurisdiction is broad—minerals and mining, Indian matters, power, reclamation, national parks, territories, and public lands, which comprise about one-third of the land face of the United States. Today's hearing deals with one of the chairman's new favorite bills—the National Land Use Policy Act. Some of the Republicans didn't like it. It smacked of big brother—forcing zoning laws into every level of government, all across the nation.

But Jackson, not much of a worrier about big-brother federalism, thinks the time has come for regulations over how man uses the land surface—rules which are consistent from county to county, city to city, and state to state. Something to control the disorderly, anarchistic way the nation is using its land as it grows. Jackson leads into a question of a witness with a brief speech about the pressures of American life. He talks about people scrunched together in cities of concrete. And the sprawling suburbs aren't much better, he adds. They chew into the greenery of the countryside and bury or foul the streams. When people are packed together, surrounded by asphalt, dangers develop. "The sociological impact . . . is enormous," the chairman tells the hearing room audience. "You know, experimentation has been run with animals. You put a few in an area and they can survive. But add a few more and they start eating each other.

"Well, they are shooting at each other now in large metropolitan areas and it is pretty bad.

"There is a need for better land-use planning for new towns and for revitalization of small communities. There is certainly a limitation on the proper size of the urban mass and I think it has reached the point of crisis here."

When the environment broke suddenly on the national scene as the hot new public issue in the late 1960s, Jackson already had some background in it, when the issue was called conservation.

During boyhood summers Henry Jackson went on Boy Scout hikes up into the Cascade foothills to the east of his home in Everett—to places like Monte Cristo and the Sultan Basin. Climbing toward the high country, he and his friends hiked along trails shaded by dense Douglas fir and cedar. Then abruptly they came into a denuded area where all the trees had been cut. The raw hills bristled with forlorn stumps, looking like a World War I battlefield. Scars sliced into the earth by the logging equipment deepened into gullies as they were scoured by mountain rainstorms. Creeks which flowed crystal clear out of the high mountains suddenly turned into a milky tan when they cascaded through the clearcut area.

Jackson now acknowledges he didn't understand the word conservation as a twelve-year-old. "But that one contrast made a hell of an impression on me. As far as conservation is concerned, I guess you'd call it early osmosis. These are things you retain. They stick in your mind. They devastated that beautiful stand of timber—just cut it all down."

First as a congressman, then later as a senator, Jackson specialized in land- and water-resource issues—as a minor to his political major in national defense and the atom. He worked on the projects which produced payrolls in his home state. Yet sometimes he made the dramatically opposite move. In the 1950s, he pushed for a wilderness bill which upset timbermen. Earlier he advocated a bigger Olympic National Park when lumbermen were trying to open some of the park lands for logging. Washington, like other Western states, already had too much wilderness, they said. Those were the days when a pro-conservation argument would not only provoke a stern letter from a lumber company executive; it also could provoke a punch in the nose from any of the burly loggers who knew their jobs depended on a future supply of trees.

Water fights sometimes were settled with six-shooters in the Old West, and some of the latter-day political fights over water were wild and woolly, too. Jackson got in the middle of most of them and won some of his combat ribbons as a liberal that way. The conservative Republicans opposed the federal dams, charging that the projects were socialistic. Keep the federal government out, let private power companies develop the dam sites, they urged. The network of federal power lines was socialistic, too, they said. Always Jackson was on the side of federal multiple-purpose development and he and other public-power advocates won almost every battle in Congress. Nearly always the debate during the forties, fifties, and early sixties revolved around *who* would build the dams and power lines and other projects, not *whether* they would be built.

That changed abruptly when the issue of the environment arrived. When the Sierra Club ran advertisements in *The New York Times* in 1966, tens of thousands of people suddenly became alarmed that some proposed dams might impound lakes into the Grand Canyon. The publicity exaggerated the issue: The dam-happy government engineers, it suggested, were trying to fill the beautiful canyon with water—like a bathtub. But, exaggerations or not, the campaign got results. Angry mail from Manhattan to San Francisco poured into congressional offices. The Colorado River dams were killed and the lusty political issue of the environment was born. Soon afterward two national park proposals became live issues—the North Cascades National Park, in Jackson's home state, and the Redwood National Park in northern California. They rekindled some of the old-fashioned six-shooter-hot western passions.

Each park had been talked about for years. The Redwoods sanctuary, particularly, had been the dream of conservationists for nearly a century. The Johnson Administration sent a Redwood National Park bill to Capitol Hill, but it envisioned a preserve so small it infuriated park proponents. As small as it was, it would take enough privately-owned Redwoods to knock the Rellim-Miller Redwood Company out of business. That would maim the economy of northern California's Del Norte County, so that area became the source of bitter opposition.

There was similar heat in the North Cascades debate. Park proponents wanted vast areas of the ruggedly lovely alpine country—where Jackson had hiked as a boy—put into park status. They wanted the timbered valleys added to it, too, as primitive access corridors. And they wanted the park to extend east of the Cascades to include the head of lovely, remote Lake Chelan. *They wanted everything. Those people—the birdwatchers—always want everything,* said foes of the park.

Lumbermen liked the way things were. Forest Service management permitted timber harvest and other uses. Users of the land—the hunters, campers, skiers, ranchers who leased grazing rights—and businessmen of the towns around the area agreed. Their local economy relied on the use of those hills, trees, and streams. To lock up the land for just *one* use—recreation—would be a selfish step back-ward.

But *those* people are shortsighted and selfish, the park advocates charged. *Either we save the high country now or it will be ruined forever.*

With his own stubbornness and the political style learned from Sam Rayburn, Jackson began the search for consensus on both stormy issues. He called lumbermen together for meetings. He had sessions with environmentalists. Regardless of what they *say* it is, he asked, what is the *real* impact on the lumber companies? If the Sierra Club didn't get *this* valley included in the park—or *that* stream—what would be the harm? When the sportsmen complained about the loss of hunting grounds in the Cascades, Jackson checked to find out how many hunters *really* went into that high country.

Always he seemed to be the impartial arbiter, gathering facts, but steadily pushing the adversaries inward, toward compromise. In a speech to a conservation group, he admonished them not to flatter themselves as "a valiant few in the white hats pitted against the depredations of ruthless exploiters in the black hats." In a speech to timbermen, he warned that their industry must abandon its attitude of go-away-and-leave-me-alone: Otherwise, "government is forced to act without the full benefit of industry's potential contribution."

Gradually he developed an unrelenting force behind the bills. There no longer was any doubt about *whether* the parks would be approved. Both parks were authorized by Congress in 1968. The North Cascades bill set up a two-section national park with two wilderness areas and two recreation areas. There was a little something for everyone—for conservationists, hunters, campers, sightseers, skiers, everyone. And the lumber industry wasn't hurt. The 58,000-acre Redwood National Park was smaller than the Sierra Club had hoped for, but larger than the administration proposal. Jackson maneuvered an unprecedented land swap—some federal timberland traded to the lumber companies—to preserve the payrolls.

Sterling Munro, Jackson's administrative assistant, was the chief idea-and-detail man and occasional speechwriter during the parks' legislative action. Bright, toughly political, and dispassionate, Munro typifies the Jackson staff. Munro's office, a partitioned area outside Jackson's office, is decorated with photos of the Munro family on trail hikes in the hills of Virginia and Washington State. The administrative assistant describes his boss's legislative and political style in an almost clinical way:

"You know, if you get people thinking and moving, you can get some decisions made. That works when confrontation doesn't work. Jackson tries, instead of having them deal from positions A and Z, to move toward L and M, where the differences have been mitigated rather than sharpened. If you have something moving in the direction of decision—and make it clear that it's moving in that direction—the guy who is intransigent has to get on board or he's left at the station."

Next, Jackson was pushing the National Environmental Policy Act which became perhaps his most impressive legislative victory. Because it was so sweeping, with so much impact on all the agencies of the federal government, nobody took it too seriously, particularly Dr. Lee DuBridge, President Nixon's science advisor. DuBridge, new in his job during the early months of the Nixon Administration, was summoned to appear before Jackson's Interior Com-

273

mittee to give the administration's opinion of the bill. He didn't bother to prepare a statement. DuBridge, a brilliant man, a scientist, former president of Cal Tech, casually, almost disdainfully, clicked off the reasons why the bill wasn't needed and why the administration was opposed to it.

Already there were ways to deal with the relationships of federal agencies with the environment, he said. He ended his brief testimony with an air of quiet dismissal.

Jackson, who listened quietly through DuBridge's testimony, then gave the educator a lesson in Capitol Hill procedure. In his quiet, prosecutor style, almost reminiscent of the McCarthy hearings, Jackson asked DuBridge to go with him, step by step, through the bill. Jackson reviewed the first provision. *Now tell us, Dr. DuBridge, what is your specific objection to that?* Well, no problem with that, the witness replied. *And now to the second provision, Dr. DuBridge.* The same question, the same answer. They went through the entire bill, with DuBridge agreeing to everything. That was the turning point. Thereafter, the Nixon Administration slowly turned around into a position of support for the measure. Besides setting up a presidential Council on Environmental Quality and requiring annual presidential "State of the Environment" reports to Congress, the law forced each federal agency to consider the environmental impact of each project—each dam, canal, airport, power plant, power line—every federal work and action.

For Jackson, a longtime practitioner of public works politics in his home state, his landmark legislation brought back upon him some peculiar, though expected dilemmas. His own Puget Sound area was joyfully anticipating an economic gusher because it was the gateway to the new Alaska

North Slope oil fields. In March 1969, while the bill was still pending in Congress, Jackson was the featured speaker at a ground-breaking ceremony. He praised a new Atlantic-Richfield Oil refinery near Bellingham, along the upper Puget Sound coast. It was like so many other new-project, new-payroll, ground-breaking ceremonies he attended over the years. After the construction boom, it meant 300 to 400 steady jobs for the area, he noted—a steady payroll based on the oil which was to move across Alaska by pipeline, then by supertanker to the refinery. But, months later, the whole Alaska pipeline project was stalled. It was hung up on Section 102 of Jackson's National Environmental Policy Act, the section which requires the environmental-impact review. The pipeline had to undergo scrutiny of its effect on the delicate permafrost soil. Would it be a possible barrier to migrating wildlife? A potential victim of earthquakes and landslides? Would the supertankers—and the almost inevitable oil spillages—threaten the Canadian coastline and the purity of Puget Sound? Other projects were running into the same Section 102 hangup—the controversial Florida Barge Canal, extension of runways at J.F.K. International Airport in New York, a jet-port near the Florida Everglades and some vitally needed nuclear power plants.

Jackson was a little unhappy about some of the problems his law created, especially the slowdown in delivery of needed electrical energy. But, in effect, he shrugged: The responsibility had to be imposed. The absolute conservationists would rather have none of the projects built. But most of them will be built eventually—and with more safeguards for the environment.

Rivalry inevitably arose between Jackson and Senator Edmund Muskie of Maine, a man with a national reputation as Mr. Clean as a result of his long association with environmental issues. Each was reaping credit for environmental bills—Jackson as chairman of the Interior Committee, Muskie as chairman of the Subcommittee on Air and Water Pollution of the Senate Public Works Committee. The two senators have vastly different styles. Muskie is a superb speechmaker, an individualist who works outside the Senate power circle, a man who sometimes has trouble moving his legislation. Jackson, hard-working, low-key, is a quietly effective member of the Senate Club and at times seems able to move legislation with the flick of a finger. His North Cascades National Park Bill passed the Senate quickly—so quickly, in fact, Jackson decided he wouldn't slow it down by giving it the sponsor's traditional speech.

The Muskie-Jackson collision came in 1969 after the Senate and House passed differing versions of Jackson's National Environmental Policy Act. Muskie said that measure was a hostile overlapping of his bill which was aimed at combatting water pollution. That, however, was only a technical issue. The big problem was jurisdiction: Which panel—Jackson's Interior Committee or Muskie's subcommittee—would emerge with the power over future major environmental bills? Muskie thought Jackson was making a power grab. He threatened to block conference action on Jackson's bill.

The feud simmered at the staff level, then broke out in the press. Jackson staff men were miffed: Muskie was being petty and pouty, they said. The issue wasn't that great. Muskie had been given ample notice of the Jackson bill, Munro said, and so could have appeared to testify if he chose. But Jackson wanted peace. He telephoned Muskie.

The senator from Maine was furious. He shouted his objections to Jackson's bill. The conversation ended as Jackson hung up the receiver. He muttered the supreme Jackson insult: "That guy is just absolutely hopeless."

Still wanting to settle the feud, Jackson decided to go visit Muskie at Muskie's office, even though "Club rules" decreed that a *subcommittee* chairman should come to a *committee* chairman, not the other way around. But Jackson and his aides went to Muskie. There was more bickering. But eventually compromises were reached, including an accommodation between advisory groups proposed in each of the two bills—Muskie's proposal for a White House office of environmental quality and the board of environmental advisers proposed in the Jackson bill.

Redwoods are unique among all living things on earth. All men should have a chance to stand among the ancient forests to touch the trees and reflect on how life can continue on this planet—if they are our heritage, we are their stewards. . . .

In its poetic, almost evangelical way, the Sierra Club's bulletin thus had pleaded for a Redwood National Park. Later, in March 1969, the Sierra Club bestowed its highest honor on a conspicuously non-poetic, non-evangelical politician: Scoop Jackson received the John Muir award for conservation. It was the first time the most-coveted conservation award ever had been given to a political figure.

Jackson began to receive many awards and words of praise for his environmental record. He received an implicit tribute, too, when President Nixon made it a point to sign the Jackson-sponsored National Environmental Policy bill on New Years Day 1970: *It is particularly fit-*

277

ting, the President said, *that my first official act in this new decade is to approve the National Environmental Policy Act. . . .*

But some not-so-kind things were starting to be said, too:

. . . Sludge, crud, grinch, gunk, funk, blue algae, black air, oil slicks and general industrial barf have found an advocate and defender in Senator Henry Jackson, the conservative Democrat from the State of Washington.

The growling, biting paragraph was in a column by Nicholas von Hoffman in the Washington *Post*.

The tough words were fired at the same senator who, only months earlier, was the hero in shining armor, rescuer of the Redwoods—the same senator who, also in 1969, had shared the Bernard Baruch conservation award with Charles A. Lindbergh.

Abruptly Jackson had gone from hero to hate-figure among some of the red-hot, new-wave environmentalists. In Congress he was now championing the supersonic transport and it was portrayed as an ecological disaster. Von Hoffman's tough words were return fire for a Jackson remark in Florida, where Jackson had conferred with AFL-CIO leaders, seeking support in the SST battle. When reporters questioned him after the session, Jackson attacked "environmental extremists" who were trying to shoot down the SST. He said they were making "absolutely, reckless, fear-spreading" charges. Jackson was miffed at suggestions from Senator William Proxmire of Wisconsin that the SST could alter the stratosphere and cause skin cancer. Such emotionalism, Jackson grumbled, was "a new McCarthyism."

But the SST was only one part of the new problem.

278

Jackson was irked by other emotion-filled causes of the new environmentalists who seemed to want to shut down all industry. It became a highly personal matter with Jackson, because he saw them as the same people who were so noisily opposed to national-defense policies and Jackson in particular. When Jackson talked about environment on Earth Day, the students shouted at him, "How can you be for the environment when you want to defoliate Vietnam?" He had voted to defeat an amendment which would have barred use of defoliants in Vietnam. But so had most other senators. The proposal was defeated 62-22 in August, 1970.

"I'm allegedly only supposed to be interested in military matters," Jackson complained, "but I have led the fight through the 1960s on environmental matters including the North Cascades Park. Where were all these environmentalists when I was fighting that one? And the Olympic National Park fight? You couldn't find them."

The environmental cause had lured swarms of "Johnny-come-latelies," as he called them. They seemed to Jackson to pour out of hippie communes, or they came, Cadillac-borne, from the wealthy suburbs, or they marched from the campuses to protest against every smokestack, every new power plant, every highway. *But*, he snapped, *where are their solutions?*

"It's all very well," he said, "for affluent, middle-class Americans—public officials, college students, politicians, even corporate officers—to demand that the factories be shut down, that a no-growth policy be adopted, that we adopt a new national life style which rejects the materialistic consumptive philosophy we have held dear for so long . . . but the twenty-six million people in this country . . . below the poverty line, don't share this view. Poor

279

people, black and white, do not espouse it. They want jobs."

"You can protect the environment and do it in such a way that we still have industry functioning to produce the goods and services that are needed." Save the planet and still have payrolls, said Jackson, the compromise man.

Many of the most aggressive conservationists in his home state—to whom the word *compromise* is inflammatory— are critical that Jackson never has really inflicted hardship on the lumber companies. "With the power he has, the North Cascades could have been a national park twice the size it is," one of his critics muttered.

Jackson's stubbornness and compromising inevitably invites that kind of criticism. He also suffers sometimes in an audience of avant-garde environmentalists with their new concepts and their sometimes elitist vocabulary. When he appeared before the Metropolitan Democratic Club in downtown Seattle, someone in the very liberal, dovish crowd asked him about research on recycling. "Recycling?" replied Jackson, hesitantly. He wondered if the question had to do with recycling water at nuclear power plants. The word *recycling* then was the newest word in the environmentalists' solid-waste-issue vocabulary. And Jackson didn't know it. Two men in the crowd exchanged disgruntled looks.

When environmentalists in his home state sought to recruit Jackson's powerful support for some of their local causes, he usually demurred on jurisdictional grounds. A meticulous federalist, he almost never steps into a state issue, although a conspicuous exception was his hard prolabor stand when the right-to-work measures were on the Washington State ballot. When ecologists fretted about the danger of oil or gas drilling in Puget Sound, his colleague, Senator Warren G. Magnuson, came out publicly against it. Jackson's silence was conspicuous. But it was a state issue.

A lively cause erupted in Seattle when citizens began a drive to secure Fort Lawton, a scenic military base overlooking Puget Sound, for a park. They demonstrated, held camp-ins and generated a barrage of publicity. The almost-abandoned military base was becoming surplus federal property, but the city couldn't afford to pay half the assessed valuation, which would have been the price under law.

Jackson took care of the Seattle issue with a deft federal action: He pushed through the Federal Lands for Parks and Recreation Act. That made surplus federal property available to major metropolitan areas for park purposes without cost, or at a minimal percentage of the market value. Within the first year after its passage, the law allowed other cities to obtain more than one hundred parcels of federal property for parks.

There was a subtle imagery benefit for Jackson in the Fort Lawton action: Arranging for a military post to be converted into a park was a political variation on the swords-to-plowshares theme. With a re-election campaign approaching in 1970, it was more helpful to be thought of as an environmentalist than a hawk. It was through the time when criticism of the Vietnam war grew louder that Jackson worked hardest on his environmental measures. His environmental good works took some of the edge off his political opposition and helped in his ultimate re-election sweep in 1970. Tom Wimmer, then president of the Washington Environmental Council, was a longtime conservationist and a liberal Democrat. He admired Jackson and appreciated his record on the environment. But Wimmer was agonized by the war.

On a morning in 1968, after both men had attended a breakfast meeting where Jackson gave a speech, they strolled together from Seattle's Olympic Hotel toward the senator's office in the U. S. Courthouse. Wimmer told Jackson he thought the then-pending North Cascades National Park ought to be bigger. "I think the boundaries ought to come all the way down to Twenty-Five Mile Creek on Lake Chelan. It's land that just ought to be in the park," Wimmer said. The senator listened to that and other park ideas. He asked Wimmer to send a map with some suggested boundaries to his office in Washington. Then Wimmer turned the conversation to the war in Vietnam and military policies. The time had come, Wimmer said, for the nation and, hopefully, Scoop Jackson, to "get off this military kick . . . Forget this militarism." It was advice from one Democrat to another, from one environmentalist to another. "But, Tom, what are we going to do about Russia?" Jackson replied. He told Wimmer he couldn't retreat from his tough defense positions. Jackson almost pleaded: "Tom, I've got to be honest with myself."

"He'll give you a pretty damned direct answer," Wimmer reflected later. Jackson didn't change on the national-defense issue. He didn't stretch the national park boundary lines to suit Wimmer. But Wimmer nevertheless worked for Jackson's re-election in 1970, observing, "His environmental record is pretty damned good."

In an election-year appearance before the environmental council, Jackson was slightly apprehensive: Many of the environmentalist members also were vocal critics of the Vietnam war and Jackson was getting edgy about hecklers. But when he was introduced, more than half the crowd rose to give him standing applause. Nearly all the others stayed in their chairs, but applauded.

One observer remarked: "You can tell how they are with Scoop. Those standing up and applauding are with him on both the environment and his national-defense ideas. The ones sitting down and clapping are with him on the environment. And the others . . ." The man looked around the crowd of more than one hundred and saw two young men in the back row who neither stood nor applauded.

The three-story white colonial house, the Jackson home in Everett, reigns atop a bluff overlooking the stinging-cold waters of Puget Sound. The house once owned by William Butler, the town banker, came onto the real estate market in 1967, and Jackson, a frugal man, got it at a bargain—$65,000. It is the western retreat for the family, away from the hot summers of Washington, a place where the senator says he will retire some day.

The sweeping view is westward across the Sound where ocean-going freighters and tankers plying between Sound ports and the Orient and Alaska pass slowly beside the quiet, wooded islands. Gulls wheel and shriek behind the fishing boats among the small craft which crisscross the harbor. The backdrop for the marine panorama is the silhouette of the Olympic Mountains, a range of steep granite peaks, their ankles in the cool cedar and fern thickets of the Olympic rain forest.

Jackson takes visitors out to the edge of the bluff to look down on the harbor of Everett. With an expansive gesture, he recalls, "all this was just a series of lumber mills all along the waterfront here." The mills spewed cinders and belched their smoke all through his growing-up years. Most of the mills now are gone. Some of the remains are

283

there—only the bones, a few timbers mulching at the water's edge. In their place Man has inflicted a new environmental nuisance. Smelly pulp mills dominate the waterfront today. Motorists passing Everett on a freeway more than a mile away sniff the glunky atmosphere on a westerly wind and speed up a little. The place where Jackson learned to swim as a kid is unswimmable now. Its water is polluted.

Jackson is not apologetic about the fact that his hometown port is one of the most unpleasant blemishes that Man has inflicted on the lovely Puget Sound shoreline. For decades Everett's citizens thought only of jobs and livelihood. The more industry that could be piled into the waterfront the better. It still is a working-man's town and the traditional thinking is slow to change. But there were skirmishes in Everett, too, as the battle of the environment washed over the nation. The pulp mills are under state order to clean up smoke emissions. Some environmentalists challenged a plan to fill much of the harbor to create a new tract of land for more industry. Jackson used his influence to secure a pilot study funded by the Department of Housing and Urban Development. "That jetty out there has some really nice beach," says Jackson, pointing. "It seems to me that it'll be possible to put something together where there'll be room for industries and some recreation areas, too. But you've got to get people together and talking about it. You've got to get the adversary's proceedings going so you can get some decisions made."

CHAPTER 13

CITIZEN POLITICS

THROUGHOUT THE FIFTIES and early sixties the pages of the Seattle *Times*, the Seattle *Post-Intelligencer*, the Spokane *Spokesman-Review*, all the smaller daily newspapers and the countless weeklies in Washington State invariably seemed to carry a stock story from the nation's capital.

The opening line of the story was routinely and unimaginatively the same: *Senators Henry M. Jackson and Warren G. Magnuson today announced in Washington that.* . . .

After the opening the news differed, but it always was good news—more federal money to build an irrigation canal in arid Eastern Washington, a lucrative contract for Todd Shipyards in Seattle, a Small Business Administration loan for an applesauce cannery in Wenatchee, a multi-million-dollar contract for The Boeing Company or the announcement that a new job-producing aluminum plant was coming to Washington State to capitalize on the low rates for electricity generated by the federal dams on the Columbia.

In certain years the order of the names was reversed in the stories. It became *Senators Warren G. Magnuson and Henry M. Jackson.* It was quietly understood that the senator who next was up for re-election got top billing.

It was a game that all politicians tried to play with the

bundles of federal cash that flowed regularly out of the capital. But none seemed to play it as well as Jackson and Magnuson. Their press secretaries bolted to the telephone with each news gem—whether it be a tiny sewer grant or a massive military contract. Often, the word from Jackson and Magnuson arrived in newspaper city rooms mere seconds before their scrambling competitors got on the phone. But Jackson and Magnuson almost always were first. Republican congressmen, methodically elbowed out of all the good news, grumbled unhappily that they were left with slim pickings—the contract cancellations, the bad news. Jackson and Magnuson assiduously avoided the bad news.

The senators had little trouble finding good, job-producing announcements to make to their constituents. In some years during their powerful reign, the amount of federal money that flowed into Washington State was three times as much as their constituents sent back to the capital in federal taxes. Local newsmen dubbed Jackson and Magnuson the Gold Dust Twins and sometimes complained because it wasn't easy to squeeze both names into the lead paragraph of a news story. But the names showed up anyway, because the Gold Dust Twins were the conduit for all the pork-barrel news from Washington.

A growing state, hungry for even more growth in the postwar era, was blessed with two senators who had fashioned a remarkable coalition of political power. Besides their important subcommittees, Magnuson was chairman of the Senate Commerce Committee and Jackson was chairman of the Interior Committee. At a Democratic dinner a master of ceremonies once gloated through the list of things over which those committees have jurisdiction—air transportation, railroads, ocean shipping, mines, public lands, water resources, and on and on. So, the emcee said, "if it has anything to do with the surface of the earth, the valleys, the hills, or below the earth, or on the water, or in the air, we here in Washington State—because of Maggie and Scoop—have something to say about it." Even Republicans sometimes laughed and applauded.

Oregon's Republican governor, Tom McCall, once told of trying to persuade an official of the Dow Chemical Company to locate a plant in Oregon. Midway through their conversation the Dow executive expressed a common corporate concern: "If we locate in Oregon, how will I ever explain it to Senator Jackson and Senator Magnuson?" Oregonians became sensitive about the move of federal-office payrolls to their neighboring state to the north. When introducing Jackson at a political banquet in Portland, the master of ceremonies once quipped, "Senator Jackson has informed me that if we give him a nice reception here tonight he won't take any more federal offices away from us." The crowd rose, cheering, and Jackson grinned sheepishly through one of the most prolonged ovations he ever had.

Then, suddenly, the joyous world of bring-home-the-bacon politics changed. Inspired by mass demonstrations against the Vietnam war, citizen groups began to act to protect the environment against governmental and industrial assaults. Citizens abruptly seemed to be demonstrating against almost everything. Jackson's constituents, beneficiaries of so much federal largesse, began acting *en masse* to *stop* things from happening—to reject the federal bacon, to challenge once-sacrosanct government decisions, to turn down the economic benefits of industrial expansion.

After the Northwest Aluminum Company announced it was going to build a $100 million plant on Guemes Island in picturesque, upper Puget Sound, the unheard-of occurred: People objected. They organized a citizens committee to protest against the environmental impact on the pastoral, little island. Discouraged by the uproar, the publicity and a lawsuit, the corporation abandoned Scoop Jackson's baili-wick and took its plans and payroll to Oregon.

Often the protests were over military activities and so Jackson, a man who by nature disdained protests and mass actions, the longtime Cold Warrior and defender of the military establishment, found the going uncomfortable at times.

The Gold Dust Twins only announced good federal news. So they let the Defense Department make the less-than-happy announcement that a shipment of several thousand tons of nerve and mustard gas would be arriving in Washington State in late 1969. It would move, the Army explained, by ship from Okinawa—where its presence provoked bitter demonstrations—to Bangor, site of a military ammunition depot on Puget Sound. From there the gas would be shipped by railroad car across the southwestern part of the state, into Oregon, to be stored in a depot at Hermiston.

There was an immediate outcry. Governor McCall declared in his booming voice that he didn't want the gas coming into Oregon. Magnuson, growing weary of the Pentagon, opposed it, too. What's the sense, he asked, of "maintaining stockpiles of chemical warfare agents when we have the nuclear capability of wiping out entire populations?"

Typically Jackson stayed out of the hubbub although, privately, he stubbornly defended the shipment. President Nixon only weeks earlier had repudiated the use of biological weapons in the United States arsenal. That left only nerve gas and other chemical weapons as a deterrent against Russian use of such weapons, Jackson reasoned. Besides, the public outcry smacked of the emotionalism of the student riots, demonstrations, and other uprisings of recent years—all of which caused Jackson to move instinctively into a tougher position.

As the citizenry objected to the shipment, the Army moved in with some heavy reassurance. After all, the military spokesmen said, the gas really was no more of a menace than other explosives and dangerous materials—both military and commercial—which move on trains and along highways every day. The Army issued some reassuring words about the safeguards which were planned: As the gas moved by rail southward from Bangor, there would be three trains: the first to determine that the track is safe; the second carrying the gas; the third loaded with decontaminants, medics, and guards.

The reassurances were so ominously descriptive they gave the already-worried public new shivers of concern.

Under pressure to raise some criticism of the shipment, Jackson came as close to a rebuke of the military as his stubborn nature allowed: He charged the Army with being guilty of poor public relations.

Citizen politics was in full swing. A Committee for the Abolition of Weapons of Gas and Germ Warfare was organized. So, too, was People Against Nerve Gas. PANG turned out to be a highly effective protest group, with chapters in both states. Liberal groups passed stop-the-nerve-gas resolutions and an elderly woman in a wheelchair staged a sit-in in Olympia on the steps of the State Capitol.

The Defense Department meanwhile held up plans to load the gas aboard the first ship in Okinawa. The controversy was destined to rage through the spring of 1970.

While Oregon's governor was objecting loudly, Governor Dan Evans of Washington was more restrained. He was unhappy about the gas shipment, but he accepted the Army's reassurances that there was no undue danger. Evans tried to talk the Army out of the shipment, urging that it go somewhere else in the Pacific or, better yet, that it be detoxified in the ocean. But the military men were adamant. During a briefing one of them pointed out that the state had the responsibility for preparing the standby plan to evacuate about 1,300 square miles of the state—just in case something did go wrong. Alarmed, Evans figured that this could mean evacuation of about 150,000 people along the rail route. The state couldn't possibly give that assurance. The governor tried again to get the Army men to change their mind. He failed, then publicly opposed the shipment and asked the White House to cancel the plans.

University of Washington professors issued grisly descriptions of the kind of death brought on by nerve gas and some PANG members staged a "die-in" at a downtown Seattle intersection, sprawling in the street in a mock death scene. Protestors lay in the streets and sidewalks, tying up traffic, symbolizing the dead bodies which would result if the shipment sprang a leak.

The usually patient, jocular Magnuson fumed as the controversy rumbled into April and the Pentagon continued to persist with the plan. The military's bullishness, he said, "was just plain stupid . . . The Pentagon does some stupid things, but they're getting a monopoly on it now." The gas easily could be destroyed. Yet, Magnuson grumbled, the military was obstinately trying to push the shipment into an area which was becoming more frightened each day. "But the important question is why this risk need be taken at all. There is no meaningful justification for maintaining these weapons or bringing them back to the mainland. This whole thing just doesn't make any military, economic, or public-safety sense."

Clearly Magnuson and Jackson were a long way apart on the issue. Jackson sounded like he was arguing with himself when, the day after Magnuson's outrage, he grudgingly declared, "I cannot support the movement until the Department of Health, Education and Welfare says that proper precautionary steps have been taken." Jackson refused to question the shipment. He talked about the dangers in non-military shipments of various kinds, as though that would mitigate the public fears. He suggested a task force to study all the shipments of all hazardous materials. And he warned that radicals could cause sabotage.

It was one of the rare times that Jackson was awkwardly out of step with a local issue. The emotionalism went beyond the radicals or antiwar activists who bothered Jackson. Middle-class Americans were apprehensive, too. Public attention had suddenly been focused on one of those nasty, terrifying, little-talked-about horror weapons in the American arsenal.

But Jackson quickly caught his stride. In a deft compromise move, he quietly sent a letter to President Nixon, pointing out that the shipment had not undergone the review required under his bill, the National Environmental Policy Act. It was a near-perfect political approach: If the shipment had to be stopped, then it would be better to have it halted by the Jackson bill.

On a Saturday in May Jackson was in Wenatchee for a meeting of the Washington State Law Enforcement Officers Association when he received the word by telephone: President Nixon told him the decision had been made to cancel the shipment.

291

Quickly, Jackson summoned a press conference to announce the news. The two Republican governors were furious when they heard that the Republican President had given the news first to a Democratic senator. One of McCall's aides tried frantically to get confirmation from the White House. He got in reply only an infuriating question from a White House staff member: "Has Senator Jackson held his press conference yet?"

Meanwhile no one told Magnuson what had happened. He was at home in his Shoreham Hotel apartment in Washington. "I was around here all day and nobody called me," he mourned later to a reporter.

Evans was incensed by the White House handling of the announcement. Here were two Republican governors—both opposed to the shipment, pleading for White House help—and the word was given to a Democratic senator. "McCall, particularly, was one of the earliest critics and he deserved better," Evans said.

Jackson shrugged off the Republican protests. "Well," he said, with an almost defensive grin, "I was the only one who went to the President personally." Later in the year, Evans and other Republicans would continue to wince at Nixon's obvious willingness to help Jackson during an election year. It stirred bitterness within Republican loyalists in the state, but it made Capitol Hill political sense for Nixon. Ever since the President offered Jackson the job of Secretary of Defense, they had remained close on national-security and defense issues. Besides, Jackson had been the force behind the environmental act which Nixon had come to embrace as his own.

Thereafter Jackson sometimes was introduced to audiences along the campaign trail as "the man who stopped the nerve gas from coming into the state."

"Jackson didn't stop the nerve gas," Jackson's primary-election opponent, Carl Maxey, angrily retorted. But the issue was gone. After being so stubbornly insistent that the nerve gas *had* to be moved through Washington and stored in Oregon, the Army eventually hauled it to tiny Johnston Island, an isolated atoll in the Pacific.

Jackson was stung a little in a postscript to the fight. In the Senate Mike Gravel, Alaska's freshman Democrat was, with Magnuson, pushing an amendment which would prohibit such a shipment to any point in the United States. Gravel also added funds to destroy the gas. As the Senate considered Gravel's proposal, Jackson was fighting it. It was, he said, tantamount to unilateral disarmament. Paradoxically, Jackson was fighting his Gold Dust Twin, Maggie, and at the same time losing a battle with a freshman. Gravel's amendment was adopted.

During the debate Magnuson, exasperated, used one of his favorite senatorial gimmicks—a rumbling stage whisper, not intended for *The Congressional Record*, but easily heard throughout the Senate chamber and in the galleries: "Goddammit, Scoop, what's wrong with you?"

Fort Lawton sits high on one of Seattle's western bluffs overlooking the chilled-green waters of Puget Sound. The thousand-acre tract was given to the Army in the late nineteenth century because of its commanding view of the Sound. From there the Army's cannons could protect Seattle against the marauding gunships of any foreign power. But, in all its history, not a single enemy ship exposed itself to the fort's firepower. And now the commanding view from the scenic bluff is more likely to frame a picturesque ferry boat against the jagged Olympic Mountains, an occasional Japanese steamer nudging into Seattle's port or a chug-chug-a-chugging fishing boat heading north to the bonanza waters off Alaska.

It probably can be said that the fort's most serious brush with trouble came on an otherwise peaceful day in March of 1970. On that day the lightly defended fort was invaded and the invasion made headlines around the world.

Seventy-two Indians, including women and children, scaled a cliff at the rear of the fort and tried to penetrate her defenses. They carried sack lunches and a teepee. Meanwhile, in a carefully synchronized action forty miles to the south, Jane Fonda, the actress, led another warband that tried to storm Fort Lewis.

At Fort Lawton the Indians erected their teepee near the border fence and Bob Satiacum, leader of the Puyallups, began reading a proclamation: "We the native Americans reclaim the land known as Fort Lawton in the name of all American Indians by the right of discovery." Satiacum's words soon were drowned out by the growling voice of a military-police sergeant: "Move in and take them away." The invasion was short-lived.

One of those arrested was Bernie Whitebear, a Colville who blamed the whole scene on Senator Henry M. Jackson. The Army had decided to give up the fort, rationalizing that cannon defenses of Puget Sound were somewhat outdated. Now the Indians and the city of Seattle were competing to see who would get the prized land. The Indians sought it for an Indian cultural center; the city for a park.

The Indians had taken their case to Jackson because he is chairman of the Senate Interior Committee, which oversees Indian problems. According to Whitebear, Jackson tersely instructed them to "go through federal channels," which meant struggling with the bureaucracy of the Bureau of Indian Affairs. In almost the next breath, according to

Whitebear, the powerful senator assured the mayor of Seattle that the city would get the land for its park.

Whitebear, an unrestrained activist, called Jackson the mayor's "stooge."

Jackson retorted that the land "should be for all the people."

"Do you see the precedent here, if we turn this over to the Indians? Think of it. We'd be turning property over to all kinds of special groups. The blacks would be saying, 'We deserve this property because this is where we landed when we were brought over in chains.'"

Whitebear, not to be outdone, replied that, "Senator Jackson is like the man who helps a little old lady across the street and then, when they get to the other side, steals her purse."

And so it went. The Indians perhaps were not typical of the citizen-action groups that sprouted up to challenge governmental decisions in the late sixties. But the Indian invasion was not the first time that Jackson, a man who likes problems handled neatly and officially, had trouble with activist citizens at Fort Lawton.

In late 1967 Seattle received word from Washington that it would be the site of an antiballistic-missile installation. The city also learned that the missiles would be planted in the middle of Fort Lawton, which Seattle already was coveting for a park. In a different era, perhaps only a few years earlier, this federal largesse would have been eagerly revealed to the public by Jackson and Magnuson. The announcement would have been replete with the number of jobs created, the total millions of dollars expended and the spinoff benefits that would be realized by the community.

But the times, as the folk song put it, they are a-changin'.

The senators ducked the announcement, sensing perhaps that Seattle's citizenry would not consider atomic-war-headed missiles as the best of possible presents from the federal government. If they did sense that, they were right.

The reaction was immediate and bombastic. Seattle's Mayor Dorm Braman, a man who had developed a reputation for accepting federal funds with open arms, was leary of this latest government program. He suggested that the Army look elsewhere in the Puget Sound area. The Army replied that it already had examined alternative sites and had rejected them. Almost overnight a plethora of angry citizens' groups sprang up to fight off the Army and its missiles. At first the Army was caught by surprise, dumbfounded by the ruckus. *But these are defensive weapons,* the brass insisted, *and they are there to protect you.* But the seething citizens scoffed at the logic, arguing that they didn't want *any* missiles, defensive or offensive, in their backyard. The very presence of the missiles, they said, would make Seattle a prime target for a Russian or a Chinese attack. Protests began in other ABM cities—especially in Boston and Chicago—and the Army fell back on the defensive with its defensive missile. In Seattle the battle raged on for a year, with environmentalists, allied-arts groups, and the League of Women Voters joining in the crusade. By the end of a year the citizens were questioning not only where, but also why, the ABM had to be deployed.

The ABM furor in Seattle placed Henry Jackson in an awkward political position. As he had been more than a decade earlier with the Polaris submarine and the ICBM, Jackson was one of the Senate's earliest advocates of an antiballistic-missile system.

In early 1967, as the Johnson administration agonized

over the decision to go ahead with this new, expensive, untested weapon, Jackson came out four-square for the ABM. He recommended a $5 billion, limited system that would protect America's Minuteman ICBM bases from a nuclear attack. Such an ABM system, he said, was essential to protect the "credibility" of the American nuclear deterrent. Without it, Jackson said, as he had said so many times before, the United States would be vulnerable to "nuclear blackmail" by the Russians.

Eventually, President Johnson decided to go ahead with an ABM—but one that was far different from the system envisaged by Jackson. The Johnson Administration program also called for a $5 billion, limited system, but one that would protect American cities rather than the nation's offensive-missile sites.

Jackson liked President Johnson's proposal considerably less than his own. But nevertheless Scoop Jackson became the Senate's leading defender of the ABM. By mid-1968, while the opposition was reaching its height in Seattle, Jackson was championing the ABM on the Senate floor. There was a "humanitarian" aspect to the ABM proposal, Jackson said. It would save lives. Some estimates were that 120 million Americans might die in an all-out atomic attack. With the ABM, it was said, the figure could be cut to sixty million. "That," one congressman said sardonically, "is progress." But the ABM slipped narrowly through the Senate in 1968, and much of the credit for its success went to Henry Jackson.

Meanwhile, in one of those paradoxes that occur often in politics, Jackson gradually began to give more aid and comfort to the irate citizens who did not want missiles planted in the middle of Seattle. The senator made few public statements about the controversy. Instead, he cast

297

himself more in the role of intermediary between the public and the Pentagon. That cautious role irritated some. But it was typical of Jackson. He would sit back and watch the way the tide was running.

By the middle of December 1968 the Seattle ABM battle had been raging for almost thirteen months. The citizen activists were approaching the boiling point.

"Friends of Senator Henry Jackson would like to see him immortalized in sculpture at the Fort Lawton missile site," Lorenzo Milam, an eccentric young millionaire, wrote in one of his occasional columns for the Seattle *Post-Intelligencer.* "A popular suggestion is to have the missile itself constructed in the exact likeness of the senator, with the nuclear warhead in his head. An alternative is to set Jackson himself in epoxy at the site."

Four days later—and surely not because of Lorenzo Milam's writings—Jackson announced that there would be no missiles at Fort Lawton. The Army, he said, had chosen two other sites across Puget Sound in Kitsap County. One would be located on quiet, little Bainbridge Island; the other near the tiny town of Port Gamble.

It seemed to be an almost ideal compromise, a perfect Jackson solution. The missiles had been moved out of the populated area, yet they still were close enough to do their job. Furthermore, Kitsap County seemed an ideal political location. The county was loaded with military installations—a NIKE missile base, a Polaris submarine base, the Bremerton Naval Shipyard. Surely, Kitsap County wouldn't object to one more military installation. The people might even welcome it. It meant, after all, six hundred new jobs and $100 million in construction work.

But once again the reaction was immediate—and negative. During the Christmas-New Year's week six hundred persons from Bainbridge Island turned out to protest the Army's decision. And grumbling began around Port Gamble. The same outspoken Seattleites who had opposed the Fort Lawton site now joined their country cousins in opposing the compromise. "ABM—Not Where, But Why?" became their theme. Politically, Jackson seemed to be no better off than he was before.

As President Nixon took office in January 1969, the public protest against the ABM was cresting. Most of the controversy centered on the sites, all of which were near major cities. Within days after entering the White House Nixon met with the man whom he had asked to be his Secretary of Defense. The President sat attentively, taking notes on his usual yellow legal pad, while Henry Jackson spelled out his proposal on the antiballistic-missile system: Forget the city-defense plan, humanitarian as it sounds, and place the ABMs around America's Minuteman-missile sites in the plains of Montana and the Dakotas. This, Jackson reasoned, would take the heat off politically by removing the missiles from the cities. But, more importantly, it also made more sense from the standpoint of America's nuclear deterrent. Grim as it sounded, in terms of preventing war the protection of America's deterrent was more important than the protection of her cities.

Within days of that meeting, the Army announced that it was delaying the acquisition of missile sites. Shortly after that, Defense Secretary Melvin Laird revealed that the new Nixon Administration was taking an overall look at the ABM program.

Then on March 7, while visiting Seattle, Jackson gave the first hint that President Nixon was moving away from the city-defense program. Jackson predicted that the administration would opt for a system that would protect some Strategic Air Command bases, some command facilities, and "certain Minuteman sites." Jackson, as he usually is in these predictions, was entirely right. President Nixon announced the decision several days later. It meant that there would be no missile sites at Bainbridge Island or Port Gamble, either.

President Nixon's changes took some of the steam out of the opposition—but not as much as might have been expected. The outlook still was for a very tight Senate vote, with the opponents taking the tack that the United States should continue research and development of the system but not yet deploy it.

Jackson quickly became the chief Senate spokesman for the program and warned that the President had told him there would be no compromising on his plan. Jackson worked closely with the Republican administration, and that upset some Democrats. On one occasion Herb Klein, Nixon's communications director, set up a television-panel appearance for Jackson to use as a pro-ABM forum.

But, at the same time, Jackson was becoming somewhat isolated in his own congressional delegation. The heated controversy in Seattle had riveted most Washington State congressmen into anti-ABM positions. It also caused Jackson's Senate colleague, Warren Magnuson, to take a long, hard look at deployment of the controversial missile system. It was an odd switch, because, in the past, the Washington delegation, including Magnuson, usually had played follow-the-leader with Jackson on defense issues.

Jackson could afford to ignore the congressmen, because approval of the ABM was almost automatic in the House. But, as the showdown neared in July 1969, Jackson concentrated heavily on wooing the Senate votes of Magnuson and a freshman Democrat from Alaska, Mike Gravel. He escorted Gravel down to the White House for a quiet half-hour talk with President Nixon. The pressures were intense on the young Alaskan. "I'm the only freshman who's still uncommitted," he told the *Wall Street Journal*, "and everybody seems to think that because I'm a freshman, I can be muscled around." Gravel was leaning against voting for the ABM, but he liked Jackson. He waffled for a while, then came out against the program.

Magnuson also was called down to the White House for a quiet, one-on-one meeting with the President. Or, at least, so he thought. As the meeting got under way, his Gold Dust Twin, Scoop Jackson, also walked into the President's office. Magnuson bristled some at that, because, after all, he still was the senior senator from the State of Washington. Magnuson also was invited out on the Presidential yacht for a cruise on the Potomac. There was no arm-twisting, but Magnuson found himself surrounded by people who were talking up the ABM. Magnuson can get testy—and he did, finally, when he started receiving pro-ABM telephone calls from some of his old friends in Seattle. Magnuson suspected that Jackson had put them up to it. Magnuson waffled for a while, then came out against the program.

There were some in the Senate who said that Jackson was too pushy on the ABM, that he pushed so hard that it would hurt him later. Some predicted that his direct lobbying for the missile program would cost him votes later on his state's pet project, the supersonic transport.

But, as the day of the showdown arrived, Jackson predicted that the ABM would squeak through the Senate by a 51 to 49 vote. And he was exactly right.

Scoop Jackson had won his victory in the Senate, but

301

some wondered if it might not prove to be a Pyrrhic victory. The ABM, like the SST, still had years of congressional hurdles to clear. And, as Jackson entered his 1970 election year, the ABM had given his antiwar antagonists one more target at which to throw their darts.

PURGE

MIDTOWN MANHATTAN WAS tinsel-bedraped for Christmas and the shoppers, even in their winter greatcoats, bustled to keep warm. The toys danced enticingly in the windows of F.A.O. Schwartz and the almost obscenely rich gems twinkled innocently through the plate glass of Tiffany's.

It was six days before Christmas. Among the bustling shoppers were those who were, of all things, on their way to a political meeting. The setting was unusual—the mod, radical-chic East Side apartment of Gloria Steinem, occasional author, occasional political activist, and constant, outspoken advocate of the women's liberation movement.

The visitors to Miss Steinem's apartment on the evening of December 19, 1969, were welcomed into what essentially was one large, stylish room. The ceiling was twelve to fourteen feet high. On one wall was a Cesar Chavez poster, on another a Bob Kennedy placard. Off to one corner of the room was an entrance to the kitchen. Off to another a platform had been built out from the wall, about halfway between the floor and the ceiling. A series of steps led up the platform, which served as Miss Steinem's bedroom. Beneath the platform was a cubicle that was decorated almost like a sultan's den—rich drapes, fluffy pillows, and weird, off-color lighting. Perfect, one of the guests observed, for smoking.

About thirty-five people were expected, so there was no chance to stand on formality. The guests would sit on the floor, but no one would object to that in this kind of meeting. As the guests began to arrive, their names read like a *Who's Who* of the Establishment of the political Left—those who still chose to make their moves within the system . . . .

John Kenneth Galbraith, a former Kennedy ambassador, hardly a youngster now, but a man who was striving to establish his credentials as the resident intellectual of the Movement.

Sam Brown, a young antiwar activist who had achieved a national reputation for his organization of the two Vietnam Moratoriums just months earlier.

Allard Lowenstein, an antiwar crusader, just elected to Congress from New York, the man most generally credited with engineering the fall of President Lyndon Johnson in 1968.

Peter Edelman and Adam Walinsky, two of the late Robert F. Kennedy's brightest and more left-leaning assistants.

The list rambled on through Ted Van Dyk, a former Hubert Humphrey aide, who had decided it was time to turn further left; Don Green, an organizer of Referendum '70; Curtis Ganz, Stanton Gottlieb . . . .

They were gathered together now in the unlikely setting of Gloria Steinem's posh pad to map political strategy for the congressional elections of 1970. Disorganized, hamstrung by their own petty, intramural dissensions, they nevertheless had felt the euphoria of near-victory in the strange political year of 1968. The Left had elected few of its own, but it had felled the mighty, sent its hate symbol into exile on the Pedernales. Banishing a President of the United States had been no mean accomplishment. Organized now and backed by sufficient money, who was to say what could be accomplished in 1970?

This was not a meeting of wild-eyed radicals. No one, surely, would put mild-mannered Ted Van Dyk in that category. Nor Don Green, who was an organizer not a disorganizer. Nor any of the others. No revolutionaries here. But they were of varying degrees of militancy. Some talked about electing their own in 1970. Others spoke of purging their hate symbols—without regard to whether their replacements would be better or worse.

Sam Brown was among the militants. He spoke of defeating Hubert Humphrey, who would run for the Senate in 1970. Humphrey, the great liberal leader of the 1950s, had supported the war. *Hateful man*. And Brown spoke of opposing Adlai Stevenson III, liberal son of a great liberal, who was running for the Senate in Illinois. Stevenson had opposed the November Vietnam Moratorium, a protest that had been taken over by the radicals. *Hateful man*.

John Kenneth Galbraith, a towering man who seemed to dominate the meeting both physically and verbally, was among the militants. He had been talking for some time about purifying the Democratic Party. The party had come to greatness in the 1930s because it had opened its arms to a vast cross-section of the American electorate. It had taken in the poor, the deprived, the workers, the Southerners, and the left-intellectuals who wanted to build a new world. But now, in the waning years of a terrible war that seemed to be the product of the great Democratic coalition, Galbraith wanted a purge. He wanted a new party, built along ideological lines. Fit the mold of its ideology, or get out.

It was inevitable, in this kind of meeting, that the name of Henry M. Jackson would be mentioned. "Scoop Jackson is one of my best friends," Galbraith intoned, pausing for emphasis, his perpendicular form looming over the rest of the group. "That's what politicians say when they are about to stab somebody in the back."

Scoop Jackson, supporter of the New Deal and the Fair Deal and the New Frontier and the Great Society, marked now for a purge from the Left? Not everyone in the room agreed with that logic. Van Dyk, asked later what he would think of Lowenstein establishing residence in Seattle to run against Jackson, had a caustic reply: Lowenstein could be assured of 2½ percent of the vote. And Green, looking around for profitable places to invest Referendum '70s meager finances, rejected Washington State. Jackson, he concluded, looked like an 85-15 winner. But even among the less militant, the rejection of the Jackson purge came more out of frustrated realism than it did out of philosophical disagreement. Jackson looked unbeatable and, in some ways, that intensified the Left's animosity toward him. So did the fact that he was a liberal. Green would say later that Jackson, the liberal warhawk, was "the most hateful" of them all. L. Mendel Rivers, Strom Thurmond and their ilk were hopeless. But Jackson was a liberal and *still* he thought all those awful thoughts, all those awful Cold War, hot-war thoughts. To the Left, Jackson personified the classicly evil Democrat—so deceptively liberal on some issues, so strong in his support of the war. They would have relished defeating Jackson, above all others, in 1970.

After about two hours of meandering talk—and few, if any, hard conclusions—the meeting broke up for a buffet dinner. Then, after climbing the stairs to the platform bedroom to retrieve their overcoats, the participants pushed back out into the cold Manhattan night.

CHAPTER 14

THE YEAR OF THE
MARSHMALLOW

THE MAN'S VOICE was half-shocked, half-pleading as he spoke into the microphone, trying to reason with the emotional convention crowd. "If you reject Senator Jackson, you will throw out eighteen years of seniority in the United States Senate. It will make us, not him, look like a jackass."

There were groans, applause, derision. The din increased and, shouting above it all, other delegates at other microphones in the hall clamored for recognition. *Mister Chairman. Mister Chairman!*

Democratic conventions, especially those in Washington State, have a tradition of raucousness and unpredictability. But as it unfolded in Seattle that May afternoon, the angry 1970 King County convention was making startling history. Democrats of the most populous county in the state were inflicting a stinging blow on Henry Jackson, the most popular politician, the greatest vote-getter in his state's political history.

The vote was on a resolution to endorse Jackson for re-election. As it went down to defeat, the new liberals were chanting its joyous requiem: *Peace! Now! Peace! Now!* With an elated flourish, they administered the *coup de grace* to tradition: They voted, 508 to 485, to endorse

Carl Maxey, the man opposing Jackson in the Democratic primary election for the Senate.

Two middle-aged women delegates could stand it no longer. Fury in their faces, they flounced out of the convention hall even before the voting ended. "Just ridiculous. Just absolutely ridiculous," snapped one. Behind them a teen-age delegate stood and grinned toward the balcony, flashing the peace sign and a great grin of triumph to a half-dozen long-haired friends watching from the gallery.

Jackson wasn't in the midst of the public agonies of 1968. When the bitter juices spilled over, rising from the assassinations, the war frustrations, the ghetto bitterness, other politicians like Hubert Humphrey became the targets of the vituperation. Spasms of the agony recurred in 1969 and late that year there were massive moratorium demonstrations to protest the persistent killing in Vietnam. But when spring crept out of the winter of 1970, with about 450,000 United States troops still in Vietnam, Sam Brown, young coordinator of the Vietnam Moratorium, theorized that street-protest demonstrations were losing their effectiveness. The election year of 1970 was to be a year for political action.

Brown, the boy-general of Gene McCarthy's frustrated young army, went into Spokane in March to tell a New Left gathering at Gonzaga University that Jackson should be defeated. The senator, he said, gave unlimited support to the Vietnam war and encouraged a war-based economy in his home state.

Already there was anti-Jackson political action simmering in the state, born of the McCarthy campaign. Antiwar political activists were organized in the Washington Democratic Council. Mostly they were young, but there were veteran, dedicated liberals among them, too. They had already criticized Jackson for, as the WDC put it, his dedication "to keep alive a fearful mood of Cold War confrontation and his eagerness to feed the military-industrial complex a lion's share of the available resources."

Locked out of a convention hall in Chicago in 1968, the New Left was moving into the political system and, in Washington State, it was well organized and clearly targeted on Jackson.

Some of the students were awaiting Jackson when he went into the home state of Gene McCarthy and Hubert Humphrey that spring. The occasion was a routine speech at Mankato State University about the military-industrial complex. In his earnest, straight style, Jackson talked about the Russian menace, meanwhile trying to ignore some of the contemptuous sardonic sounds from students in the front row.

During the after-speech question-and-answer session, one of the students stood and ceremoniously read from a scrawled indictment written in the dogmatic language of the new campus radicals: "Senator Jackson," the young man began in a pompous jury-room tone, "you represent The Boeing Company. We the people of the United States find you guilty of aiding and abetting inflationary war policies . . . "

Jaw set, Jackson stared into space, his face a portrait of cold impatience and boredom.

" . . . and present American priorities, which put profits above the needs and desires of United States citizens and other peoples around the world, no matter how much suffering results. You are guilty!"

Then it began: One, two, then several tiny white missiles arced toward the speaker. They landed with fluffy little bounces around Jackson. *Marshmallows*. The students in the front rows were tossing *marshmallows*, pulling them out of bags carried into the auditorium. During the barrage, the kids began their standard antiwar, antidraft chant. *Hell, no! We won't go!* Jackson, the Senate's powerful advocate of the ABM, raised his personal missile defenses: Elbows and forearms lifted to shield his face from the marshmallow blizzard. It ended in seconds. The front row students arose and left the hall, while some of the back row students muttered angry sounds at them.

The senator got in a parting retaliation as they stalked out: "I'll defend your right to do that, but in the Soviet Union, I'd like to see you have the opportunity to do what you just did to me."

Earth Day came in April, a day to salute and exhort the cause of environmental protection. As father of important national parks and author of the bold new National Environmental Policy Act, Jackson expected and got special attention. But the day was stained by dissenters again. As he talked to some high-school students on the University of Washington campus, some older students pushed into the hall and heckled him. At Washington State University at Pullman, near Spokane, he was marshmallowed again. A girl at the door of the auditorium explained the significance of the marshmallows she was handing out: "They're to fight noise pollution. It's better to throw marshmallows than bombs."

He was under a stinging political attack now, too. "The enlightened and creative work of the young Henry M. Jackson of years ago, who cared for people and their environment, is only a memory," said Carl Maxey. "Senator Jackson is pampered by the Pentagon and coddled by big business. He has become another power-oriented politician." Maxey was the announced challenger for the Democratic nomination for Jackson's Senate seat. There were assorted other candidates, but Maxey, a 45-year-old black attorney from Spokane, was the principal threat if, indeed, Jackson had any threat at all. The Spokane man resigned as chairman of the Washington Democratic Council to wage the campaign. "I kind of like the guy," Maxey said of Jackson at the outset. During Jackson's 1952, 1958, and 1964 campaigns Maxey had worked for the senator. Thereafter he split with Jackson over the war- and defense-spending issues.

Reared in an orphanage, Maxey worked his way through school, attended Gonzaga University where he was a light-heavyweight collegiate boxing champion, then finished law school at Gonzaga. With his graying hair, chocolate skin, and broad smile, he had a deceptive Uncle Tom appearance. But his talk was tough. His "I-kind-of-like-the-guy" comment was quickly forgotten. He raked Jackson with sometimes brutal criticism. "There is an old saying that even a cat can look at a king," he said, "and this black cat has looked at King Henry Jackson and seen a political schizophrenic. His advice to bomb North Vietnam, to send more troops to Southeast Asia, escalated the war from 30,000 or so advisors to over one-half million men. It has meant to the American citizens over 40,000 men killed, 275,000 wounded."

Political reality said that Maxey was, indeed, looking at a king in his own world of politics. Jackson was virtually unbeatable. Even Maxey acknowledged that, although he held the new wishful hope of the New-Left underdog: "Remember what happened to Lyndon Johnson."

Jackson seemed always to be campaigning at home, if

not in person through his ministrations and the work of a loyal, efficient staff in Washington. When the federal government decided to retreat from its Atomic Energy Commission activities in the Tri-Cities, in the southeastern part of the state, Jackson put together an atomic-industrial diversification plan which put private corporations into the area to take over government facilities. It saved the economy of the region. He had a similar hand in good works everywhere in the state—dams, irrigation projects, parks, industries, roads, federal power. When the proposed nerve-gas shipment stirred sharp controversy, other political figures protested loudly. But it was Jackson who announced that the shipment was canceled. He was the architect of the plan to enable the city of Seattle to acquire Fort Lawton as a park. Jackson obviously worries occasionally about his military image; at Fort Lawton he converted a military base to a park.

All across his diversified state Jackson built a lively personal identification. He regularly went into the little towns of the cattle country east of the Cascades, the mining districts, the fruit-growing valleys, and wheatlands. West of the mountains he toured the lumber and fishing communities and the industrial centers. When an eastern newsman went west to cover Jackson's campaign, he was startled by the informality. Small-town voters showed no deference to the vast political power of one of the Senate's most influential men. When he strolled down the street or rode in a parade, they greeted him—"*Hi Scoop*"—as though he were a neighbor.

During a campaign stop at his Everett home, Jackson invited the reporter into the kitchen for a piece of hot apple pie. Mrs. Solie, the Jacksons' maternal Norwegian housekeeper, bakes "the best apple pie in the world," the senator

312

said. The newsman found himself sitting in the kitchen eating apple pie and listening to Scoop Jackson talk about his boyhood. For a cynical eastern newspaperman it almost was too rich a dose of Americana. But it was the *real* Jackson, he concluded. When everyone had left the kitchen, Jackson, unnoticed, slipped back into the pantry to give Mrs. Solie a hug and a kiss—and tell her the pie was better than ever.

During an election year Jackson is a regular passenger aboard the "Red-Eye Special": The evening jet flight whisks him from the end-of-the-week business in the Senate to a busy weekend of appearances and politicking in his home state. Late Sunday night he is flying eastward again to an early-morning arrival in Washington and another week of business. He uses the time-zone change for one of his rare lines of humor during a speech at home: "You know, when I get up out here, it's six o'clock by my watch, but it's only three o'clock by your time. And you know there's nothing more frustrating for a politician than to go outside in the morning and find there's nobody to shake hands with."

Through the years Jackson's political coattails became magical. In 1964 he spent most of his re-election campaign working for a slate of Democrats seeking seats in the House of Representatives—Floyd V. Hicks of Tacoma, Lloyd Meeds of Everett, Brock Adams of Seattle, and Tom Foley of Spokane. Each won. Each acknowledged that Jackson's help was a major factor in his victory. For the first time since the Truman years, Democrats thus won a majority in Washington State's House delegation.

Foley said later that Jackson's help to the candidates that year was greater than anyone knew. Jackson used his own scheduled television time on Spokane TV stations to plug Foley's candidacy in the Fifth District. After Jackson sent out word he wanted financial help for the young candidate, Foley began receiving checks from donors in New York of whom he'd never heard. Foley tied his little-known name to the well-known name of Jackson in litera-ture and posters. For months after his election, Foley's office received mail addressed to "Congressman Jackson Foley." Yet, said Foley, Jackson never sought to extract anything in return from the new House members—"not even a vote on the ABM." Jackson's code is never articu-lated, but it is certain: He gives loyalty and he expects loyalty. He can forgive a vote opposite to his own ideas, just as the Southerners understood his liberal votes in his early days in the Senate. But he becomes impatient if the defector is noisy about it. When Brock Adams, one of the beneficiaries of the Jackson coattails, became an outspoken dove on Vietnam, the Jackson-Adams relationship became strained.

In more placid campaign years one of the nastiest things critics said about Jackson was that he voted liberal in Washington, then came home and talked conservative. But Maxey's rhetoric was roasting in 1970: "Our destiny is in the hands of fat contractors, bellicose generals, and a Na-poleonic little senator who can juggle bombs and ballots, conservation and nerve gas, on a platform of a continued draft that kills sons and brothers . . . The big issue is peace. Leaving peace in the hands of Henry Jackson is like leaving a lion to guard the Sunday roast."

Maxey's audiences were small and often too young to vote—until the movement of United States troops into Cambodia stirred new disorders and demonstrations. Na-tional Guard gunfire killed four students at Kent State and the never-healed wounds of American society were bleeding anew. Protest marchers moved in waves into downtown Seattle through a week of turbulence. Nearly ten thousand people converged in front of the United States Courthouse for a day of mourning of the Kent State victims. They cheered Maxey as he urged the impeachment of President Nixon and Senator Jackson. But, instead of growing into a new-direction political wave, the agony days of spring, 1970, turned out to be only an emotional spasm which gradually ended with the end of the military incursion into Cambodia.

Kent State had been the prelude to the King County Democratic convention which repudiated Jackson. Afterward he angrily dismissed the endorsement given his opponent. The convention, he said, had been rigged. "The real convention will be held in November and I have no doubt about the outcome."

In reality, the county convention was not rigged nor was it an emotional binge. Most of the regular Democrats underestimated the antiwar Democrats and the organizational determination of the Washington Democratic Council. The dissenters moved aggressively into precinct caucuses—in much the same way Barry Goldwater's people worked in 1964—and seized a surprising block of power in several counties.

In Kitsap County, home of the big Bremerton Navy Yard and a Jackson political stronghold, the Democratic convention approved a resolution which subtly needled Jackson on civil rights: It denied support to any candidate belonging to an Elks Lodge or any group with a whites-only membership policy. Its backers made a point of the fact that Jackson was an Elk.

The state Democratic convention in Spokane that July

was, for Jackson, an event that he would just as soon have avoided. The antiwar movement was making gains and, although he had no real political trouble, the inevitable squabble could be another embarrassment. But he went to deliver an introductory speech for his longtime colleague, Warren Magnuson, the convention keynoter. The schedule was changed to allow the two senators to appear on Saturday, rather than Friday as originally planned. A Friday appearance would have put Jackson and Maxey on stage the same day and Jackson was doggedly following a plan to avoid any joint appearance with his caustic foe. The schedule-juggling was one of those awkward little maneuvers which sometimes become conspicuous and Maxey exploited it. Standing alone on the stage that Friday, he asked mournfully, scornfully: "Where is Henry Jackson? Henry, wherever you are—let's debate the issues."

Police in civilian dress were backstage and in the gallery of the convention hall to keep an eye on the action when Jackson was introduced the next day. There was the explosive sound of shouts, chanting, and band music. Jackson demonstrators, joined by Maxey demonstrators, were surging in the aisles and then some were on the stage, chanting, surrounding the senators and their wives. Magnuson grinned. He reveled a little in the old-style political fun. Maybe this was the New Left versus the Establishment, but it was like other Democratic conventions to Magnuson —fun. Jackson's face was a frozen mask. Doves pushed in front of him and chanted. *Peace! Now!* Rival demonstrators elbowed each other and there was a brief moment of tension. But then they were hoisting and pumping their Maxey and Jackson signs for the TV cameras. When the cameramen had enough footage, the TV lights went out and so did the enthusiasm.

316

Magnuson's rollicking, avuncular come-together speech ended in a fumbling, afterthought endorsement of Jackson. Jackson, unhappy that Maggie hadn't given him ringing praise, had a look of frozen fury on his face as they left the stage, past backstage police wearing "Pigs is Beautiful" sweatshirts.

Through the rest of the day in the Spokane Coliseum, perspiring delegates struggled over planks in the party platform, fighting issue after issue which all seemed to indict Jackson. The senator's lieutenants lost every skirmish. Antiwar delegates were there in surprising strength in many of the thirty-nine county delegations. They voted for a troop pullout from Vietnam by June 30, 1971, and urged amnesty for draft-dodgers. They even approved the "Elks Club Resolution" which would withhold support of Democrats who belong to organizations with a membership policy of racial bias. "I'm an Elk and a good Democrat and, goddammit, I'm going to stick with both," grumbled a state legislator.

Ultimately the state convention meant little. Its platform, like other platforms, would not have any impact on any great issues. But Maxey embraced the peace-now, antidraft actions and said the party had, in effect, endorsed him. A convention rule had prohibited an outright endorsement of either Maxey or Jackson. As the day's battles ended, the Democratic "regulars" were seething, just as they had been at the King County convention in May.

A tall, gray-haired man, skinny-legged in Bermuda shorts, ran to a microphone and explained joyously: "It is a great victory." He was John Stenhouse, Maxey's successor as chairman of the Washington Democratic Council. It *was* a victory. Two years after Chicago, critics of the war and defense spending had gone into the political system and

317

scored a great psychological victory over their hated hawk.

But their day of victory was in time forgotten by nearly everyone—except Jackson.

Angered by rebukes from within his own party, Jackson wanted a big win—a crushing victory. It appeared possible that he might get it, too. Moderates and many Republicans —who can cross over to vote for Democrats in Washington's blanket primary election—thought Jackson was getting shabby treatment from the dissidents.

When Jackson and his wife rode in an Olympia parade, a young man ran up to their convertible, splattered them with liquid garbage and ran away. "Now what's the sense of that?" Jackson asked later in his typical schoolmarmish way. "Just no manners at all."

When he showed up for a dinner appearance in Centralia one night, police had a ring of protection around the senator and his wife and officers patrolled outside the restaurant during Jackson's speech. The newspaper office in Centralia had received a telephone call that there would be an attempt on Jackson's life. Days later the telephone caller, a one-time mental patient, surrendered at Western Washington State Hospital. The man also had written a letter to the *Daily Olympian*, describing a plot to assassinate seventy-two American political leaders, the "ardent advocates of militarism." For days afterward, though, a police officer spent several nights on guard in the Jackson home in Everett. "It didn't worry us, really," Mrs. Jackson said, but life was far from pleasant.

The heckling, the abuses, the exasperating marshmallow incidents, the guerrilla political tactics, were commonplace in America's 1968 campaign, but they were unprecedented insults to Jackson in his home state. His view of dissenters grew more bitter.

Extremists, he said more frequently, were threatening the democratic process—taking the law into their own hands. It became, he said, a tyranny of the minority over the majority. He told the State Labor Council convention that the New Leftists were hostile to organized labor because "they feel you aren't as well educated and informed as they are." He added that "this small, tiny group does not speak for the majority. It's time for you to stand up and be heard." The labor council stood up and voted Jackson a labor endorsement. Such appeals jangled the ears of the liberals in the state, echoing President Nixon's "silent majority" strategy, but Jackson would make the same point over and over again—or adapt it—in speeches along his own Presidential campaign trail starting a year later.

"I have said over and over again that I'm proud of the fact that during my term in the Senate I opposed both McCarthys."

That was Jackson's proud claim to political moderation.

That first McCarthy—Joe—went into Seattle to speak against Jackson only days before an election in 1952. Dark-jowled, menacing, ascending to the zenith of his power, Joe McCarthy sought to beat Jackson with charges that he was soft on communism.

Now, days before Jackson's 1970 primary election, Gene McCarthy stood onstage in Seattle, to attack Jackson for leading the United States down a road of militarism with a blind fear of the Russians.

Gene McCarthy had been introduced to the crowd and it was like 1968 all over again. The youngsters stood and cheered, shining faces turned upward toward their handsome, gray-haired, poetic leader. He looked back at them with a melancholic smile. Two girls laid their flowers on a chair, to free their hands for clapping. The master of ceremonies had said it was unusual for a senator to come into a state to campaign against another senator of his own party, but in this case it was Henry Jackson—a special menace. The kids' cheers lapsed into their peace chant, then they quieted as McCarthy began to speak.

He was here, he said in his soft voice, because "the campaign against Henry Jackson is one that has some very special significance, I think. The decision to go into Vietnam was not one that was made in a vacuum. It was not one in which he or I or anyone in the Senate was in any way consulted, so far as I know. So then why should he, in any way, be held responsible?

"Well, for two reasons: One, he more or less endorsed it after the act. But more serious than that, I think, is that we have had going on for nearly twenty years in the Senate of the United States, in the Congress of the country, and in politics, the building of a kind of climate and a complex out of which the decision to go into Cuba very easily arose; out of which the decision to invade the Dominican Republic very easily arose, and out of which the decision for an escalated war in Vietnam also arose.

"A pattern of thought and a pattern of action for which I think anyone who is in the Congress those roughly twenty years—and I was there for twenty-two of those years—must bear some responsibility—either for his failure to see what was happening and raise a challenge . . . Or for his contribution to its development."

The buildup went on, McCarthy said. "ABMs, ICBMs, C5As, and TFXs—almost anything you give an initial to, some people will vote for." The new name of the game is defense. And the argument is deterrent. And protecting the deterrent.

"Henry Jackson and some others in the Senate would

not feel safe if the sky was black with strategic bombers, if there were so many nuclear submarines in the ocean that they were running into each other . . . They would still say they were not enough."

But, McCarthy confided in a quiet voice, there still are other gaps. Amazon Indians have more blowpipes and poison darts than we do. The audience was laughing. " . . . We're short of catapults, short of crossbows. And pikes and shields and any number of things." But don't tell Henry Jackson or he'll worry, or, worse, he'll offer an amendment to a defense-spending bill.

McCarthy's speech trailed off in bitter whimsy to an uncertain ending, as McCarthy's speeches often did. He looked tired. It was after ten P.M. on the Pacific Coast and after one P.M. by his watch. It also was very late for Carl Maxey. Only about 2,500 people had turned out to hear Gene McCarthy and Carl Maxey that evening. McCarthy was politician enough to know that nothing much was going to happen to Scoop Jackson this year.

Maxey had said that his "referendum for peace" in 1970 might make a good showing against the invincible Jackson. His forecast grew gloomier as the election day neared. He confided privately on election day he might do no better than fifteen percent of the vote. His estimate was close. Jackson's crushing victory count was 497,000 to 79,000— an 87 percent victory.

The antiwar critics' barrage of fury had bounced off Jackson's political fortress like marshmallows.

With the primary election over, the only thing left was a race against a Republican and, for Jackson, that was easy. The winner of the scarcely noticed Republican primary election was Charlie Elicker. Likable, bouncy, easygoing

Elicker, a 43-year-old state senator, wore a moustache, metal-rimmed glasses, and he looked strikingly like Theodore Roosevelt. But he hadn't charged into the race against Jackson. He was dragged into it by Republican State Chairman C. Montgomery (Gummie) Johnson and by Dan Evans, the young liberal Republican governor.

It wasn't easy finding a candidate. And once a candidate was found he seemed more hampered by Republicans than Democrats.

Johnson, the chairman, was an ardent liberal Republican, with deep misgivings about the Vietnam war. So he was especially eager to have a candidate oppose Jackson and, hopefully, keep Jackson tied up through the general election campaign so that the senator's coattails wouldn't carry too many Democrats into office.

Art Fletcher, an assistant secretary of labor and onetime Republican candidate for lieutenant governor, turned down a request that he run against Jackson. "That," quipped Fletcher, "would be like trying to climb Mount Rainier barefoot."

While the state Republican party was frantically trying to raise some money, Johnson learned to his horror that some of the top party men were putting up money for Jackson. Clandestinely, they agreed to raise $100,000 for the senator, Johnson grumbled. But a major Republican money-raiser, William Reed, top executive of the Simpson Logging Co., said it was only about $50,000 and it was intended to ensure Jackson's renomination. Reed said many Republicans liked Jackson's views on defense and foreign policy. It was not a traitorous act to help Jackson, Reed insisted: Donors were guaranteed Jackson wouldn't use any of the money to help Democrats in other races. (Eventually Jackson turned most of the funds, unused, back to the G.O.P. donors.)

Gummie Johnson was no admirer of Spiro Agnew, but the state chairman badly needed money for the state G.O.P. treasury. He tried to get Agnew to come into Washington State. Agnew's "effete snobs" and "supercilious sophisticates" speeches were inflammatory, yet they lured crowds and party money to Republican banquets. But Agnew declined to go into Washington State, saying his schedule was too crowded. "He's been to Wyoming at least three times since then," Johnson ruefully complained later.

Early in the year President Nixon lavished praise on Jackson at a banquet of the Veterans of Foreign Wars. Presenting the VFW congressional award to the senator, Nixon enthused to the audience that Jackson was "a man who understands the threat to peace and freedom in the world as well as any man I know . . . He understands national defense and is not afraid to speak out for it, understands national security and is not afraid to speak out for it . . . He is a man who is a great credit to his party and to America."

Such celebration from the Republican President caused the state chairman and the governor to wince. Johnson, a tough, plucky politician with a bright sense of humor, confessed later that he was getting a little paranoid about it all. He told the story of a frustrating day he spent in Washington . . . .

. . . Walking down the corridor of the Old Senate Office Building, Johnson encountered Senator John Tower, a Texas Republican and a great pal of the Pentagon.

"Hi, Gummie, how are you?" said Tower. "Haven't seen you in a long time . . . Say, you're not running anybody against my buddy Scoop, are you?"

Later in the day Johnson was at the White House talking with John Ehrlichman, a former Seattle attorney, the President's chief domestic advisor. "Say, you're not running anybody against Scoop are you?"

That evening, at a White House reception, Johnson came before President Nixon in the receiving line. The President greeted him and asked, "Gummie, you're not running anybody against my buddy Scoop are you? . . ."

Any humor in the situation faded for local Republicans when Jackson made the announcement that the nerve gas would not be shipped across the state. The governor had, along with Republican Governor Tom McCall of Oregon, been the first to protest the shipment. Other public officials, both Republicans and Democrats, had protested, too. Jackson was conspicuously quiet, yet when the President decided to cancel the shipment, he telephoned Jackson, allowing Jackson to make the joyous announcement to the press— and in an election year.

Johnson murmured unkind words about "the illicit love affair" between Nixon and Jackson.

"It's frustrating to have a guy like Jackson get news announcements and breaks when he just hasn't been involved to any great degree at all in the issue," the governor said. A governor's aide told of complaining to Herb Klein about it: "Klein told me we've got to take good care of Jackson. He's our friend among the Democratic senators. Evans snapped that Nixon, by his solicitude, might inadvertently be building his Democratic pal in the Senate into a possible Presidential opponent.

State Republicans dredged up $25,000 in cash and $25,-000 in pledges for the hopeless race against Jackson. With that as his meager campaign kitty, Elicker reluctantly agreed to take on Jackson.

Elicker was an articulate, quick-witted, Phi Beta Kappa

sacrificial lamb. A law-school graduate, he had decided to give up the practice of law and chose instead to run a nursing home on quiet Bainbridge Island, near Seattle. Many young people who worked for Maxey during the primary election campaign came over to help Elicker. With their help, with the help of other doves and, with maybe a wayward Republican who still wasn't for Jackson, Elicker figured he might make it a contest.

Capitalizing on his resemblance to Teddy Roosevelt, Elicker wistfully adopted the obvious one-word campaign slogan: "Charge!" He charged at Jackson the best way he could, with some serious campaigning, but mostly humor.

Seriously, he said, Jackson has outlived his political usefulness. For years he brought home the public works, advocated the military hardware to stop the Russians, and still the American economy expanded. Now the economy is hurting and national priorities are warped. "When you can't find the money to carry out adequate health programs and meet the problems of the cities and the poor, but you can afford to spend one million dollars per bombing sortie in Vietnam, I think a lot of people are beginning to say, 'There is a limit to what we can do,' " Elicker said.

Tongue in cheek, Elicker poked fun at Jackson's opposition to revenue sharing and the senator's enthusiasm for defense. Perhaps Jackson would go for a compromise, he suggested: federal strategic weapons for local governments —"weapons systems . . . for beefing up our local first-strike defense." If a crowd at a Lawrence Welk music festival got out of hand anywhere in the State of Washington, he mused, "missiles armed with nitrogen oxide could be launched from as far away as Puget Sound to deal with this threat to our statewide economy."

Because Jackson avoided the marshmallow threat of college audiences, Elicker made it a point to get to almost every campus in the state. He opposed oil drilling in Puget Sound on the grounds that it posed an environmental threat. After Jackson declined to take a stand on the grounds it was a state issue, Elicker tweaked the senator's painful memory. At a press conference the Republican handed out marshmallows. Jackson is like a marshmallow, he said— "round and firm on the hero issues, but when you squeeze him on the hard issues—like oil drilling in the Puget Sound —you don't get a sound."

A tense campaigner during the primary campaign, Jackson grew more relaxed and affable in the race against Elicker and became almost amiable toward his opponent. Once Elicker's lonely campaign trail took him to Wenatchee, where he had few friends and no apparent support. It was solid Jackson country. When Elicker arrived at a reception honoring Hu Blonk, managing editor of the Wenatchee *Daily World*, the man near the door who greeted Elicker was Jackson. The senator put an arm around Elicker's shoulder and took him around to introduce him to everyone. "This is Charlie Elicker," said Jackson. "He and I have a little race going on."

Jackson ploddingly campaigned against President Nixon's economic policies and for his own environmental ideas. He advocated a standstill ceasefire in Vietnam. Meanwhile, a well-financed, well-organized mechanical campaign went on for Jackson. Campaign TV spots featured Jackson and Grand Coulee Dam, Jackson and the Columbia River which he helped save from the threat of diversion to the Southwest; and Jackson and his family strolling through the lovely forests which he helped save.

Jackson campaign brochures were laced with solid middle-class appeals. "A quiet, hard-working studious man . . . Maybe it's because of his Norwegian ancestry. Or because he grew up in western Washington where the land was a living and making a living was a tough, full-time job...."

An array of special citizens' committees for Jackson sent out tens of thousands of letters to selected mailing lists. The Residential Construction Committee sent letters to home-builders, the Veterans Committee, the National Service Committee, the Sportsmen Committee, and others wrote to their constituents, telling how Scoop Jackson served them. Simultaneously, Jackson's Forestry Resources Committee wrote to timber-industry leaders about Jackson's interest in them, while his Conservation Committee wrote to environmentalists about the man who sponsored and supported "the major environmental and conservation legislation of the decade."

Near the end there was a marvelous moment along the campaign trail which suggested to Jackson that he was, indeed, the man of all the people—or all the political people, at least. During a testimonial luncheon sponsored by the Teamsters Union in Seattle he stood there while the men serenaded him. They sang special lyrics to the tune of Hello Dolly: "You do it big, Henry. This we dig, Henry . . . . " The voices, mixed faltering tenors and wobbling baritones—but all fortissimo—came from an astonishing assortment of political VIPs. Arnie Weinmeister, burly ex-pro football player and boss of the Teamsters, was elbow to elbow with Norton Clapp, top man of the Weyerhaueser industrial complex, a Republican fat cat. And Brock Adams, the liberal Democratic dove congressman, sang on with Charles O. Carroll, longtime king of King County Republican politicians. *Hello Henry. Well, Hello Henry. . . .* They sang on—political tigers of the left, right, middle. Jackson—architect of consensus, middle-ground, something-for-everyone, Mister Straight, personality politics in his state—beamed. The grinning impresario of the remarkable show was Ed Donohoe, the mischievous Teamster journalist who once peevishly had branded Jackson as Senator Hotspur.

Before the polls closed election day, the quotable Elicker issued a tongue-in-cheek reassurance to everyone: "I don't intend using the United States Senate seat as a step to higher office." As the polls closed at eight P.M., he opened a beer at the Elicker "victory" party in downtown Seattle. He took a sip. At 8:03 P.M. network television carried a bulletin: the NBC computer had just "re-elected" Henry Jackson of Washington to another term in the Senate by a seventy percent margin. Elicker shrugged at the electronicized wonders of democracy. He had another couple sips of beer. A local newscast said the Jackson victory margin was climbing past eighty-three percent. "Well," grinned Elicker, "it looked good there for a while."

After his usual election-night victory-appearance rounds of the television stations in Seattle, a happy Senator Jackson walked into one of his campaign workers' cocktail parties in the Olympic Hotel. Empty mixer bottles were stacking up behind the portable bar. Ashtrays overflowed. A spilled drink pooled on the coffee table. It was a scene typical of Democrats, crowded together, cocktails in hand, rejoicing in the victory of an election. Scoop's margin was going over 700,000 votes, someone said. Bigger than 1964. And that was a record for the state. Jackson eased through the sardine-pack of humans, shaking hands, beaming his boyish grin. Such a pleasant, engaging guy, they said. No one who *really knew him* could have said such nasty things about him as *they* had said this year. Someone offered him a drink.

Even those who have known him for years, never get quite used to Jackson's unchanging straightness. "No, thanks, no. Well, do you have some diet soda of some kind? If you've got it. No? Well, that'll be OK. I've got to be going. Thank you anyway."

He has a standardized maneuver at a cocktail party. After a late arrival, Jackson goes directly to the center of the room and does a slow rotary movement in the crowd, shaking hands. You never get trapped in a corner in an unending conversation that way, a Jackson-watcher once explained. Then he quickly departs. Jackson was on his way out when a reporter at the doorway asked him for a comment on his overpowering victory. His angry emotions had been held in check through the painful moments of the campaign. Now, in total triumph, he kept his exultant emotions in check. Jackson spoke slowly, quietly: "This wasn't a referendum on the war or a referendum on peace. Obviously thousands of people voted for me because of their judgment on several things. It had to be that way. I know there are more people than that who are very concerned about the war."

His voice grew very soft, almost inaudible over the noise of the cocktail party behind him. "I know a lot of, I suppose you'd call them, doves, voted for me."

He turned and quick-stepped down the hotel corridor, hurrying as though he were in mid-campaign.

Back in the room someone shushed the cocktail crowd. Another vote count was coming on television. Jackson now was an eighty-three percent winner—the biggest margin given to a senator in any contest in the nation. The Democrats reamplified their noisy political conversation again, talking about Jackson—cautious words, now—for higher office.

CHAPTER 15

TO NEVER BE PROVED
RIGHT

PLUNKING INTO A chair, one sportshirt collar poking out of
the neck of his light-blue pullover sweater, Henry Jackson
apologizes to the three television men for being late. He
had to go to the funeral of an old friend this morning, he
explains.

"Did you fellows get some cake and coffee?" The television crew nods. Mrs. Jackson had greeted them and served
them while they waited here in the glassed-in porch, a sun-
drenched place of lawn furniture, glass-topped tables, pot-
ted ferns, and flowers. "Did you get enough cake?" Yes,
plenty, they assure him.

The TV crew had been sent to Everett, to the senator's
home, from CBS, Los Angeles. Jackson is in the news these
days. His big re-election victory of 1970 catapulted him
into the group of men considered possible Democratic
nominees for the Presidency in 1972.

A compulsive organizer, Jackson outlines his ideas for
the day's filming—a few scenes around the house, "and
then I thought we'd take the kids down to the beach and
play catch. We can toss a ball back and forth. You know.
That'll give you some good pictures." The director winces
a little. It is a pretty corny idea.

"Peter." The senator calls his five-year-old son to him

and puts a hand on the boy's shoulder. "Peter, go find the ball, will you?"

Photographers like the Jackson face because of the way it can light up. It has been lighting up with almost unfailing precision through more than thirty years of public life—whenever a camera appears. In his steady war against overweight, he sometimes loses a skirmish with the lure of whipped cream. Then he becomes jowly and the face grows moon-shaped. But even then, there is the boy in the face—the evenness of eyes, nose, and mouth which inspired the Jimmie Stewart comparisons back during the McCarthy hearings in the early days of television. His hair is graying a little, but the hairline—as though he *wills* it to do so—refuses to retreat.

His eyes turn to his daughter, pretty Anna Marie, now eight. She sits solemnly, holding her cat, Punkin. Punkin examines the senator through unblinking green eyes. "It's a stray cat that Anna Marie found," he explains to his visitors. "A free cat. But do you know how much that free cat cost us, by the time we got through with its shots and medical bills and everything?" Eyes mirthful, his smile begins, signaling the approaching punchline. "A hundred and fifty dollars!" He laughs and the smile is finalized—seemingly ear-to-ear, dimpled, his narrowed eyes filled with giggles. Charlie Elicker, the Republican victim in Jackson's latest political victory, described it as "almost like an Eisenhower smile. It's that infectious." *A hundred and fifty dollars!* The TV crew is laughing along.

They haul cameras, mikes, and lights into the wood-paneled den where Jackson's desk sits before the inevitable backdrop of bookshelves. The titles are all politics and geography—*Alaska, The Vulnerable Russians, The Last of the Redwoods, Dateline Vietnam, Strategy for Tomorrow.*

331

Under the glare of the lights, Jackson fusses with some papers and the telephone rings, as though on cue. His home telephone number is unlisted, but somehow the caller has dialed it. It was a constituent with a routine question, so the senator asks the caller to phone his office in Seattle.

Mrs. Jackson arranges Scene Two for the camera: Peter does his "act"—a series of somersaults up the carpeted stairs. "That's the way he goes to bed every night," his mother explains. Her voice is a quiet one. There is a slight touch of a Texas accent in her speech. On camera, the little boy starts at the bottom step. He does a slow-bending somersault upward two stairs. Grinning, he hoists his body up the two steps and repeats the process. The scene ends as his father walks on camera, beaming at him, carrying the ball. Jackson ad libs a line of his own shooting script. "Let's go down to the beach and play catch."

When it was built, the house had a massive grand stairway, Jackson explains. But it was torn out by another owner, who installed a more compact stairway. "We kind of like the old things," he says, hands in pockets. Jackson's conversational style is relaxed and straight at the listener. Neither up nor down, his chit-chat with the cameramen is as it would be with the president of a corporation.

Over the mantel of the gracious white-and-gold living room is a framed photograph of the senator's father— Peter Jackson. Handsome, stern, the immigrant laborer has moved posthumously, in portrait, into the biggest home in the town.

Scene Three will be the family emerging from the house, through the sliding screen door of the sun porch. In the shooting script, they are on their way to the beach. The TV crew is outdoors setting up its gear in the driveway when three teen-age boys in denims, their hair rather long, stop on the distant sidewalk to watch. The director beckons the boys to cross the forty feet of lawn to the house. He wants them to move on camera to talk with the senator.

The family emerges from the house, Jackson carrying the ball, shepherding the children toward the car for the camera. "Senator," the director calls, "why don't you talk with those boys over there?" The director waves the boys to get into the scene. They approach. Then they are stopped short as the senator shouts, "Here, let's play catch," and abruptly throws the ball at one of the boys. A hard toss. The boys, twenty feet away, defensively join in a game of catch. The senator returns each throw with the ferocity, if not the grace, of a major-leaguer. The despairing cameraman has long since turned off his camera. The senator's impromptu throw kept the boys out of lens width.

But the director persists, urging Jackson and the boys to come together. They move warily into close range. Since the marshmallowing, the picketing, the obscenities, and the abuses of 1970, Jackson seems wary of young people— particularly those with long hair who may be loitering around his house. He isn't sure who they are or where they came from.

Stiffly he asks, "Are you boys from Everett?" They nod mutely. "What are you doing this summer?" *Mowin' lawns.* "Mowin' lawns, huh? You know, I used to have a paper route here. I delivered papers for years here in Everett." One of the boys said he had a paper route for a while. "Are you in Boy Scouts?" Two reply, *Boys Club. We're in Boys Club.* "Boys Club, huh? Well, that's the same thing. That's fine."

The teen-agers passed Jackson's test.

Ball tucked under his arm, the senator chats more easily, smiling, telling them about his Youth Conservation Corps bill and jobs for kids in the forests. . . .

. . . On the wall above his desk in the den, apart from all the books, the conservation trophies and the other political miscellany, is a small frame with a browning newspaper clipping under its glass. The article is from the July 2, 1927, Everett *Daily Herald*

> *Herald Carrier Has*
> *Perfect Record for 2*
> *Years; Wins Prize*
> *Henry Jackson, 15-year-old Herald Carrier, today was awarded his second prize for perfect service—service which The Herald believes has established a record for the Northwest and perhaps for the entire country. Henry delivered 74,880 Heralds without a single complaint for nondelivery. Furthermore he was never late calling for his papers . . . .*

Beyond the joy and pride that article brought to his parents, the clipping became a life manifesto of discipline and industriousness for the boy. Soon thereafter, he was the determined, earnest high-school commencement speaker lecturing about law enforcement, and later, the 26-year-old prosecuting attorney running gamblers out of the county.

In one corner of the county a group of pro-Hitler Silver Shirts were distributing hate-the-Jews literature, so the young prosecutor ran them out, too. "My mother always felt very strongly about the Jews. She said they were a minority and should be protected." As a young congressman he saw Buchenwald and as a senator he champions a militarily strong, independent Israel in a Middle East threatened by the historically persistent Russian appetite for influence.

"My two years as prosecutor had a profound influence on me in my analysis of people," he says. "It left me being suspicious of people. Not that I don't like people, but I learned to ask the tough questions. I found out that some of the people in town that I thought were the best turned out to be pretty bad eggs.

"The first case I handled was a classmate of mine . . . I sent him to the penitentiary, charged with embezzling funds from the Great Bear Logging Company—about $6,-000. He was a very fine guy. I went up to the jail and we talked it out. He pleaded guilty . . . After he got out of prison, I got him a job.

"You handle everything in the prosecutor's office. I always felt that one has to be just cold-blooded in analyzing people and what they're up to and what they're apt to do. Well, I think I have an inner toughness. I can be pretty tough when I want to be . . . Not everyone's an S.O.B. You've got to decide who really is. You don't listen to those people who come in and say, 'I demand this' or 'I demand that.' You don't just listen because they raise their voice. . . ."

Bobby Kennedy lay dying in Los Angeles and the news of the shooting, rousing Jackson from a deep sleep, jolted him into that rare emotional exclamation: *Oh, my God, the world has gone mad*. Even with the shock of that moment, it was an almost unbelievably passionate quote from Jackson, a steadfastly dispassionate man.

Months earlier the military operation known as the Tet offensive earned a place in military history books: It erased any last uncertain thought of military victory in Vietnam.

335

So the nation—or most of it, the polls said—began after 1968 to make a grudging accommodation with Vietnamization, Richard Nixon's gluey, prolonged political creep-out which, to frustrated opponents of the war, seemed only to compound the insanity. So the agony persisted. Concerned for years about the emotionalism of the rising peace movement, Jackson recoiled at the draft-card burning, the sacking of ROTC buildings on the campuses and the other upheavals which defiled traditions. The longhairs sometimes wore old army jackets, to mock the military—and waved Vietcong flags. And they called the police "pigs."

Only days after President Kennedy entered office in 1961, Jackson went to the White House to talk over a Russian problem which bothered him. Instead, he found the young President preoccupied about the Communist threat in Indochina. "I thought that the Russians would renew nuclear testing . . . But Kennedy turned the conversation to Vietnam . . . Maxwell Taylor had told him it was deteriorating." Constantly Vietnam seemed to grip the American attention through the years and deflect it from the constant threat—the Russians. "I still think what we tried to do out there in Southeast Asia was the right thing," Jackson said later. But Jackson despaired that Vietnam was encouraging neo-isolationism and compounding the abuses the military had to take. . . .

. . . On a Saturday night in late summer, 1970, Jackson strayed a little from his re-election-campaign trail. He might have gone to any number of events around the state where he could have wooed more registered voters. But instead he went to the officers-club banquet-hall at the Whidbey Island Naval Air Station on upper Puget Sound. After sipping a soft drink through the usual cocktail reception at the admiral's home, he went to the club where he was greeted reverently, as always, by the officers in their dress whites and gleaming gold trim and wives in formal gowns. Jackson's after-dinner speech was like a pep talk from a beleaguered coach to an embattled team at halftime of a game that's going very badly. "Some of us in Congress are willing to take the heat and see to it that the nation is kept strong," he said. "We are the trustees for those who serve our nation in uniform. You're not able to participate in the decisions. But we are there . . . We are proud of each and every one of you for being able to take it when you shouldn't have to take it."

They gave him his umpteenth Henry-Jackson-Appreciation Award and he handshook his way through the beaming crowd, through the club doorway, into the night. Jackson dropped into the rear seat of his sedan and sighed, "Some of these officers—the young ones, particularly— catch a lot of hell, you know, from the other guys their own age. You know, they just give the military a hell of a time. These guys feel it and it's really a morale problem."

During his ill-fated "referendum for peace," Carl Maxey said some hateful things: "Every time I see Jackson in that television commercial, walking in the woods with his child, I see the trees and I'm reminded of the coffins they are sending our children home in from Vietnam."

Attacks like that sharpened Jackson's hostility toward the dissenters. Within weeks after his re-election, while the national press watched his ascendancy as a Presidential contender, he said some tough things, too—both on foreign policy and on home issues.

The Russians are building up their stock of land-based ICBMs, he warned. And they're catching up to the United

States in Polaris-type missiles. "What the Soviets are designing is a nuclear straitjacket in which our hands are tied, while they are free to twist arms elsewhere in the world." It was the line he has used often. And to some listeners, the words were echoes of warnings about a missile gap a little more than a decade earlier when John Kennedy began a Presidential campaign. Jackson's audience this day was the World Affairs Council of Los Angeles. Ironically it was a luncheon at the Biltmore Hotel—the same hotel where almost a decade earlier exactly, Jackson waited hopefully for a call to be John Kennedy's running mate.

On a warm May evening in San Diego, he opened a campaign of stinging criticism against party leaders who, he said, "are having trouble hearing the voice of the people because the noise from the Absolute Left is so loud . . . I have fought extremists and totalitarians . . . As a liberal Democrat, I have fought the Radical Right . . . In my book those of the Absolute Left, who sneer at the common sense and ideals of the common man, are just as anti-liberal as the extremists of the Right and I don't intend to let them destroy the Democratic party."

The speech had been delivered in a raspy voice, because Jackson was suffering from a spring head cold, but the words reached and inflamed antiwar liberals everywhere. Later he struck the same note again—harder and louder— in a speech to labor leaders in New York. "Throughout my career I have been deeply concerned with the preservation of civil liberties and the right to dissent." He fought repression for years, he said. Now the repression is on campuses where the radicals break up classes and drive professors from the classrooms. There is repression in the neighborhoods where the elderly, the poor, the black, and other minorities are repressed by fear of lawlessness and disorder. The speech was a wholesale rebuke of radicals, disturbances, and the intellectuals and other Presidential Democrats, who, Jackson said, pander to them. It was his call for a return to good, old-fashioned values and old-fashioned law and order.

It was a cynical echo of Vice-President Agnew's inflammatory knock-a-few-heads-together rhetoric, Jackson's critics grumbled.

"It's a hard-hat kind of appeal to the 'real majority' of Middle Americans," wrote Richard Wilson in The Washington *Evening Star*. ". . . the un-young, un-poor, and un-black who account for 70 percent of the vote in Presidential elections. Thus Jackson can say he has no time for people who wave Vietcong flags and hail Vietcong victories, no patience with Left Wing intellectuals who have forgotten about the working man's interest and no sympathy for colleagues who scoff at law and order for the common man as merely a ruse for racism."

That San Diego speech, and *that New York speech*. Allard K. Lowenstein sat, chin in hand, and slowly wagged his head as he spoke the words. Lowenstein: Intellectual, liberal, antiwar Democrat. He had never met Jackson, but they knew of each other. Jackson acknowledged he was talking about people like Lowenstein. Perhaps it was Lowenstein more than anyone else who brought on the new political turbulence, the criticism of national defense, the talk of new priorities. The former New York congressman had been the man who began the dump-Lyndon-Johnson movement. Commiserating with his President through those tough, dark days, Jackson felt the antiestablishment upheaval personally.

It was one thing, said Lowenstein, for Jackson to gleefully embrace and advocate every weapons system the

Pentagon could dream up. That bellicosity was at least understandable because that was *Jackson*. But now to re-open a slowly-healing factionalism within America and the Democratic Party. . . .

"The Democratic party will be committing suicide if Henry Jackson gets on the national ticket," Lowenstein declared. Lowenstein sat in a restaurant in Seattle. He was in Jackson's home state to see if he could do *something* to block Jackson's aspirations for higher office. The dump-Johnson man now was thinking dump-Jackson.

Emmett Watson, writing in the Seattle *Post-Intelligencer*, responded to the new Jackson utterances with just one tiny, hurtful sting. He wrote *Spiro M. Jackson*.

Scoop Jackson, battler against the Right Wing of the fifties, thus was saluted as having come full cycle.

Almost unnoticed during the reaction to Jackson's Middle-Americans talk during 1971 was one of his typical countervailing actions. While raking the intellectuals and dissenters and extremists from other platforms, he delivered a quiet civil-liberties lecture in a Law Day speech at Wayne State University in Detroit. In the effort to control dissenters in the streets, government, often at the urging of the people, has a tendency to "twist old and cherished traditions of the law," he warned. Jackson criticized the District of Columbia Crime Bill and especially its preventive-detention provisions. "The illusion that we can buy social order at the expense of civil liberties has already been translated into statute by Congress," he complained.

The notion that preventive detention is aimed only at criminals and thus should be of no concern to law-abiding citizens is an example of "Orwellian Doublethink," Jackson said. Instead, it is "alien to all the principles of the rule of law . . . Such power is the first power of tyranny

. . . The power to detain citizens for crimes which they might commit is not far removed from the power to detain citizens for words they might speak or thoughts they might be thinking. . . ."

Thinking thoughts of running for the United States Senate, Henry Jackson, a solemn 39-year-old congressman, defined the central issue in 1951: *The greatest problem of the last half of the 20th century is to avert and avoid World War III.*

He won his victory the next year and entered the Senate. And, while other issues came and went, Jackson's Cold War philosophy about the Big War never changed, even though such political phrases became less fashionable. Not everyone—perhaps fewer than ever today—agree with his methods to "avert and avoid" war. Some people think his philosophy of the powerful military deterrent perpetuates a gripping war-fear hysteria which begets danger. But he has not changed.

Through his years in the Senate, the political memorabilia has accumulated in his office, Suite 137, Old Senate Office Building, giving it an old-shoe decor. The red-leather chairs are government issue. A nicked and scarred desk is piled with mail, clippings, and memos. In a slowly-automating Senate, where robot typing machines grind out letters to constituents and a machine signs a senator's name in ink, Jackson personally fusses with a great percentage of his mail.

More than a dozen photos hang on the office walls: His family . . . a favorite photo of Jackson swinging a bat toward the blur of an approaching softball with John Kennedy as catcher and Mike Mansfield as umpire . . . a warty picture of Abe Lincoln . . . one of those big, drab, bureaucratic photos of a Columbia River Dam. There are a few plastic models—surprisingly few—from the military-industrial complex—a Boeing helicopter and models of the SST, the B-52, and the Nautilus.

In the outer office is his staff of men and women. Like Jackson, they are loyal, efficient, hard-working, and pleasantly dispassionate. A secretary enters his office and serves his tea at the low table beside the chairs where he sits to chat with visitors. He thanks her, then fusses because he's mislaid his favorite cup, but a substitute cup is found. Staff can sometimes be a tough jury and Jackson office workers are steadfastly fond of and protective of their boss.

The days of the Trans-Lux with its all-newsreel shows are gone. So now he sees almost no movies. Occasionally there are private showings for VIPs, but they are infrequent. "I like Westerns—you know, good action." He doesn't watch late-night television—any television, for that matter. He *listens* to the news on the morning *Today* show while shaving.

A total preoccupation with politics and government makes life joyful for him, but it is a totally serious business. The anthology of Jackson humor is practically a barren tract. The sparse Jackson humor is *about* him and his preoccupied life style, rather than *from* him. Like the morning in 1968 after Jackson, Congressman Tom Foley, and their aides spent the night in the small town of Chelan. The others gathered outside the motel in the quiet dawn, awaiting the senator, noticing that a bakery was just opening across the street. Clad in a T-shirt and jockey shorts, Jackson appeared on the motel balcony, obviously in the midst of shaving and between telephone calls to Washington. He carefully recited the morning schedule for the men below, even though they already knew it. Then Jackson directed them: "Why don't you fellows go on over to the bakery and have a cup of coffee and I'll be ready in about ten minutes." A woman opened the bakery door for them and Foley, in mid-campaign, thrust out his hand: "Hi, I'm Tom Foley and I'm running for re-election." The woman replied drolly, "Well, I dunno if I'll vote for you, but if that tiger over there in the jockey shorts ever runs for anything, I'd vote for *him*."

He is not a man to sit around, feet propped up, drink in hand, philosophizing about the meaning of life, so Jackson's innermost self is a source of fascination to friends. Even John Salter, his longtime personal friend and for years Jackson's closest political confidant, says he doesn't know the inner man.

"I have an inner toughness," Jackson says. And those who know him politically enthusiastically confirm that. But also he is a man with an inner squeamishness about violence. "As a little boy we had some rabbits," he recalls, "and I had my pets. And the rabbits were killed and then we were to have rabbit meat for dinner. Well, that just sickened me." There was, too, the golden-gloves boxing tournament at Everett when a friend was hit at a precisely deadly point on his chin. "He died right in front of me. That was in 1929. I'm all for sports like basketball and football, but, what the hell, when they're just out to bloody up the other guy I just can't see that."

He remembers, as a young senator, going to a bullfight in Juarez, Mexico, and being sickened by the killing of the bull. "To me it was a ghastly business with no purpose— this deliberate killing. The whole purpose of the operation was to me just sickening." His voice becomes slow, faltering, as he talks about it.

During a battle at an old French plantation in Vietnam

343

in 1965 he "was right up there with the First Division. They were firing all around us and they were bringing the wounded right in. We were watching them come in—the wounded." His voice drops—again slow and uncertain. If an inner instinct wants to cry out against war and a vision of khaki soaked by blood, the inner toughness and discipline fights back. A wall of antiemotionalism seems to descend behind his eyes. Jackson says, "I feel very strongly about one day being able to stop all this business. But you know . . . if you're honest with yourself . . . you know man continues to sin and commit these acts of war. You keep striving that much harder to resolve these things."

Jackson agrees with the occasional student of the Senate who views him as the last of a special political breed, the Cold War liberal. The classic Cold War liberal was Paul Douglas, a former senator from Illinois. "We were close friends. I thought a lot of Paul."

Politically, they had much in common even if they were dissimilar in other ways—the older, scholarly Douglas and the younger Jackson a fervently hard-working Norwegian who usually disdains intellectuals. They fought for the classic domestic liberal issues—monopoly controls, repeal of the Taft-Hartley Act, federal aid to education, broader Social Security, civil rights, and the Marshall Plan. Then, because of Douglas' advocacy of a strong military defense, the New Left of the day—the Progressive Party of Henry Wallace—attacked him: "We believe that he is a man who parades as a liberal but is, in point of fact, one of the most open Red-baiters and warmongers in the nation."

"Now I get it from the other side, too," says the last of the Cold War liberals.

Douglas had a tough early life, too. As did Jackson, he waited on tables as a youth and labored as a concrete mixer. "Paul was a civil libertarian in that great tradition. He hated the Commies and he fought totalitarians at the University of Chicago. I didn't agree with Paul on some of his crusading in the economic area. In his later years he got a little too doctrinaire and a little too rigid.

"You know Carl Sandburg once was told: 'You were a socialist and you fought for all these things and now you've become a conservative.' And he said, 'The trouble with some people is that they don't know when a crusade is over.' Carl Sandburg was a great liberal. He fought against the bad aspects of big business. He wasn't against all big business, you know—just the bad practices of big business in some sectors. He said that crusade is over. They (the liberal critics) feel that if you've fought for these things that you have to keep spinning wheels . . .

"It's curious how fast labels can be readjusted on people without substantive justification. Here I am labeled a conservative and conservatives really believe it. And the liberals, so called, put this label on you. And what's it based on? It's all based on foreign policy."

As the master of coalition politics, Jackson doesn't mind it too much when he is occasionally referred to as a conservative—particularly if it happens before the right kind of an audience. He even smiles a little if the adjective is tossed into one of his introductions to a Rotary Club in his home state.

But he becomes angered when anyone says he is *not liberal*. When a newsman asked him about the *Spiro M. Jackson* line he snapped "no comment," his face darkened in anger.

He was mischievously miffed one day when he heard that Senator J. William Fulbright referred to him as a conservative. Fulbright, arch-critic of Vietnam policy but a domestic-issues conservative, made the reference in one of his caustic critiques of defense policy. So, the story goes, Jackson telephoned his colleague. "Bill, is it true you called me a conservative?" The report confirmed, Jackson retaliated: "OK, Bill, I'll get even with you. I'm going to start calling you a *liberal*."

Jackson's usual response to the slur that he is not liberal is to point out that "I fought Joe McCarthy back in the days when the other so-called liberals couldn't be found." Yet now the critics say that is not an impressive medal of liberal valor: Taking on Joe McCarthy during the time of the Army-McCarthy hearings was as dangerous as drinking a morning cup of coffee. "Well," Jackson retorts, "*They* —whoever said that—couldn't have been *around* then." Besides, he adds, he had criticized McCarthy in 1950.

On a new political stage, tilted slightly by the turmoil of the 1960s, Democrats jockey for position on their new scale of liberalness by debating *when they* first spoke out against the Vietnam war. Liberalism is built on shifting sands. Even Lowenstein, in Seattle, to begin his stop-Jackson movement, was heckled by the Left. Longhaired Progressive Labor Party radicals handed out leaflets charging that Lowenstein and the Gene McCarthy organization he helped put together "was backed by the ruling class—people who made money off the war."

A nagging question among Jackson-watchers is why he became so deeply absorbed in national defense and national security, rather than other issues. When he went to Norway at the end of the war, two conspicuous things happened: He witnessed the persistence of the Russian presence; and he almost died of pneumonia. The close brush with death might have caused Jackson to become a leading advocate of medical research and national health care. That would have been highly compatible with his early-day experience with welfare and with his own personal Norwegian view of government and its responsibility to people. Instead, though, Jackson became the national-defense man.

"Well," he says, "first things first. We're dealing with survival. You can't talk about a better United States, if the country can be destroyed. That's what happened to Norway. Norway had a thousand years of freedom. They had clean air, clean water, clean land, a great environment. They had one of the highest standards in the world. They had one of the first health programs, dating back to the turn of the century. What good did it do them when the hobnail boot took over in the spring of 1940?"

The timing of his career also thrust him into his specialty on defense. He entered politics during the Depression years when the hot issues were human and economic. But as he was sworn into office as a 28-year-old congressman in 1941, America's political attention was abruptly swinging outward to the menace of fascism and the worldwide threat to freedom. In 1952 while he was campaigning for the Senate, Jackson talked about the *external* menace of Communism and through the years he rose in stature in the Senate, the confrontation with the Soviet Union *was* the overriding national issue.

Yet even in foreign policy, Jackson had his encounters with the conservatives. When, in 1956, he advocated giving the islands of Quemoy and Matsu to Red China in exchange for assurances of Formosan security, the conservative press charged him with advocating "another Munich." "We are selling to all other Communist countries and we are only fooling ourselves refusing to trade with Red China on nonstrategic materials," he argued in 1958. Even with his state's Puget Sound ports interested in increased Orient trade, those were bold positions for the 1950s. "It is pretty obvious," he said in 1969, two years before President Nixon's historic China moves, "that some time, somehow, the mainland Chinese regime will have to join in the negotiations of arms control if it and the rest of the world are going to have peace and security."

"A lot of people think I have an obsession about the Russians. I get this thing constantly. But I don't have an obsession. It's just that Russia is the only country in Europe that's never known freedom.

"That's why during the first ABM debate . . . I pointed out that the Russian leaders were the product of the Stalin terror and that seventeen million died and they, the leaders, knew what was going on . . . They only went up the ladder to leadership by walking over the dead bodies of their comrades."

The Cold Warrior tells of visits he has had with Russian newsmen, one in particular. "You know they tell you how independent they are. Well, about three weeks later I saw (Ambassador Anatoly) Dobrynin and he said, 'I hear you had a very interesting discussion with *our man.*' "

Jackson emphasizes it: "*our man!*" After another visit from another Soviet newsman, Jackson said, "I got a report back through intelligence sources. He (the newsman) was really impressed. He said Jackson was tough. But he said I was the only one he could make any sense out of. They have no respect for people who put out a lot of mush."

An Atlanta newspaperman related to Jackson the conversation during a visit by some Russians who, when asked about potential United States Presidents, replied, "They're all acceptable except Senator Jackson. Dangerous man."

With a grin, Jackson delivers those words a second time, too, in mock Russian accent: *Veddy dendjurous man.*

"With the passage of time there is the tendency to believe that, because something didn't happen, therefore there is no problem. The reason why NATO is in trouble is because it has been so successful. After all, they say, why do you need NATO when nothing has happened? But the reason nothing's happened is because of NATO. . . . in the postwar period Churchill said, in effect, that America is a great country and a great people, 'but I have only one question: Do they have the will to stay the course?'

"When I talk to the Russians, I talk about our inner toughness. And that the fact that we have these demonstrations and disturbances here at home is not to be construed as weakness. The greatest danger would be for them to conclude that we're coming apart . . . I say we could be unified overnight when a real threat appears. . . ."

As chairman of a special subcommittee of the Senate Armed Services Committee, he keeps a close eye on the Strategic Arms Limitation Talks. "The time will come," he says. "But you have to be patient. I've supported all arms-control moves that made sense and that provide stability rather than instability. Some arms-control agreements would cause greater instability than no agreement at all, if they were based on a false set of assumptions." His approach to SALT is hard-nosed, reminiscent of his stubborn insistence on safeguards during the 1963 Nuclear Test Ban Treaty debate. If it means no agreement, if it means less than an ironclad break-even result for the United States, Jackson would rather wait.

"I would say that a politician would be in real trouble if he has taken a—quote—soft position—end quote—on defense and something blows up . . . I have to take these risks as a politician. What you want, of course, is to never be proved right."

Driving down the hill from Everett toward the beach at Mukilteo, the senator is at the wheel of the family's gray Oldsmobile, the television crew following in a rented red Ford. Although he has an astonishing layman's grasp of the technology of the atom and other mysteries of science and industry, Jackson can't understand the automobile. He seems oblivious to such needs as gasoline and maintenance. Because he has partial red-green color blindness and because he usually is preoccupied with thought, he also is a poor driver. The Oldsmobile makes an abrupt stop about fifty feet short of an intersection. Then it starts again and moves swiftly through a stop sign, turning right into a flow of traffic toward the beach.

In the bright sunlight, the senator and his family walk along the beach, hair rumpled by the southerly wind which puts a chop on the dark blue water of Puget Sound. In the background a gleaming white ferry, trimmed in green, slides past the lighthouse on the point, toward its berth at Mukilteo. Anna Marie leaps nimbly over a whitening driftwood log, slowly being buried by the sands-pushing high tides. Carrying the ball in his right hand, the senator extends his left to hoist his short-legged son up and over the log. The TV crew is getting some good footage.

"Now," wonders the senator, "would you like to have us play catch with the ball?" "No," replies the director. He still isn't interested. "Well, I guess they don't want us to play catch," Jackson says and he tosses the ball up on the sand. "Here, I'll teach you to skip rocks," Jackson says to the children. "I used to do this all the time as a kid. Let's find a flat rock." Eyes turn downward looking for a flat rock. As his sweater hikes up, the senator's blue pants are revealed to be bunched in pleats under the belt. They're old pants and he has lost fifteen pounds, he explains, pleased.

"Can't find a very flat rock," he says. But he has a sort-of-flat rock in hand. Beginning with a ferocious expression on his face, he puts his whole square frame into the throw. No natural athletic grace. Almost a little awkward. But the whip throw sends the rock—*spat, spat, spat, spat, spat, spat*—across the water.

Six skips. *Six! Hooray*, shouts his wife.

The kids seem unimpressed, but they couldn't realize that, considering the rock wasn't flat and smooth, a six-skipper was a pretty good toss.

INDEX

INDEX